THE ORDNANCE SURVEY GUIDE TO

GREAT
BRITISH
RUINS

THE ORDNANCE SURVEY GUIDE TO

GREAT BRITISH RUINS

BRIAN BAILEY

CASSELL

Cassell Publishers Ltd
Villiers House, 41/47 Strand, London WC2N 5JE

First published 1991

Distributed in the United States by
Sterling Publishing Co. Inc.
387 Park Avenue South, New York, NY 10016–8810

Distributed in Australia by
Capricorn Link (Australia) Pty Ltd
PO Box 665, Lane Cove, NSW 2066

British Library Cataloguing in Publication Data
Bailey, Brian J. (Brian John), 1934–
Great British ruins.
1. Great Britain. Ruins – Visitor's guides
I. Title
914.104859

ISBN 0–304–31855–8
ISBN 0–319–00262–4 (Ordnance Survey)

Typeset in Monophoto by August Filmsetting, Haydock, St Helens
Printed in England by Clays Ltd, St Ives plc

Contents

KEY TO LOCATION MAPS

RELIEF

Feet	Metres
		·274 Heights in feet above mean sea level
3000	914
2000	610
1400	427
1000	305	Contours at 200ft intervals
600	183
200	61
0	0	To convert feet to metres multiply by 0·3048

TOURIST INFORMATION

- ✝ Abbey, Cathedral, Priory
- ₥ Ancient monument
- 🐟 Aquarium
- ⋏ Camp site
- 🚐 Caravan site
- 🏰 Castle
- 🕳 Cave
- 🏛 Country park
- Craft centre
- ❁ Garden
- ⚐ Golf course or links
- 🏠 Historic house
- Information centre

- 🏎 Motor racing
- 🏛 Museum
- ❗ Nature or forest trail
- 🦅 Nature reserve
- ☆ Other tourist feature
- ✕ Picnic site
- 🚂 Preserved railway
- 🏇 Racecourse
- ⛷ Skiing
- Viewpoint
- 🦌 Wildlife park
- ▲ Youth hostel
- 🐘 Zoo

ROADS Not necessarily rights of way

- Motorway with service area, service area (limited access) and junction with junction number
- Motorway junction with limited interchange
- Motorway under construction with proposed opening date where known
- Trunk road with service area
- Main road
- Roundabout or multiple level junction
- Secondary road
- Road under construction
- Toll   Road tunnel
- Narrow road with passing places
- Other tarred road   Other minor road
- Gradient 1 in 7 and steeper
- Distances in miles between markers

The representation on this map of a road is no evidence of the existence of a right of way

GENERAL FEATURES

- Buildings
- Wood
- Lighthouse (in use)   Lighthouse (disused)
- Windmill   Radio or TV mast
- Youth hostel
- ⊕ Civil aerodrome { with Customs facilities
- ✦ { without Customs facilities
- Ⓗ Heliport
- ☎ Public telephone
- Motoring organisation telephone

ANTIQUITIES

- ✳ Native fortress   𝕮𝖆𝖘𝖙𝖑𝖊 · Other antiquities
- ⚔ Site of battle (with date)   Roman road (course of)
- CANOVIUM · Roman antiquity
- ₥ Ancient Monuments and Historic Buildings in the care of the Secretaries of State for the Environment, for Scotland and for Wales and that are open to the public.

WATER FEATURES

- (boat)   (hovercraft)   Ferry routes for vehicles (subject to change)
- Canal   Short ferry routes for vehicles
- Lake   Bridge   Ferry
- Marsh

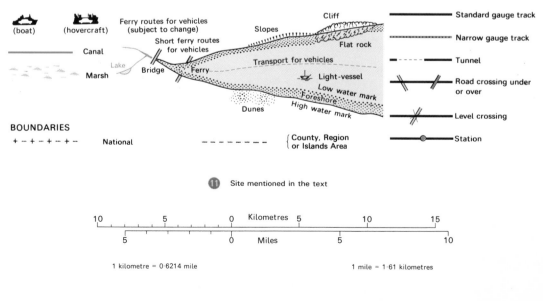

RAILWAYS

- Standard gauge track
- Narrow gauge track
- Tunnel
- Road crossing under or over
- Level crossing
- Station

BOUNDARIES

- + – + – + – + –   National
- – – – – – – –   { County, Region or Islands Area

⑪ Site mentioned in the text

| 10 | 5 | 0 | Kilometres | 5 | 10 | 15 |

| 5 | 0 | Miles | 5 | 10 |

1 kilometre = 0·6214 mile   1 mile = 1·61 kilometres

Introduction

The fascination that ruins hold for a great many people seems to others perverse: it can certainly be melancholy. But nostalgia is not entirely negative. There is a great deal more to admiring ruins than dwelling uselessly on the past; otherwise the modern olethrophile (connoisseur of ruins) would not have such a long pedigree. Shakespeare had made reference to gazing on ruined monasteries within half a century of the Dissolution, and in Webster's *The Duchess of Malfi* (1623) Antonio declares, 'I do love these ancient ruins.' The sentiment has been echoed through the centuries with few dissenting voices.

The excitement generated by picturesque ruins reached its climax with the Romantic movement of the eighteenth century, when landscapes with moonlit ivy-clad towers or prominently sited battlements were perceived as 'sublime'. Poets and artists, with other inspired sightseers hot on their heels, sought out ruins with what the Germans aptly called '*Ruinenlust*'.

Was all this perverse? I think not entirely. What Rose Macaulay called 'a morbid satisfaction in images of decay' is only one aspect of a human reaction to ruins which is very complex. I believe ruins can often prompt our self-awareness and sometimes fuel our self-respect, as well as our dreams, which are not necessarily bad because they are

An abandoned farmhouse at Whitwell-on-the-Hill, in North Yorkshire

A leafy corner of Waverley Abbey, Surrey

exercises in escapism. And they can undoubtedly help to form our aesthetic sense.

Nor do all such worthwhile ruins have to be great abbeys or mighty castles. These are naturally the ones which have received most attention, as dramatic witnesses to earlier ways of life which, though destroyed by a violent past, have helped to shape our own lives. But it is possible to derive as much aesthetic satisfaction from a ruined farmhouse, say, and arouse our curiosity about more recent social history. I still recall with pleasure my discovery, quite by accident, of a tiny ruined church (Bix Bottom) in an Oxfordshire lane on a hot summer afternoon many years ago. It was almost hidden by vegetation. I wondered about the disappeared community that had once worshipped in it and then abandoned it, and found only later that this derelict church had been the subject of a hysterical outburst, nearly 40 years before, by H. J. Massingham, who had compared the ivy clinging to its walls with Germany crushing Poland. What diverse emotions ruins can arouse!

My object in this book is to draw the traveller's attention to as many of the good ruins of all types throughout Britain as space will allow. I have included some that are no more than fragments, as well as the great and famous such as Fountains Abbey and Kenilworth Castle. Although the book is comprehensive, it is by no means exhaustive. It would require a volume at least double this size to catalogue the ruins of every Welsh or Scottish castle, every Norfolk church, and every prehistoric megalith that may qualify as a ruin. So there is much for the enthusiast to discover for himself.

What exactly *does* qualify as a ruin? The one essential ingredient, for the purposes of this book at any rate, is evidence of architecture. A knowledge of architecture is not in the least necessary in order to enjoy ruins, but something that could never have been called architectural cannot be called a ruin. So prehistoric stone circles are not ruins. Nor, of course, are mere earthworks – so Norman mottes are only mentioned when they have the remains of stone-built castles on them. I have generally avoided fragments of ruins which have been incorporated into later buildings and can only be understood by the expert. And I have not generally included ruins which are on private land to which

there is no access and which cannot even be glimpsed from a nearby road, although there are one or two important exceptions to this rule for the sake of completeness. As for industrial ruins, I have approached them with extreme caution in this book, because they are much more liable than others to be restored or moved wholesale into industrial museums, if they are not demolished altogether. This latter liability applies even more to ruined barns and other non-historic houses and buildings. Follies, of course, do not count, and the enthusiastic ruin-hunter should always be aware that this country is littered with relics of the Romantic period which are not genuine ruins at all.

Many real ruins are hardly distinguishable from follies today, alas, due to the current policy of carrying out extensive cosmetic work on ancient monuments. In the age of Wordsworth and Turner, ruins evoked strong sensations by their very air of neglect – crumbling walls covered with ivy, and carved stones lying on the ground where they had fallen long before, had aesthetic qualities only rarely encountered today. Ruins ought to be exempted from the 'Keep Britain Tidy' exhortation. The argument is that ruins which are open to public inspection must be made safe, preserved from further decay, and rendered intelligible by removing the camouflage of vegetation and the untidiness of scattered and meaningless fragments. The current passion for wholesale preservation is used to justify excavation and even restoration work. I am against all this except for the safety aspect. It is conservation gone mad, to my mind. It falsifies history and tries to reverse evolution. Is it not rather like confining wild animals in zoos as opposed to protecting them in the wild?

I have not allowed my own feelings to intrude on the visitor's own reaction to each ruin described, however, except for an occasional remark about a particularly outstanding example. Whether you want to examine a minute architectural detail revealed by science, or take in the atmosphere as a whole, and day-dream of horses' hooves clattering on a castle's cobbled courtyard, or see the ghosts of white-cowled monks moving silently in a moonlit cloister, is entirely up to you. I have merely tried to provide some basic facts, and occasionally legends, about the ruins included.

Practical Details

At the top of each entry is a section giving practical information. Each ruin is numbered on one of the location maps.

Directions are given for reaching the site with the National Grid reference for each ruin. Ordnance Survey 1 : 50 000 maps are strongly recommended for finding the less famous ruins, which although interesting, are not always well signposted, if at all. The distances given in the directions to each ruin are as the crow flies, not road mileages. Then there is a symbol indicating opening times, as follows:

* Standard. These are all-year-round opening times maintained more or less the same by English Heritage, the National Trust, Cadw and SDD, and generally mean every day except Christmas, though Sunday mornings are often still excluded, and English Heritage properties are now usually closed on Mondays in the winter months. In the vast majority of these cases there is an admission charge.

** Summer Standard. This means that properties are open every day through the 'summer' months only, usually April to October inclusive, but not necessarily on Sunday mornings. There is almost always an admission charge.

*** This symbol means that opening times are less regular than those above, and may be confined to only two days a week, for instance. In these cases, telephone numbers are given when possible so that enquiries can be made before travelling. There is invariably a charge for admission.

+ This symbol means that the property is accessible at 'any reasonable time', which is taken to mean during daylight hours. Access to most ruins in this category is free of charge, though a few have an 'honesty box' at the gate where you are asked to deposit the stated entrance fee. In a few cases, ruins marked thus can only be seen from outside, because of the danger of falling masonry or for some other legitimate reason.

⊖ *No access* ⊖ indicates that there is no access to the property at any time.

At the foot of each entry is the name of the body responsible for administering the ruin (not necessarily the owner). SDD is the Scottish Development Department; Cadw the Welsh equivalent of English Heritage. AM signifies a scheduled ancient monument that may be in private or public hands.

It is inevitable, in a book of this kind, that a few errors of detail creep in, due to changes in ownership and administrative responsibility, and so on. The publishers and I would be glad to have such errors brought to our notice for incorporation in future editions.

NOTE ON ILLUSTRATIONS
Photographs of all the ruins in England and Wales are by Rita Bailey. The photographs of ruins in Scotland were supplied by the J. Allan Cash Photolibrary, London.

England

Waverley Abbey, Surrey

1 Avon

See top map on page 14

1 AQUAE SULIS
Bath city centre, near Abbey

[ST 7564] ★

It was not until the nineteenth century that the remains of the Roman spa at Bath were properly excavated, to reveal a site unmatched in western Europe. More than 1500 years before Bath became a fashionable modern health resort, Romans had luxuriated here in the water from the hot mineral springs, building five baths and two swimming pools, with hypocausts, steam rooms, cooling rooms, and so on. They dedicated the place to Sulis, a local Celtic goddess of the springs. The remains are part of the Museum adjoining the Pump Room.

City of Bath

2 HINTON CHARTERHOUSE
Off Trowbridge road from village centre

[ST 7758] ⊖ *No access* ⊖

The largely excavated remains of a Carthusian priory are in the grounds of Hinton House. The priory was the second-oldest house of the order in England, founded in the thirteenth century by Countess Ela, the widow of William Longespee. A three-storey building which remains here consisted originally of the chapter house on the ground floor, with a room above it, and, on the top of that, a dovecote. There were 14 separate cells for the monks round the cloister. Can be seen from the road.

Private

3 TEMPLE CHURCH, BRISTOL
Temple Street, ½ mile (0.8 km) E of city centre

[ST 5972] + *(exterior only)*

The gutted church of the Knights Templars, with a leaning tower, dates mostly from the fifteenth century, but its oldest parts go back to the late thirteenth century. It originally had an oval nave. The church is in Victoria Street, and was bombed during the Second World War.

English Heritage

The Roman baths at Aquae Sulis (Bath)

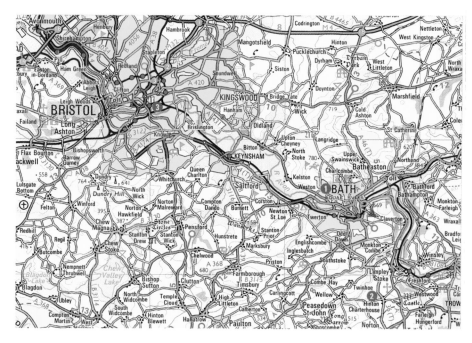

chancel was rebuilt as recently as 1819, but it stands in a field, isolated from the modern village, having been built originally for an earlier community which migrated ½ mile (0.8 km) away to the main road, possibly as a result of devastation by the Black Death. The new village continued to use the old St Mary's church and its graveyard until the nineteenth century, however, for it was not until 1849 that it got a new one. This bit of English village history should on no account be allowed to fall into further decay.

Church of England

2 DUNSTABLE PRIORY
Close to parish church

[TL 0121] +

The nave of the abbey church was taken into parochial use after the Dissolution, but nothing else remains of the house of Augustinian canons except a guest-house subsequently built into a modern house

2 *Bedfordshire*

See map below

1 CLOPHILL CHURCH
By track N of A507 E of village centre

[TL 0938] +

Its brown ironstone walls and tower remain remarkably intact, and indeed its

The church at Clophill

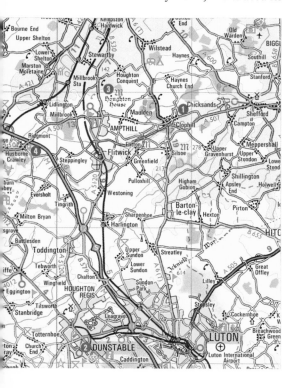

and the ruins of the fifteenth-century gatehouse, standing south-west of the church.

AM

3 HOUGHTON HOUSE
E of A421 1 mile (1.5 km) N of Ampthill

[TL 0339] +

Built around 1615, Houghton House was the property of Sir Philip Sidney's sister Mary, by this time Dowager Countess of Pembroke. It was a characteristic Jacobean two-storey mansion, built of brick with white stone dressings on an H-plan, with mullioned and transomed windows, tall chimneys and Dutch-style gables. The countess spent £10,000 on it, bringing artists and craftsmen from Italy, and allegedly basing it on a house described in her brother's poem *Arcadia*. But Houghton was hardly finished when she died, in 1621. The house was altered afterwards, Inigo Jones being said to have redesigned the west front, with its classical centrepiece of Tuscan columns. It was finally dismantled by the Duke of Bedford in 1794. John Bunyan is said to have based his 'House Beautiful' in *The Pilgrim's Progress* on Houghton House, from the top of which Christian was shown the 'Delectable Mountains'. But what dominates the view from the present ruins is the belching forest of chimneys of the Bedfordshire brick factories.

English Heritage

4 SEGENHOE CHURCH
Off A507 near Ridgmont, 3 miles (5 km) E of Woburn Sands

[SP 9835] +

It is a sorry sight nowadays, with its ugly crumbling buttresses, patched-up walls and rendered upper tower, standing in an overgrown churchyard, with the M1 motorway making its tottering stonework tremble still more. But it was once the church, built in the eleventh century, of the village of Segenhoe, which no longer

Donnington Castle, near Newbury

exists, the population having migrated at some stage to the more economically viable site now called Ridgmont, ¼ mile (0.4 km) away.

Church of England

---

3 *Berkshire*

See map below left

1 DONNINGTON CASTLE
Off B4494 1 mile (1.5 km) N of Newbury

[SU 4669] +

The fairly sparse remains of the fourteenth-century castle near Newbury depend heavily for their surviving interest on the tall twin-towered

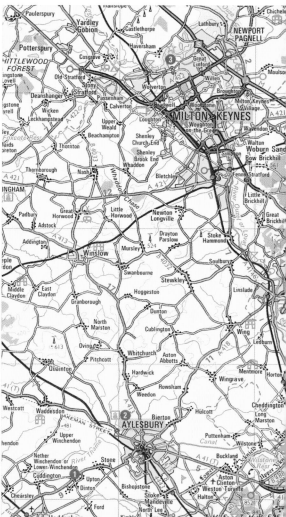

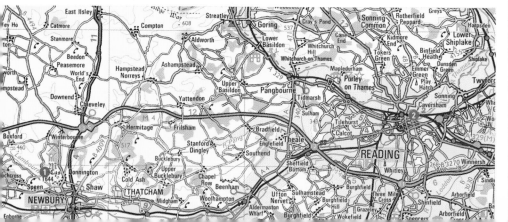

gatehouse, standing on rising ground above the River Lambourne. The castle was built under licence by Sir Richard Abberbury, and was contemporary with Sir Edward Dalyngrigge's building work at Bodiam (q.v.), but Donnington was smaller, without a moat. The castle's history was uneventful until the Civil War, although Elizabeth Tudor owned it at one time and retired here on occasions during her half-sister's tenancy of the throne. The castle was twice besieged during the Civil War, and on the second occasion heavy bombardment reduced it to ruin. One of the stone gatehouse towers shows a patch of brick repairwork where a hole was blown by a mortar in this attack.

English Heritage

2 READING ABBEY
Near Forbury Gardens, town centre

[SU 7273] +

Very little remains of the great Benedictine establishment begun as a Cluniac house founded in 1121 by Henry I, who was buried in the abbey church in 1136. What there is is very fragmented, with parts incorporated in other buildings and parts in the local museum. But the monastery once stretched north from the banks of the Kennet to the area now known as Forbury (from faubourg, or outer court), and was one of the three or four richest and most powerful religious foundations in England. Only St Albans and Glastonbury took precedence over Reading among the mitred abbots in the House of Lords, and many pilgrims came to Reading to venerate its most treasured, if gruesome, relics – the alleged left hand of St James the Apostle and the head of St Philip the Apostle. Reading Abbey was also the source of what might be called the first English popular song, 'Sumer is icumen in'. Its church was consecrated by Thomas Becket in the presence of Henry II, for it was not completed until 43 years after its commencement. John of Gaunt's marriage to his first wife, Blanche, took place here in 1359. At the Dissolution, the abbot was hanged in front of the main gateway, and the abbey was converted into a royal palace, but gradually fell into ruin from the seventeenth century, much of its stone being used in other town buildings. The ruins of flint and rubble, which have as their close neighbour the melancholy Reading Gaol, are well signed.

Reading Corporation

4 Buckinghamshire

See map on page 15, bottom right

1 DINTON CASTLE
Off A418 3½ miles (5.5 km) SW of Aylesbury

[SP 7611] +

Although I have excluded follies from this volume, Dinton Castle may be permitted as it was built for a practical purpose and, whatever it may have looked like originally, it is now a genuine ruin. It stands beside the main road near Dinton Hall and was built by Sir John Vanhattem in 1769 to house his fossil collection. It was a stone hexagonal building with two turrets.

AM

2 QUARRENDON CHURCH
Beside footpath between A41 and A413, 1½ miles (2.5 km) NW of Aylesbury

[SP 8015] +

All that remains is a fragment in a field in what is now a suburb on the north-west side of Aylesbury, on the line of the Roman road known as Akeman Street. Quarrendon was a medieval village, which migrated to a new site more than once before finally becoming deserted altogether, and its church of St Peter, built in the thirteenth century, was already described as a 'melancholy object of contemplation' early in the nineteenth century. Earthworks of the former village surround the ruin, including the moat and fishponds of the former manor house of Sir Henry Lee, who entertained Elizabeth I here and was given a magnificent funeral in this church. Reached on foot by paths east from the A41 or west from the A413.

AM

3 STANTONBURY CHURCH
Off minor road N of Wolverton, Milton Keynes

[SP 8342] +

Close to a Roman site near the village of Haversham (and also near the M1 service station at Newport Pagnell), St Peter's is again the former church of a lost medieval village. It is rather pathetic now, but it once had a fine Norman chancel arch and was described, even at the beginning of the present century, as a 'beautiful little building'.

AM

5 Cambridgeshire

See map on page 18

1 BLACKFRIARS, CAMBRIDGE
Second Court of Emmanuel College

[TL 4558] +

Around the so-called Second Court of Emmanuel College, fragments remain of a large priory for Dominican Friars founded about 1238. It was a place of study for the English branch of the order. When Emmanuel was founded in 1584, it was built on the site of the priory which had been suppressed nearly half a century earlier. There is nothing to make much sense of, however.

University of Cambridge

2 CAMBRIDGE CASTLE
Castle Street, NW of city centre

[TL 4459] +

Fragments of the curtain wall and bastions remain of a castle which Edward I intended to be one of the strongest in the country, but his ambition apparently dwindled, and the stone was already being plundered by the fourteenth century. What was left was refortified for the king during the Civil War, but afterwards fell victim to Cromwell's demolition gang.

City of Cambridge

3 ELY ABBEY
S side of cathedral

[TL 5480] +

Attached to the magnificent cathedral at Ely are the ruins of the cloister of a Benedictine monastery which preceded it. Founded in the tenth century, it became a cathedral priory early in the twelfth. It had itself succeeded a Dominican friary founded in the seventh century and destroyed by the Danes. The later monastery was suppressed in 1539 and the cloister pulled down, other buildings being taken over by the cathedral.

Dean and Chapter

4 RAMSEY ABBEY
Town centre

[TL 2985]

Once a Benedictine foundation of considerable size and importance, all that remains of the abbey now is its former gatehouse, standing beside the green at the centre of the small market town of the same name. But even in the ruins of this you can see how splendid the otherwise vanished monastery buildings must have been, for it is an ornate piece of Decorated architecture, with a two-light oriel window over a doorway, panelled buttresses and ornamental stonework. It was founded in 969 by a nobleman named Ailwine, whose Purbeck marble monument is now kept inside the gatehouse. By the time of the Norman Conquest, the abbey already had a school of high reputation and extensive fenland estates on which it bred sheep and cattle and grew rich crops. At the Dissolution it was dismantled, mainly for other building purposes, and some of its stones now form Cambridge colleges.

National Trust

Wothorpe Lodge

5 WISBECH CASTLE
W of parish church

[TF 4609] +

Scant remains of the stone castle where, after the Civil War, a mansion was built

The gatehouse of Ramsey Abbey

with the same name, this also having been erased by demolition in the nineteenth century, leaving only gate piers and garden walls.

AM

6 WOTHORPE LODGE
Off A43 ¾ mile (1.2 km) S of Stamford

[TF 0205] ⊖ *No access* ⊖

Thomas Cecil, 1st Earl of Exeter and disappointing eldest son of Lord Burghley, built this house early in the seventeenth century, 'to retire to', according to Thomas Fuller, 'out of the dust while his great house at Burleigh was a-sweeping'. It is a little south of Stamford and west of Burghley House, and was built in the form of a Greek cross. Although it has been in ruins since the eighteenth century, it still stands to its full height, having four square towers with octagonal tops, and is a very curious building, sometimes known as Wothorpe Towers, but now, alas, in a sad state, serving as a farmyard building. Visible from the farm lane at Wothorpe-on-the-Hill.

Private

6 *Cheshire*

See top map on page 19

1 BEESTON CASTLE
Minor road W of village centre, off A49 S of Tarporley

[SJ 5359] ★

This fragmentary ruin was already a wreck at the end of the Tudor period, for despite its impregnable-looking site, on a cliff-edge high above the Cheshire Plain,

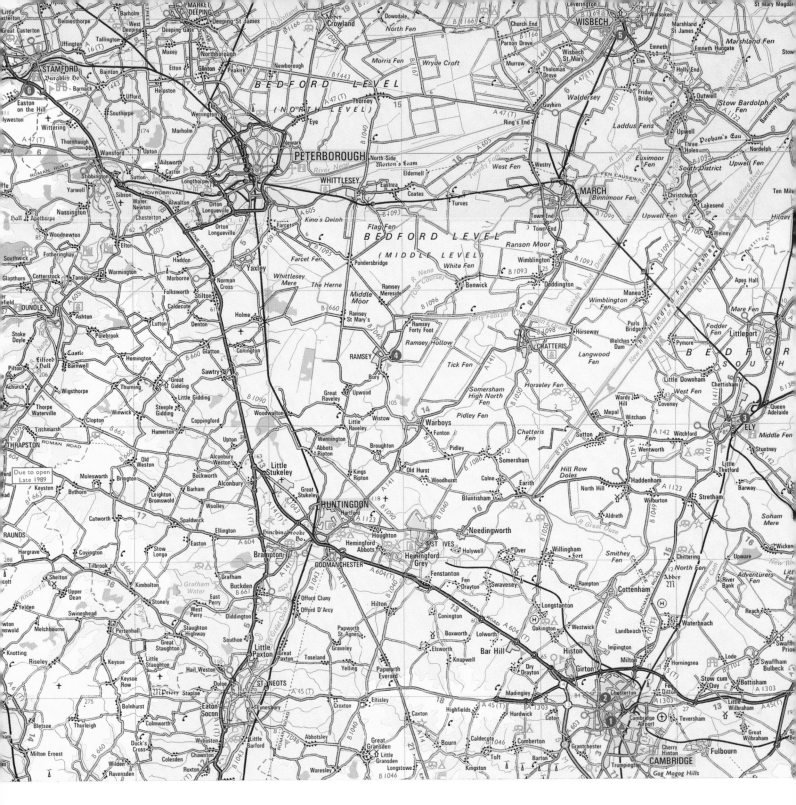

it has been taken several times and reduced to ruin twice in its lifetime. It was built in 1220 by Randulph de Blundeville, Earl of Chester, and it featured in battles between the king's forces and those of the barons at the time of Simon de Montfort, and again during the Wars of the Roses. It was rebuilt and strengthened, but was then besieged by Cromwell's troops during the Civil War, when it finally succumbed after holding out for four months, the castle's cats being consumed by the occupants when no other food was available.

English Heritage

2 ECCLESTON CHURCH
In village churchyard, off A55 S of Chester

[*SJ 4162*]   +

In the churchyard of the present parish church of St Mary is a fragment of a former church built early in the nineteenth century, and then demolished when the Duke of Westminster rebuilt the ancient church in the town.

Church of England

3 HALTON CASTLE
Near Castle Hotel at Halton, Runcorn

[*SJ 5381*]   ★

Close to the Mersey and now embraced by Runcorn, the fragmentary remains of this eleventh-century castle stand on a rocky hilltop, accompanied by the village church. The castle was built by Nigel, the 1st Baron Halton, to whom the manor was granted by his cousin Hugh Lupus, Earl of Chester. It eventually passed to the Duchy of Lancaster, and John of Gaunt used it as a hunting lodge, but under Elizabeth I it was in use chiefly as a prison for recusants, and it was already in ruins by the time of the Civil War.

AM

4 TABLEY OLD HALL
Between M6 and A556 2 miles (3 km) W of Knutsford

[SJ 7177] ⊖ *No access* ⊖

The brick manor house and chapel were built on an island in the mere for the Leicester family, and were reached by a stone bridge, but the house was replaced in the eighteenth century by the new mansion to the north, the birthplace of John Byrne Leicester Warren, the poet and botanist and 3rd and last Baron de Tabley. Subsidence led to the gradual disintegration of the Old Hall, but the chapel was dismantled and re-erected adjacent to the new house. The brick ruin is just visible from the A556.

Private

5 TOWN WALLS, CHESTER
Surrounding city centre

[SJ 4066] (Tower) +

Most of the walls which enclosed the

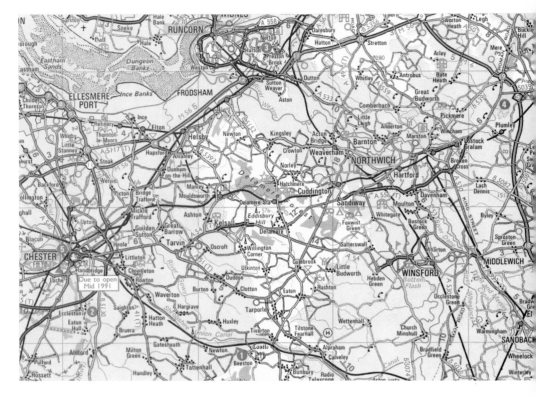

medieval town of Chester survive, partly built on the foundations of defensive walls of the Roman town, Deva. Some of the original gates and towers also remain. There is not space in this volume to cover the walls, 2 miles (3 km) in circumference, in detail. They were mostly built in the thirteenth century, in brown sandstone, and though considerably damaged by Cromwell's troops, were later repaired to some

extent. One of the most interesting areas is near the Water Tower, built to defend the former river port around 1325. Standing in the Water Tower Gardens, close to the River Dee, the Water Tower is linked by a spur wall to the so-called Boneswaldesthorne Tower, at the north-west angle of the town's defences.

Chester Corporation

Beeston Castle

Gisborough Priory

7 *Cleveland*

See bottom map on page 19

1 GISBOROUGH PRIORY
Close to Guisborough town centre

[NZ 6116] ★

Founded for Augustinian canons by Robert de Brus in the twelfth century, but partly destroyed by fire in 1289, so that the remains are largely fourteenth-century work. But the east wall of the priory church's chancel, the only part of the ruins still standing to a substantial height, is of the thirteenth-century rebuilding. The only pre-fire remains are the gatehouse, and an octagonal dovecote, which provided the canons with eggs and meat and is a rare survival.

English Heritage

8 *Cornwall*

See maps on pages 22 and 23

1 CARN EUNY
Minor road between Grumbla and Brane, 1 mile (1.5 km) W of Sancreed

[SW 4028] +

This first-century BC village is less impressive than the marvellous remains at Chysauster (q.v.), but it does have one remarkable survival that should not be missed. A fogou, or underground passage, 65 feet (20 m) long, with granite lintels supporting its roof covering, leads into a circular chamber which is probably of Bronze Age date, and which had a corbelled roof of granite boulders. The purpose of neither passage nor chamber is clear, but secretion was obviously an important motive.

English Heritage

2 CARN GLOOSE
Minor road W of St Just in Penwith

[SW 3531] +

The poet Walter de la Mare was driven

away from Cornwall by sensitivity to what he perceived as its pagan spirit, and many of the century's prehistoric remains have what might be called sinister associations in popular belief. Beside the long-distance coastal footpath, between St Just and Cape Cornwall, is this labyrinthine chambered tomb which was excavated in the nineteenth century. A round barrow, it is steeped in local legend. Some say that fairies danced on its dome of earth; others that it was connected with rituals in honour of the underworld powers.

AM

3 CHAPEL OF ST THOMAS BECKET
Bodmin parish churchyard

[SX 0767] +

It stands forlorn in the churchyard of St Petroc, the parish church of Bodmin. It was built in 1377 as a chantry chapel, and although precious little remains of it, the ruin serves to remind us of Bodmin's Catholic tradition, for the town rebelled against the Protestantism of Edward VI and the mayor was hanged after unwittingly building his own gallows and entertaining his judge to a sumptuous dinner.

Church of England

4 CHUN CASTLE
Off minor road ¾ mile (1.2 km) S of Morvah

[SW 4033] +

On a hilltop south of Morvah is an Iron Age fort, unusual in having a circular double rampart of dry-stone granite walling, the inner of which stood 12 feet (3.5 m) high as recently as the mid-nineteenth century. The diameter of the outer wall was 280 feet (85 m), and excavation revealed the foundations of huts or houses within the fort, which may have been built to protect early exploiters of the area's tin deposits. Nearby, to the west, is an even earlier ruin, the remains of a Neolithic tomb, Chun Quoit, with its massive capstone supported on four granite boulders.

AM

5 CHYSAUSTER
Off minor road N of village, between New Mill and Nancledra

[SW 4735] ★

Celtic settlers of the Iron Age came here to mine tin, and built themselves a

The prehistoric village of Chysauster

Launceston Castle

21

ISLES OF SCILLY

Restormel Castle

village of closely grouped oval-shaped houses flanking a wide street. The houses of these first Cornishmen had dry-stone walls of moorland granite, with drains beneath the floors, and hollowed-out stones for grinding corn. The roofs of thatch or turf were supported on single central poles set in stone sockets, and each of the nine houses had a garden and courtyard. The village was deserted nearly 2000 years ago, but many of the walls still stand to a height of 6 feet (2 m). The remains of Chysauster are certainly among the most marvellous survivals of prehistoric Britain, as evocative of the past in their own way as the grandest ruins of medieval architecture.

English Heritage

6 LAUNCESTON CASTLE
Town centre

[SX 3384]   ★★★

Set on top of a man-made conical hill which the antiquary John Leland

described as 'large and of a terrible height', the castle was built by Richard, Earl of Cornwall, titular head of the Holy Roman Empire, but it only partly replaced the castle built here originally by William the Conqueror's brother, Robert of Mortain, who was granted Cornwall as his share of the spoils of war. Its history is not distinguished. It was already in a poor condition before the Civil War, when it was hastily repaired for use as a royalist garrison, and its upkeep was not long maintained. Part of the castle was afterwards used as the notorious town prison, commonly known as 'Doomsdale', where the eighteenth-century reformer John Howard found prisoners chained together in a damp dungeon without sewers or a water supply. The outer bailey, now a public park, was long used as a place of execution.

English Heritage

7 MOORSWATER VIADUCT
Near A38 W of Liskeard

[SX 2364]   +

When the Great Western Railway was extended from Plymouth into Cornwall in the 1840s, Brunel built a viaduct to cross the East Looe River near Liskeard. The massive stone piers, 147 feet (45 m) high, carried a wooden deck across the valley. The viaduct was replaced by a new one in 1881, and the wooden structure was eventually dismantled,

but Brunel's original piers remain alongside the new viaduct.

8 RESTORMEL CASTLE
Minor road 1 mile (1.5 km) N of Lostwithiel

[SX 1061]   ★★★

The fascinating remains stand above the River Fowey near Lostwithiel, and are enclosed by a circular shell-keep, 30 feet (9 m) high, characteristic of the south-west, and surrounded by a wide moat. The first castle was built around 1100, but this may have been a timber castle rebuilt in stone soon afterwards. It appears to stand on an artificial mound, but in fact earth was piled up against the walls after completion, increasing the depth of the ditch. The remains of two-storey domestic buildings surround the inner courtyard, their windows looking inward on the ground floor and outward on the first. Richard, Earl of Cornwall, and his son, Edmund, were owners of the castle, and one of them no doubt rebuilt the castle to this excellent plan. The Black Prince was a guest here for Christmas in 1362, but the castle was in poor condition, if not actually ruinous, by the Civil War, though it was defended for Parliament for a time. The castle was described at the turn of the present century as 'rendered picturesque with creeping ivies'. Now it is almost hidden by a circle of trees.

English Heritage

Restormel Castle: the main gate and stairs to guest chamber　*Tintagel Castle*

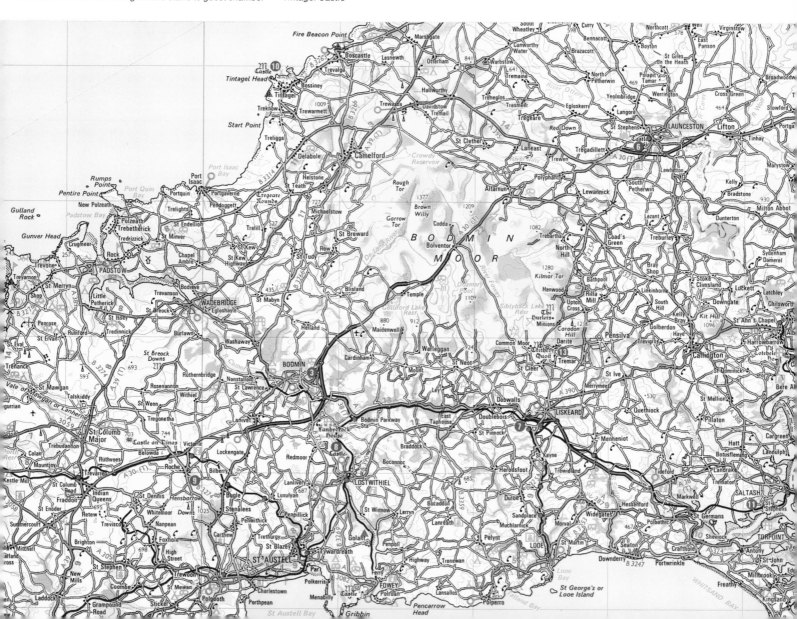

9 ROCHE CHAPEL

Off minor road to Bugle, ¼ mile (0.4 km) S of Roche

[SW 9959]   +

South-east of Roche, at the edge of a huge area turned into a lunar landscape by china clay workings, a cliff of granite rises against the background of white spoil-heaps, and at its peak is this amazing little granite chapel, looking as if it is growing out of the rock. It was built in 1409 and dedicated to St Michael, and consisted of a tiny chapel above a priest's or anchorite's cell, the whole supported by a substructure which seems almost welded to the natural rock. A flight of steps leads up to the roofless ruin, but you need stamina to reach it.

AM

TIN MINES

The ruins of Cornish tin mines are far too numerous to list individually. The chief areas where they can be seen are around Camborne and Redruth and on the Land's End peninsula. The remains above ground level are the stone-built engine-houses with their characteristic round chimneys topped with red brick, often clad in ivy, and looking for all the world like small medieval castles. The shaft-mining of tin began in the fifteenth century, but started to decline in the nineteenth, when the importation of cheaper tin began. Cornwall's tin deposits were the most important in Europe, and copper deposits were often worked in the same mines, their galleries going deep into the earth and beneath the sea. Botallack Mine, near St Just, had galleries going ⅓ mile (0.5 km) out to sea, and Levant Mine nearby, went ½ mile (0.8 km) out beneath the Atlantic Ocean, 2000 feet (610 m) below sea level.

10 TINTAGEL CASTLE

Path to coast from village centre

[SX 0589]   ★

I am all for a little romance in life, and especially in ruins, but at Tintagel romance has gone quite mad. What we actually have here are the scant remains of a twelfth-century castle variously owned by the earls of Cornwall and the Black Prince, and built on the site of a former monastery. But what the thousands of annual visitors pour down the headland slopes to see is the enduring myth of the Celtic twilight; the place where Uther Pendragon fathered on Igraine, the Duke of Cornwall's wife, the once-and-future king named Arthur,

who was delivered into the hands of the wizard Merlin while waves lapped the shores of Lyonesse. The real castle was in ruins by 1540, but its dramatic site fuels the Celtic dream, for it stands on an isthmus which was once higher and wider, but has been broken down by the relentless Atlantic so that the ruins are split in two and can only be reached by a rock-hewn stepped path across a precipitous ridge.

English Heritage

11 TREMATON CASTLE

In village of that name, SW of Saltash (not Trematon to NW)

[SX 4158]   ⊖ *No access* ⊖

It was already in existence at the Conquest, for it is mentioned in the Domesday Book, and eventually grew to become one of the largest castles in Cornwall, passing to the Duchy in Edward III's time and remaining with it still. It had a shell-keep with a fine thirteenth-century gatehouse. But early in the nineteenth century the castle was partly demolished for conversion into a dwelling house. The shell is visible from the road, south-west of Saltash.

Private

12 TRESCO, ISLES OF SCILLY

[SV 8914]   ★★★   *(Abbey)*
[SV 8815-6]   +   *(Castle)*

On the island of Tresco are three ruins, none of them substantial. In the island's famous sub-tropical gardens are fragments of walls and arches of the thirteenth-century Benedictine Priory of St Nicholas, disbanded in 1539. Further north on the island's west coast are the remains of two castles – King Charles Castle, built around 1550 (but given its present name later, after it had been held for the king for a time in the Civil War), and Cromwell's Castle of 1651. This is the best preserved, with a cylindrical tower which had no access from the ground floor. It was built to guard the island against Dutch naval attack.

Abbey Gardens: Private
Castle ruins: AM

13 TRETHEVY QUOIT

Minor road between Tremar and Darite

[SX 2568]   +

This is one of the best of the many megalithic tomb remains in Cornwall, standing on Bodmin Moor 3 miles (5 km) north of Liskeard. Six massive upright

slabs, the tallest of which are nearly 15 feet (4.5 m) high, support a gigantic capstone over 11 feet (3 m) long. The tomb was originally divided into a main chamber and a small antechamber, and apart from its covering of earth, it has stood here more or less intact for something like 4000 years, its Celtic name meaning 'place of the grave'.

English Heritage

14 ZENNOR QUOIT

Footpath S from B3306, ¾ mile (1.2 km) E of Zennor

[SW 4638]   +

South-east of the village, the capstone of this dolmen is one of the largest in the country, weighing around 12 tons. It was supported by 10-foot (3-m) high boulders, with two great slabs forming a portal to the chambered tomb. Georgian farmers ruined it, and the capstone is no longer in position, but when the burial chamber was examined, cremated bones were discovered in it.

AM

---

9 Cumbria

See maps on pages 26 and 30

1 ARNSIDE TOWER

Off minor road between Arnside and Silverdale

[SD 4576]   +

South of the village, this is the ruin of a fifteenth-century peel-tower, five storeys high, and was one of a chain of defensive forts against the Scots. It belonged to the Stanley lords of the manor once, but was burnt down in 1602. There are no floors in the shell now, but it stands in attractive country, flanked by National Trust woodlands.

2 BROUGH CASTLE

S of town centre

[NY 7914]   ★★★

Not to be confused with Brougham Castle (q.v.) near Penrith, this one is at the village of Brough on A66, nearly 20 miles (32 km) to the south-east. But, like Brougham, for a long time it was in the hands of the mighty Cliffords, and the indefatigable Lady Anne of that ilk was the last restorer. It had been built originally on the site of a Roman fort soon after the Conquest, but was destroyed by the Scots in 1174 and was then rebuilt, and survived Robert the Bruce's attacks on the town. The keep remains to a substantial height, and you can climb to the top and look down on the castle's plan, with its moat surrounding other buildings and a cobbled courtyard. Lady Anne Clifford's repairs did not last long. Within a few years there was another serious fire, and after that the castle was left to rot.

English Heritage

3 BROUGHAM CASTLE
Minor road off A66 1½ miles (2.5 km) SE of Penrith

[NY 5329] ★★★

The original castle here was built in the time of Henry II, but in the following century it came by marriage to the Clifford family, and its fame is all in connection with them. One of them was the Baron Clifford known as 'the Butcher' because of his cruelty in the Wars of the Roses, and who features in Shakespeare's *Henry VI, Part III*. In the seventeenth century the castle was largely rebuilt by his descendant Lady Anne Clifford, later Countess of Pembroke, a formidable builder who also owned the castles at Appleby, Pendragon, Skipton and Brough, her family having lorded it over much of Cumberland and Westmorland for four centuries. She called her keep at Brougham 'Pagan Tower', for the castle had been built within the ramparts of a Roman fort. But it did not long survive her death, falling into dereliction and losing its lead, stone and oak wainscoting to the builders of other houses.

English Heritage

4 CALDBECK MILLS
Footpath to 'The Howk' from village green

[NY 3139] +

A path across a field from the village green leads to an eerie limestone gorge known as 'the Howk'. Before reaching the gorge itself, you pass a derelict woollen mill where John Woodcock Graves, author of the song *D'ye ken John Peel?*, worked. Farther along, where the river has created swallow holes strong in local superstition, there are scant remains of a stone-built bobbin mill, part of a once-thriving Cumbrian coppice industry which supplied bobbins to Lancashire's cotton mills.

Brougham Castle

5 CALDER ABBEY
Off minor road ½ mile (0.8 km) NE of Calder Bridge

[NY 0506] ⊖ *No access* ⊖

It keeps questionable company nowadays, being only a stone's throw from Sellafield, but it was founded by William de Meschines in 1134 as a Savignac monastery in what was then a solitary spot by the banks of the River Calder. It had 12 monks, who were dispossessed of the property by Scottish raiders, but the abbey was later repossessed by monks from Furness. After the Dissolution, parts were incorporated into a private house, but the ruins of the abbey church remain, and are very picturesque. Not yet given the usual cosmetic treatment, this is a ruin that deserves to be better known.

AM

6 COCKERMOUTH CASTLE
Near town centre

[NY 1230] ⊖ *No access* ⊖

It dates mostly from the thirteenth and fourteenth centuries, although there are fragments of an earlier castle built by one Waltheof in 1134. Its history is one of seemingly constant beleaguerment, from the Scots under Robert the Bruce, from the Yorkists in the Wars of the Roses,

and from the Royalists in the Civil War, after which it fell into ruin until, in the nineteenth century, it was partly restored to habitable condition again.

Private

7 DUKE PIT ENGINE-HOUSE
[NX 9618] +

South-west of Whitehaven along the clifftop is this ruined fan-house, looking like a stone medieval relic because of the high architectural finish the local landowners put into the buildings of the Cumbrian coalfield. This one was owned by the Earl of Lonsdale. Built around 1862, it housed a wooden fan, 36 feet (11 m) in diameter, which blew fresh air into the mine.

8 EGREMONT CASTLE
S of town centre

[NY 0110] +

Built by William de Meschines around 1140, and brought to ruin in the sixteenth century, its remains consist chiefly of a rectangular gatehouse, with herringbone masonry and a rib-vaulted ceiling, and parts of the curtain wall and domestic buildings, standing on a hill on the south side of the town. The castle is associated in legend with the 'Horn of Egremont' – a symbol on the coat of

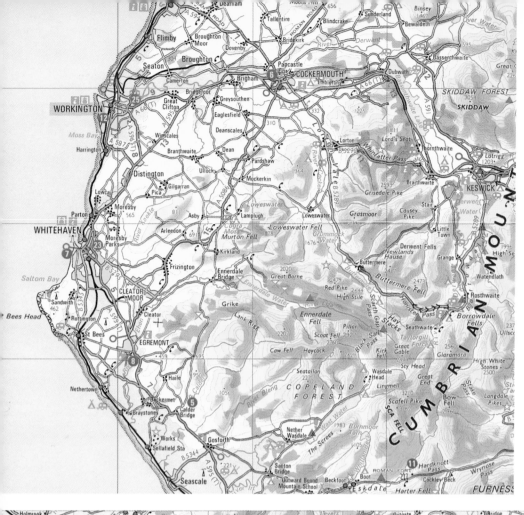

arms of the Lucy family, who were hereditary local foresters. It is said that Hubert de Lucy usurped the barony while the true lord of the manor, his brother Eustace, was on a Crusade. But when he returned, Eustace blew the horn at the gate which could only be sounded by the rightful lord, and Hubert fled, but the brothers were subsequently reconciled. The legend is the subject of a poem by Wordsworth, one hardly need say.

Private

9 FURNESS ABBEY
Off A590 N of Barrow-in-Furness

[SD 2171]   ★

It hardly qualifies as the most beautiful of ruins (though it has some exquisite architectural details), but its square and solid walls of red sandstone lend credence to its reputation as an ecclesiastical powerhouse second only to Fountains Abbey as the richest and most powerful Cistercian monastery in the kingdom before the Dissolution. The abbey owned vast lands in Lancashire, Yorkshire, Ireland and the Isle of Man,

Furness Abbey

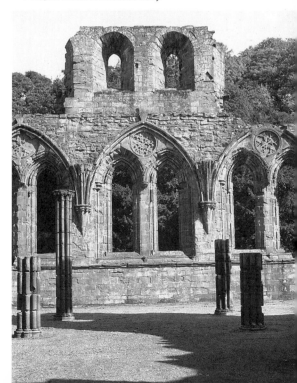

The chapter house at Furness Abbey

and capitalized on iron-founding and sheep farming. It built ships in its own dockyard and exported its wool in them. It was famed for its lavish hospitality, and so far deserted the Cistercian ideal of austerity and remoteness from human intercourse as to raise an army which fought at Flodden. It was the cradle of the heavy industry which now surrounds its still-quiet spot on the Furness peninsula, and its chapter house was a medieval boardroom with the profit motive high on the agenda. The monastery had been founded as a Savignac abbey in 1123 near Preston, but moved four years later to this 'Valley of Deadly Nightshade' and became a Cistercian establishment. It prospered for 400 years before the last abbot, Roger Pyle, submitted to the intimidation of the king's commissioners at Whalley Abbey, where he must have seen the corpses of hanged monks still dangling in the gateway, and surrendered Furness and all its possessions to the king, 'frely of

my selff and without any enforcement'. Who needed any further enforcement after the king's savage suppression of the Pilgrimage of Grace, that great northern demonstration against suppression of the monasteries?

English Heritage

10 GALAVA FORT
½ *mile (0.8 km) S of Ambleside on N shore of Windermere*

[*NY 3703*]   +

The Roman fort of Galava was originally built in the first century on a promontory at the head of Windermere, near Ambleside. Built of timber inside a double defensive ditch, it was rebuilt later with a stone outer wall, and the remains include barracks and granaries. The pleasant site should be compared with that of the next fort along the route to the coast, Hardknott Castle (below).

English Heritage

HADRIAN'S WALL: *See under* Northumberland, page 103.

11 HARDKNOTT FORT
Beside Hardknott Pass, 2½ miles (4 km) E of Boot

[NY 2101] +

The Roman governor of Britain, Agricola, probably built this remote outpost of empire in the first century AD, the middle one of three forts along a road linking Ambleside with the port at Ravenglass called Glannaventa. This fort was Mediobogdum, and was built on a dramatic triangular plateau site below Hardknott Pass and overlooking Eskdale. It had a parade ground, centrally heated barracks, baths and granaries. It must have been a grim place, especially in winter, for the 500 men stationed here at one time, and they cannot have been under much threat here from raiding parties. No doubt they spent their free time thinking of home, and sex, and slandering the cooks, as soldiers usually do.

English Heritage

12 JANE PIT ENGINE-HOUSE
Off B5296 S of Workington

[NX 9927] +

The battlemented stone chimneys and engine-house at Workington are characteristic of pit-head structures in this area. The engine house was built around 1843 by Henry Curwen of a long-established local family of landowners and industrialists.

13 KENDAL CASTLE
Off A65 E of town centre

[SD 5292] +

On a hill at the eastern side of the town, above the River Kent, fragments of three towers and an enclosing wall are the remains of a twelfth-century castle, and there is part of a later range with dungeons below. This was the birthplace of Catherine, daughter of the lord of the manor, Sir Thomas Parr. She was married first to Sir Edward Burrough and then, after his early demise, to Lord Latymer, who also died within a few years. The twice-widowed Catherine was still only 31 when she accepted the proposal of marriage to Henry Tudor, King of Great Britain, France and Ireland, himself an experienced widower. The childless widow from Westmorland was Henry VIII's last and, in many respects, most successful consort, gathering his scattered offspring to her and supervising their education, for she was highly intelligent and had a strong sense of duty. But after four years the corpulent and ulcerous monarch died, leaving her widowed yet again, and she eventually married Sir Thomas Seymour, dying herself in childbirth at the age of 36. The seat of her fathers was already in decay before the end of the sixteenth century.

AM

14 KENTMERE HALL
Minor road W of village centre, 4 miles (6.5 km) N of A591 at Staveley

[NY 4504] ⊖ *No access* ⊖

The remains of a fourteenth-century peel-tower are attached to a later farmhouse, it was built by the de Gilpin

Hardknott Fort

lords of the manor. Legend has it that a colossal oak beam in its structure was lifted into position by the so-called 'Troutbeck Giant', Hugh Heard, a man of 'prodigious strength and stature' who once told the king that he normally ate a whole sheep for dinner, and was himself a tower of strength locally in repelling Scots raiders.

Private

15 KIRKOSWALD CASTLE
Minor road E of village centre, B6413 7½ miles (12 km) N of Penrith

[NY 5541] +

Not a lot to see. A moated castle built around 1200 by Ralph Engayne, it was destroyed in the Civil War. Enclosed by its ditch are the remains of two angle-towers and a large domestic tower containing a spiral staircase.

AM

16 LANERCOST PRIORY
Minor road off A69, 2½ miles (4 km) NE of Brampton

[NY 5563] ★★

The nave of the priory church was restored after the Dissolution and has served as the local parish church ever since, but the loft choir and transepts are open to the sky, and are impressive with their Early English arcading. Little remains of other buildings, some of which were converted into a private house, and others plundered for their building material. The ruin stands in the valley of the River Irthing close to Hadrian's Wall, and Roman material was plundered by its original builders to supplement the local red sandstone. Founded by Robert de Vaux in the twelfth century, it was a house of Augustinian canons, but it enjoyed little peace, even before its suppression, when its canons were hanged for joining the Pilgrimage of Grace. It had suffered raids by the Scots, and the prior's lodging was a peel-tower.

English Heritage

17 LOWTHER CASTLE
In parkland between A6 and Askham

[NY 5223] ★★★

With a few flags fluttering on its battlemented turrets, under a clear blue sky, it could almost pass for Disneyland. It is a sham-medieval pile, built in 1806 and abandoned 130 years later, when its owners could no longer afford the

Lanercost Priory

upkeep. It looks whole from the outside, but is really a roofless and hollow shell. It was Hugh Lowther, the 5th Earl Lonsdale, who built the mock-Gothic castle on the site of an earlier seat of the powerful Lowther lords of the manor. The architect, Robert Smirke, was recommended to him by Sir George Beaumont. It was the 6th Earl who gave the Lonsdale Belt to boxing. By 1936, the family which had once ruled half of Cumberland was forced to move to a more modest home, and the contents of Lowther Castle were sold and the interior demolished. Still owned by the family, access to the ruin is only permitted during a short period each summer, but can be seen from roads through the extensive park.

Private

18 MARDALE CHURCH
On foot only, SW bank of Haweswater

[NY 4711] +

When Haweswater was turned into a reservoir by the Manchester Water Board in 1940, one of the casualties was the village of Mardale at the southern end of the lake. The tiny church of Holy Trinity, which had a square tower with a weathercock, was blown up, and the farmhouse bulldozed. But when the water level is low, in long dry summers, you can see the remains of the church beneath the surface. Local legend says that the church bells can sometimes be heard ringing under the water.

North West Water

19 PENDRAGON CASTLE
Off B6259 4 miles (6.5 km) S of Kirkby Stephen

[NY 7802] ★

One of those characteristic northern border defensive dwellings known as peel-towers, this one dates from late Norman times. It was burnt down by Scots raiders in 1541, but Lady Anne Clifford restored it after the Civil War. Little remains except the surrounding ditch and part of the rectangular keep. Legend associates it with the father of King Arthur, Uther Pendragon, but it was actually called Mallerstang Castle until the fourteenth century, when Lady Anne's ancestor Robert de Clifford,

Edward I's Warden of the Scottish Marches, apparently renamed it Pendragon.

AM

20 PENRITH CASTLE
S of town centre

[*NY 5129*]   +

Standing in a public park, the red sandstone ruins are of a castle first built by William Strickland, later Archbishop of Canterbury, at the end of the fourteenth century, improved and extended by Ralph Neville, Earl of Westmorland, and by Richard III. Abandoned after the Battle of Bosworth, it soon fell into dereliction and was then used as a stone quarry for other buildings in the town. Unlike other Cumbrian castles, it was built with ranges enclosing a courtyard, and fireplaces and an oven can be seen in the domestic quarters.

English Heritage

21 PIEL CASTLE
[*SD 2363*]   +

The tiny Piel Island in Morecambe Bay, between the crab-like claws of Walney and Foulney, has at its southern tip the remains of a medieval sandstone castle which came into the possession of Furness Abbey (q.v.), the monks rebuilding it to protect their ship-building and wool-exporting activities on the island. Access is by boat from Roa Island, tides permitting.

English Heritage

22 RAVENGLASS BATH HOUSE
By harbour, S of town centre

[*SD 0896*]   +

Locally known as 'Walls Castle' the ruin is a fragment of a Roman bath house, belonging to the coastal fort which covered 4 acres (1.5 ha) of ground. The bath house walls, built of red sandstone, still stand to a substantial height.

English Heritage

23 ST NICHOLAS CHURCH, WHITEHAVEN
Near town centre

[*NX 9718*]   +

One of Whitehaven's two parish churches, it was built in 1883 to replace the earlier church on the site. It was a large church of red sandstone with a west tower. But in 1971 it was destroyed by fire, and is now a ruin standing in public gardens.

24 SHAP ABBEY
Minor road off A6, 1 mile (1.5 km) W of village

[*NY 5415*]   +

Founded for Premonstratensian canons at the end of the twelfth century, it is a sad relic now, with only a late tower standing to any height, and little of the monastic buildings remaining except in plan. Yet it was still a picturesque ruin in the eighteenth century, as we know from engravings. After the Dissolution, the abbey came into the possession of the Lowther family, who used its stone to build their mansion, Lowther Castle, itself now in ruins.

English Heritage

25 WORKINGTON HALL
Near town centre

[*NY 0028*]   +

The home of the Curwen family, this was originally just a medieval peel-tower, but was later extended to become a fine mansion where Sir Henry Curwen welcomed Mary, Queen of Scots, in 1568, fleeing after her escape from Lochleven Castle. Work was done on the house as late as the early nineteenth century, reputedly by John Carr, but it

eventually fell into decay after several changes of ownership, and is now an impressive ruin of various periods set in a wooded park.

Local authority

---

10 *Derbyshire*

See map below

1 BOLSOVER CASTLE
Off A632 W of town centre

[*SK 4770*]   ★

There was a castle here from the eleventh century, but the present ruin is that of an early seventeenth-century mansion built with all the paraphernalia of fortification by Sir Charles Cavendish, son of Bess of Hardwick, and in 1634 Charles I and Henrietta Maria were entertained here on a lavish scale. The 'castle' was wrecked by Parliamentary troops later, but was subsequently repaired. From the eighteenth century, however, it was neglected and fell into partial ruin. The roofless long range or gallery is in picturesque architectural style, with much ornamental stonework,

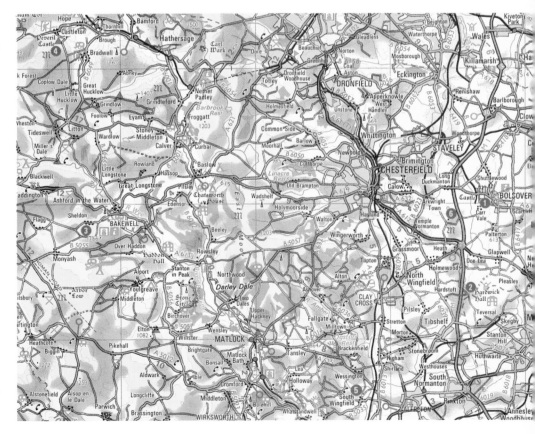

and on another side of the courtyard is an indoor riding school, one of the earliest known, built by William Cavendish, later Duke of Newcastle.

English Heritage

2 HARDWICK OLD HALL
Minor roads S from A617 at Mansfield or Glapwell

[SK 4663]   +

The house in which that great female property-developer the redoubtable Bess of Hardwick grew up still stands in ruins beside the grandiose new mansion she built when she was in her eighties. She was already over 70 when she remodelled her father's old house, employing some of the finest craftsmen of her day. But this ambitious empire-builder then decided that it was not a fit place in which to entertain the queen, whom she was fondly expecting to visit her, and she left the house, which became a servants' lodging when she embarked on the new building. But the queen never came! Bess outlived four husbands (she was first widowed at 13) and, according to legend, a soothsayer told her that her life would be preserved as long as she kept building. She died at 87, when her masons had to suspend work during a hard frost.

English Heritage
(Note: the 'new' hall is open only on certain days in the summer months.)

3 MAGPIE MINE
Off minor road between Sheldon and B5055

[SK 1768]   +

This is the finest remaining site of the extensive former Peak District lead mining industry. The ruins include an engine house and chimney, winding houses and various other buildings. The mine was worked for over two centuries. In the eighteenth century, Defoe described local men of a 'strange, turbulent, quarrelsome temper' who worked 60 fathoms (110 m) deep for 5 d. a day, clad entirely in leather. Visitors are warned to beware of uncovered mine shafts dotted about the landscape.

Peak District Historical Society

4 PEVERIL CASTLE
Off A625 just SW of Castleton

[SK 1482]   *

Set on a hilltop overlooking Castleton, and protected on both flanks by limestone gorges, the castle was built very soon after the Conquest by William Peveril, bailiff of the local royal manors, and is among the earliest castles of stone. But the Peverils' lands were confiscated in 1155 after one of them had poisoned the Earl of Chester, and the king, Henry II, took possession himself and built the square keep and other extensions and improvements. The castle was already in

ruins by the seventeenth century, and the views *from* it are more impressive nowadays than the views *of* it, but it is famous as the castle in Sir Walter Scott's *Peveril of the Peak*.

English Heritage

5 SOUTH WINGFIELD MANOR
Off B5035 through village, 2 miles (3 km) W of Alfreton

[SK 3754]   ★★★

Within two centuries, this fortified manor house of dark Carboniferous sandstone was raised by one Cromwell and reduced by another. Ralph Cromwell, Henry VI's Lord Treasurer of the Exchequer and Master of the Royal Hounds and Falcons, built the place in four years from 1441, but died just before it was completed, and it passed to the 2nd Earl of Shrewsbury, John Talbot, whose family occupied it through the reigns of the Yorkist and Tudor monarchs. George Talbot, the 6th Earl, was charged with the custody of Mary, Queen of Scots, here for a time after her confinement at Tutbury Castle (q.v.). When the 17th Earl died in 1616, the manor passed through various hands until it was partly demolished in the Civil War, and in 1774 much of its stone was taken for building a new house for the then owner, Immanuel Halton. The great hall of South Wingfield was built

Hardwick Old Hall

South Wingfield Manor

over a large vaulted undercroft to raise it above sloping ground, and the undercroft remains one of the most interesting parts of this substantial domestic ruin.

AM

6 SUTTON SCARSDALE HALL
Reached from village, N of A617 near Heath

[SK 4468]   +

This Baroque mansion was built in the eighteenth century for the Earl of Scarsdale, and was a two-storey house of brick faced with stone, with giant fluted pilasters all round and attached columns supporting a central pediment at the front. It was lavishly decorated inside. But it was eventually gutted and partly demolished, and many of its treasures taken to the United States. The ruin looks out over a landscape of opencast mining, and is too modern to be romantic. Only the exterior is accessible at present. A good distant view is from the M1 motorway, looking west just north of junction 29.

English Heritage

11 *Devon*

See maps on pages 35, 38 and 39

1 BERRY POMEROY CASTLE
Minor roads between A381 and A385, 2½ miles (4 km) NE of Totnes

[SX 8362]   **

Reputed to be the most haunted castle in England, it was in the possession of the Seymour family from 1548, when it was purchased by the Protector Somerset, and before that had been held by the de

Berry Pomeroy Castle

Pomeroys since the Conquest. The first family built the medieval castle and the second a Tudor mansion within it, but both buildings were victims of the Civil War and the castle was abandoned before the seventeenth century was out. It occupies a magnificent site in wooded country between Torquay and Totnes, above a tributary of the River Dart, its great twin-towered gatehouse still bearing the de Pomeroy arms and forming a stark contrast with the later domestic structure with its rows of mullioned windows.

English Heritage

2 COLOMBE CASTLE
Minor road off B3161, $\frac{1}{2}$ mile (0.8 km) N of Colyton

[SY 2494] ⊖ *No access* ⊖

One of the many properties of the ubiquitous Courtenays of Devon,

Colcombe was built in the thirteenth century by Hugh Courtenay, Baron of Okehampton, but passed to the Pele family after the demise of the Courtenays. They began rebuilding, but never finished the work, and in due course the 'castle' became relegated to the level of a farmhouse. The kitchen contained a 20-foot (6-m) wide fireplace.

Private

3 DUNKESWELL ABBEY
On minor road, 2 miles (3 km) N of village, 7 miles (11 km) N of Honiton

[ST 1410] ⊖ *No access* ⊖

The walls of the nineteenth-century church to the north of Dunkeswell village are actually the original walls of the Cistercian abbey's thirteenth-century church. Not much else survives, except part of a gatehouse. The abbey was founded by William de Brewer, a regent

during Richard the Lionheart's absences on Crusades, and one of the signatories of Magna Carta. It was dissolved in 1539.

Private

4 EGGESFORD HOUSE
Seen from minor roads W of A377 at Eggesford

[SS 6711] ⊖ *No access* ⊖

It is the shell of a grey stone house, built only in 1832 by the Hon. Newton Fellowes, subsequently Earl of Portsmouth, to replace an earlier mansion of the Chichester family. It once contained fine oak panelling and had a profusion of chimneys, but all that remain are its castellated outer walls. It was dismantled during the First World War. Occupying a magnificent site overlooking the Taw valley and backed

by woods, it is now totally inaccessible. It can be seen, however, looking west from several points in the vicinity of the isolated church ¾ mile (1.2 km) away.

Private

5 EXETER CASTLE
Near city centre

[*SX 9292*]   +

The eighteenth-century Assize Courts (not open) occupy much of the site, but

Exeter had one of the first castles built after the Conquest, William having driven the city's defenders from the protection of the old Roman walls and erected a timber castle at once. It was called Rougemont, for obvious reasons

35

when you see it. By 1071 a gate tower had been built in stone, and this remains, showing Anglo-Saxon influence still, but the ground-floor entrance is now blocked. Some of the later curtain walls still stand to a substantial height, as well as fragments of angle towers, all of which can be seen from the public park which now surrounds the castle.

City of Exeter

6 FRITHELSTOCK PRIORY
Behind village church, between A386 and A388, 2 miles (3 km) W of Great Torrington

[SS 4619]   Tel: 0805 23163

Founded for Augustinian canons around 1220 by one with the splendid name Robert de Bello Campo. There is an interesting story of lingering paganism here in the fourteenth century when the Bishop of Exeter was startled to learn that some of the monks were worshipping an idol like 'the unchaste Diana'. Little remains of the monastic buildings, but parts of the priory church remain on farmland adjacent to the village church. The farmhouse incorporates the former prior's house.

The ruin can be seen from the churchyard but appointments must be made for closer scrutiny.

AM

7 GIDLEIGH CASTLE
Near village church; minor roads from A30 7 miles (11 km) SE of Okehampton

[SX 6688]   ⊖ No access ⊖

In this village on the northern fringe of Dartmoor is the tower or 'keep' of a small fortified manor house of the early fourteenth century. It consisted of a solar above a cellar or undercroft, with a stair-turret on the east side of the square stone tower.

AM

8 GRIMSPOUND

[SX 7080]   +

The remains of this remarkable Bronze Age village on Dartmoor, deserted long before the birth of Christ, bear the name given to the place by Christians, who ascribed to the Devil anything they could not otherwise explain. Thus 'Grim', the old English name for Woden, was identified with the Devil, and his

'pound', a livestock enclosure, was imagined from the huge and roughly circular enclosing wall, surrounding 4 acres (1.6 ha) of land. Inside the enclosure there are two dozen huts or dwellings, circular in shape. They were built of rough moorland granite and no doubt had roofs of turf or thatch. Each dwelling had a little entrance passage, facing south-west, to form a windbreak and keep driving rain and snow out of the living quarters. Some of them had hearths for their winter fires, and a water supply, in the form of a stream, ran through the village. The remains lie about 3 miles (5 km) north-east of Postbridge above an unclassified road running south from B3212 towards Widecombe.

English Heritage

9 HALLSANDS
Minor roads S from Chillington or Stokenham, 1 mile (1.5 km) NW of Start Point

[SX 8138]   +

Near the southernmost tip of Devon are the melancholy remains of a once-thriving fishing village which was

Okehampton Castle

destroyed by the sea, following unwise human interference with nature's forces. The village stood on a narrow shelf of rock looking out over Start Bay, with a population of about 120 living on either side of a tiny village street with shop, post office and pub as well as its houses. In 1897, the Board of Trade gave permission for dredging of gravel to be carried out in the bay, for the extension of Devonport's naval dockyard, and in four years half a million tons of gravel, sand and shingle were dredged from the area, the government ignoring local warnings that the shingle bank which protected the village from the ocean's batterings was being destroyed. But considerable damage was caused by winter storms in 1903 and the following year, exposing the foundations of sea-walls, carrying away sections of the road and causing damage to houses, three of which were rendered uninhabitable. Repairs were carried out, but in January 1917 the sea bombarded Hallsands for two days and nights with a fury that destroyed the village street and 29 houses, making the population homeless. The Board of Trade said the disaster was due to natural causes. Fragments of houses still remain precariously perched on the edges of rocks exposed by the sinking shore-line.

10 HOUND TOR
Off minor road from B3387, 1 mile (1.5 km) S of Manaton

[SX 7479]   +

Unlike Grimspound, this lost village site high on Dartmoor is not prehistoric but medieval, occupied (it is believed) from late Saxon times until the thirteenth century. Excavation only took place in the 1960s. The earliest houses, or huts, were built of turf lined with wattle hurdling, and must have been regularly rebuilt until being replaced by timber and then by the stone houses whose walls we can still see. The presence of corn-drying ovens suggests extensive cultivation in this unlikely spot, but presumably the inhospitable site eventually led to desertion of the settlement, unless it became a victim of the Black Death. The village name comes from the nearby granite outcrop.

English Heritage

11 LYDFORD CASTLE
Near village church, off A386, 8 miles (13 km) SW of Okehampton

[SX 5084]   +

At first sight a Norman motte-and-bailey castle, it was in fact a tower or keep built on a site where houses were demolished to make way for the original castle in the eleventh century, Lydford being then one of the chief towns of Devon. The present square tower was built in the twelfth century, and earth was piled up against the walls later, blocking up the ground floor windows. It was not built specifically as a prison, as some say, but it *was* used as one later, when it no longer had any strategic value, and was the Stannary Prison for the county, with a bad name for rough justice, a local poet writing:

I oft have heard of Lydford law,
How in the morn they hang and draw,
And sit in judgement after.

English Heritage

12 MARISCO CASTLE
SE end of Lundy Island

[SS 1443]   +

The Marisco family ruled the island of Lundy from the second half of the twelfth century, and the ruins of their moated castle remain at the southern tip, the island's only landing point. The 9-foot (3-m) thick walls protected the lords of the isle, who lived on piracy, until William de Marisco was captured and taken to London, where he was hanged, drawn and quartered for allegedly sending one of his henchmen to cut the king's throat. That was in 1242, and afterwards the island changed hands many times, the castle finally falling into ruin. In the eighteenth century some hovels were built inside the rectangular keep – these too are now ruins. Access to this island is chiefly by steamer from Ilfracombe.

Landmark Trust

13 OKEHAMPTON CASTLE
Minor road off B3260, ½ mile (0.8 km) S of town centre

[SX 5894]   ★★★

Mightily impressive as you approach it, the castle stands high above the river in well-wooded countryside at the town's southern outskirts, its shattered walls silhouetted against the sky. Although there was a motte-and-bailey castle here in the eleventh century, the stone castle whose ruins we see now was built by the de Courtenays in the twelfth and following centuries. They held the castle for 350 years, becoming in due course earls of Devon, but in 1538 Henry Courtenay was executed for treason, and his castle was pulled down by order of the king. The keep is the oldest part of the remains, but the later works includes a banqueting hall and buttery, a kitchen with two ovens, and a chapel.

English Heritage

14 PLYMPTON CASTLE
Close to St Maurice's church, near town centre

[SX 5455]   +

Nothing much remains of the castle built in the twelfth century by the lord of the manor, Richard de Redvers, except parts of the walls of a circular stone keep, raised on a motte. The castle is said to have been destroyed in the reign of Stephen, when the rebellious Baldwin de Redvers surrendered to the king's forces. The keep was originally surrounded by a rectangular bailey.

AM

15 ST CATHERINE'S ALMSHOUSE, EXETER
In city centre off High Street

[SX 9292]   +

In Exeter, only a few yards from the cathedral, the red sandstone ruin of this charming almshouse is carefully preserved. It was founded about 1450 by Canon John Stevens, for thirteen poor men, and stood for nearly 500 years, having survived the Dissolution despite being an ecclesiastical foundation. But in May 1942 it was a victim of the *Luftwaffe*'s bombing raid on the city. The almshouse consisted of the inmates' rooms, chapel and refectory, arranged round a small courtyard. The chapel's bellcote remains intact.

City of Exeter

16 ST EDMUND'S CHURCH, EXETER
Near Frog Island SW of city centre

[SX 9192]   +

Sometimes known as St Edmund-on-the-Bridge, it is actually one ruin on top of another, and has been landscaped by the city to form a very appealing scene, though somewhat diminished by being on an island site amid hectic ring-road traffic. What we can see is chiefly the red sandstone undercroft of a thirteenth-century church which was rebuilt in 1834 but destroyed by bombing in the Second World War. The church ruin is supported by the shallow arches of a medieval bridge across the Exe, which

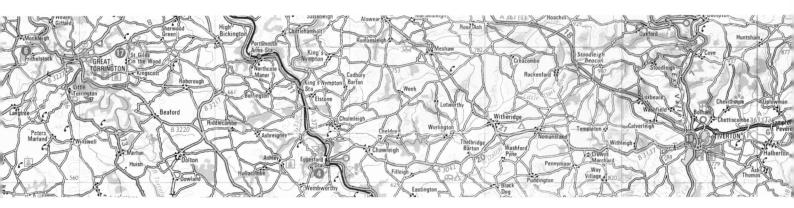

St Edmund's church and medieval bridge, Exeter

formed the main thoroughfare over the river for nearly 600 years, from about 1196 until a new crossing was made in 1778.

City of Exeter

17 STEVENSTONE HOUSE

S of B3227, 2 miles (3 km) E of Great Torrington

[SS 5219]

This house was the home of the Rolle family, the lords of vast lands in Devon from the Tudor period, and was probably the largest and one of the finest mansions in north Devon during its brief lifetime, although Hoskins refers to it as 'villainously ugly'. It was built between 1868 and 1873 by the younger Charles Barry in French chateau style, on the site of an earlier manor house, and had a fine curving stone balustrade separating its garden from the 300-acre deer park. It also had stables, tennis courts and a detached library. But after the First World War half the house was demolished to make it more manageable, the Rolles having long gone. Then it became neglected, troops were billeted in it during the Second World War, and it soon fell into ruin. It is a sad sight now, though offering tantalising glimpses of its former glory.

Mr R. W. Parnell
Strictly by arrangement with the owner

18 TIVERTON CASTLE

Close to parish church, near town centre

[SS 9512] ★★★ *Tel: 0884 255200*

Tucked in among other buildings in the town, it hardly strikes you as a defensible fortress. It was built by Richard de Redvers, whom Henry I made lord of the manor in 1106, but not much of his work remains, most of the castle being of the thirteenth century with a Tudor mansion

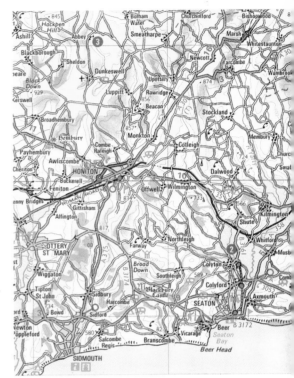

superimposed. The castle became the chief seat of the Courtenay Earls of Devon until the mid-sixteenth century, and was dismantled 100 years later when it was taken by Fairfax in the Civil War. Apart from the later mansion, the chief remains are of a gatehouse and two angle towers of the former quadrangular castle.

AM

19 TOTNES CASTLE
Minor road off A381 near town centre

[SX 8060]   ★★★   Tel: 0803 864406

Although its more or less circular shell keep is remarkably intact, and one of the best-preserved in the country with its parapet and crenellations almost complete, little else remains except fragments of the outer bailey's curtain wall. The ramparts stand high on a motte, and date from a fourteenth-century rebuilding by the Zouche family, one of the many owners of the castle, which began as an early Norman fortification on an Anglo-Saxon site. The walls of the shell keep are nearly 7 feet (2 m) thick and 20 feet (6 m) high.

English Heritage

20 WHEAL BETSY ENGINE-HOUSE

[SX 5181]   +

North of the village of Mary Tavy, below the Okehampton to Tavistock road, is this ruin of a stone-built engine-house and its chimney stack. Its job was to pump water from the workings of the Prince Arthur Consols mine, which produced lead, zinc and silver in the eighteenth and nineteenth centuries. The mine was still working as late as the 1870s.

National Trust

Wheal Betsy Engine-house on Dartmoor

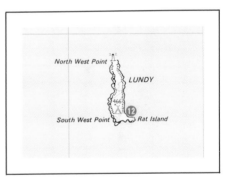

12 Dorset

See maps on pages 42 and 43

1 ABBOTSBURY ABBEY
Off B3157 near village centre

[SY 5785]   +

Very little remains of the Benedictine monastery founded about 1045 by one Orc, a steward of King Canute, and dissolved in 1539, but as the place is so well known, and its swannery and huge medieval barn so much visited, such ruins as there are deserve an entry here. Parts have been incorporated in other nearby buildings, notably Abbey House, near the church. The eastern gable of one of the conventual buildings remains.

English Heritage

England

2 BINDON ABBEY
Minor road off B3071, ½ mile (0.8 km) E of Wool

[SY 8586] ★

Robert de Newburgh founded this Cistercian monastery in 1172, but its remains are sadly sparse, though the customary layout of the order's establishments can be followed from the foundations and scant fragments of walls. The abbey was dissolved in 1539. In the seventeenth century the property came to the Catholic Weld family, who built a summer-house close to the abbey church whose ruins had already provided most of the stone for the 3rd Viscount Bindon's Lulworth Castle – also a Weld property later. Angel Clare, hero of Hardy's *Tess of the D'Urbervilles*, worked at the Bindon flour mill, and the abbey's remains feature in the novel.

Private

3 CHRISTCHURCH CASTLE
Minor road off B3059 near town centre

[SZ 1692] +

Built originally by Richard de Redvers, Earl of Devon, to whom the manor was granted by Henry I. Not much of that castle remains, however, though it was owned later by the Neville earls of Warwick. More interesting are the ruins of the so-called Castle Hall, or Constable's House, built later in the twelfth century by the second Redvers earl. This was built in the outer bailey of the castle, and is now in the grounds of a hotel. You can see a fireplace with its chimney rising above it; a garderobe with its drainage channel running to the stream; and two-light Norman windows at first floor level with carved chevron decoration above.

English Heritage

Edward the Martyr's Gate, with displaced tower at Corfe

Knowlton Church

4 CORFE CASTLE
*At N end of village of that name, 4 miles
(6.5 km) SE of Wareham*

[SY 9582] ★

In my view, Corfe is not only one of the
most spectacular, but also one of the
most fascinating of all the medieval
castles of Britain. It stands on a conical
hilltop and dominates the landscape for
miles around, its pale Purbeck limestone
gleaming white in the sunlight of
summer, or looming suddenly and
overwhelmingly out of the fog in winter.
Its origins go back to before the
Conquest, when it was built, mostly of
timber, no doubt, to guard a gap in the
Purbeck Hills known once as Corvesgate.
The Saxon king Edward, later known as
the Martyr, was stabbed to death here in
978, at the instigation of his step-mother.
A stronger castle, known then as
Wareham Castle, was erected by William

of Normandy, but its chief feature today,
the tall keep known as the King's Tower,
came later, around 1100, and King John
carried out extensive improvements to a
castle he used partly as a state prison,
starving to death in its dungeons 22
French noblemen. Edward II was also
imprisoned here before being taken to
Berkeley Castle, where he was done to
death in ghastly manner. In 1572
Elizabeth I sold the castle to Sir
Christopher Hatton, and then it passed
to the Bankes family, who owned it,
apart from the Commonwealth period,
until only a few years ago, when it was
passed to the National Trust. The
bombardment of the castle by
Parliamentary troops in 1646 must have
been witnessed by the villagers below
with disbelief, as gunpowder exploded
and brought masonry crashing to the
ground. One of the towers of Edward the
Martyr's Gate was blown from its

foundations but remained upright and
intact, and you can still see the huge rent
where it was separated from the
adjoining stonework.

National Trust

5 KNOWLTON CHURCH
*Beside minor road off B3078, 1 mile
(1.5 km) S of Wimborne St Giles*

[SU 0210] +

A forlorn small church built of flint and
of unknown dedication, Knowlton would
seem to have little to recommend it to the
notice of connoisseurs of ruins, but it is
worth travelling a long way to see. It is of
Norman origin, and stands at the centre
of a circular Bronze Age earthwork
surrounded by a ditch and bank. The
earthwork is one of the so-called
Knowlton Rings, of unknown purpose.
Many early Christian churches were

built on pagan sites, following Pope Gregory's injunction to Augustine to absorb rather than destroy places of idolatry, but few of the prehistoric sites can now be appreciated as clearly as this one. The church itself has not been in use since 1647, the original village it served having vanished, possibly because the community felt uneasy in the company of lingering pagan forces. Not surprisingly, it is said to be haunted, but no ghosts put in an appearance when I spent a night there a few years ago. There is also a legend that one of the church's bells lies in the River Stour, and that whenever attempts were made to recover it, the rope invariably and inexplicably broke. It was said that 'All the devils in Hell could never pull up Knowlton bell'.

English Heritage

6 RUFUS CASTLE
On Isle of Portland, off minor road SE of Easton

[SY 6971]   ⊖ *No access* ⊖

On the eastern side of the Isle of Portland, parts of it have collapsed into the sea as shown by the fact that the wall facing the sea is clearly a thin internal one rather than a defensive exterior wall. Consequently, the remains are dangerous. It was erected in the fifteenth century on the site of an earlier castle, and was built, naturally enough, of Portland stone, in the form of a five-sided tower. George III granted the castle to Admiral Sir William Penn, then Governor of Portland.

Private

7 SANDSFOOT CASTLE
NW shore of Portland Harbour, Weymouth

[SY 6777]   +

One of the chain of coastal artillery forts built by Henry VIII to protect the south coast harbours from the French, this one was a twin of Portland Castle, two miles south, and between them their heavy cannon could cover all of Weymouth Bay. The castle had little protection from the landward side, and was never put to the test in the Civil War, but remained as a harbour defence until coastal erosion and local builders robbed it of its masonry. The gun emplacements collapsed into the sea in the nineteenth century, and only parts of the living quarters remain.

Weymouth Corporation

Corfe Castle

8 SHERBORNE OLD CASTLE

Minor road off B3145, E outskirts of town

[ST 6416] ★

Roger, Bishop of Salisbury, built this castle, which was really more of a fortified palace, in the first quarter of the twelfth century. It was built of the glorious golden limestone from the quarries of Ham Hill, a few miles west, which lent itself to the new taste for ashlar masonry, and was erected on the same side of the River Yeo as the town. The remains of the domestic range, built within a large walled bailey and round a courtyard, have some interesting architectural details, with zig-zig decoration, vaulting, and evidence of newel staircases. Later in the twelfth century the castle became Crown property, and eventually Elizabeth I sold it to Sir Walter Raleigh, who began to modernize it, then changed his mind and built the new castle instead. The old castle was reduced to ruin in the Civil War.

English Heritage

Sherborne Old Castle

13 Durham

See map on page 46

1 BARNARD CASTLE
Near town centre

[NZ 0416] ★★★

This castle standing on a cliff above the River Tees was built by Bernard Baliol, whose father had aided the Conqueror and whose descendants include a Scottish king and the founder of Balliol College, Oxford. It eventually came into the possession of Richard III through his marriage to Anne Neville, daughter of Warwick 'the king-maker', and the castle remained Crown property until the Civil War. It was besieged in 1569 during the northern rebellion under the earls of Northumberland and Westmorland, and the occupants, under Sir George Bowes, were starved into surrender, but when the rebellion was crushed, Bowes had the satisfaction (I suppose) of hanging more than 60 of the insurgents. The castle's remains include the Brackenbury Tower, used as a prison and named after Sir Robert Brackenbury, Lieutenant of the Tower of London under Edward IV and Richard III.

English Heritage

2 BOWES CASTLE
Off A66 W of village, 4 miles (6.5 km) SW of Barnard Castle

[NY 9913] +

The massive three-storey rectangular keep, built by Henry II around 1175, is the sole feature of this castle. It was built to guard the Stainmore Pass into Yorkshire from the Pennines against Scottish raiders, and was sited in a former Roman fort, Lavatrae, some of its sandstone coming from the Roman remains. Although there are traces of an inner and outer bailey, the castle consisted of no other buildings than this

Barnard Castle

tower, which originally had a kind of porch giving access to the ground floor.

English Heritage

3 DERWENTCOTE FURNACE
½ *mile (0.8 km) E of Hamsterley, off A694 N of Consett*

[NZ 1356]   +

Also known as Hamsterley Furnace, it is the country's only remaining eighteenth-century cementation furnace, a conical building of stone in which an early technique for converting iron into steel was practised. It was in use until the late nineteenth century, when the improved 'crucible' method made it redundant.

Durham County Council

4 EGGLESTONE ABBEY
Minor road off B6277 between Barnard Castle and Rokeby

[NZ 0615]   +

Founded by Ralph de Malton in the twelfth century for Premonstratensian canons, it is unusual in being placed on a hilltop, above the River Tees. Some walls of the nave and chancel of the church remain, of substantial height, with a variety of Gothic windows. Of the monastic buildings, only the monks' refectory is still there, converted into a house after the Dissolution by Robert Strelley, and itself now a ruin, with mullioned windows, fireplaces and chimneys.

English Heritage

5 FINCHALE PRIORY
Minor road between A167 and A690, 3 miles (5 km) N of Durham

[NZ 2947]   ★

Beautifully set in a loop of the River Wear a few miles north of the city of

Egglestone Abbey: the Tudor house in the east range

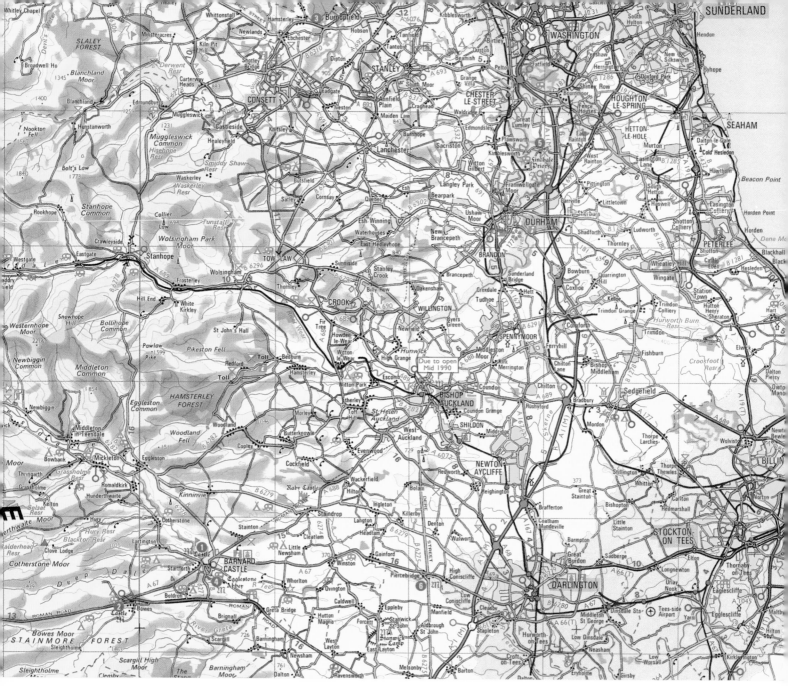

Durham, the ruins of this thirteenth-century foundation for Premonstratensian canons are still peaceful and attractive. A chapel was built here in the twelfth century for pilgrims who came to the spot where St Godric had settled until his death in 1170 at the age of 105. The monastery was begun a quarter of a century later, and the chancel of the new church took the place of the little chapel. The remains are extensive and the layout of the monastic buildings clear. From the fourteenth century to the Dissolution in 1538, Finchale seems to have been used as a sort of holiday or convalescent home for the monks of Durham Cathedral, the permanent residents here being only five in number. An oriel window in one room formerly had a window seat which was reputed to ensure issue for any sterile

woman who, 'having performed certain ceremonies', sat upon it. But the eighteenth-century antiquary Francis Grose observed slyly that when the priory was dissolved, and the monks gone, the seat strangely lost its magical power.

English Heritage

6 ROMAN BRIDGE, PIERCEBRIDGE
B6275 just S of A67 at Piercebridge

[NZ 2115] +

Although, strictly speaking, it is on the Yorkshire bank of the Tees, I have included it under Durham because that is where the village, and the fort with which it is associated, lie. You can see the southern abutment and remains of the

piers which carried a timber bridge over the river as part of Dere Street, built in the second century.

English Heritage

---

14 *East Sussex*

See maps on page 47

1 BATTLE ABBEY
Close to town centre

[TQ 7415] ★

William of Normandy vowed that if he should be rewarded with victory, he would build an abbey in thanksgiving and, true to his word, he raised this

Bodiam Castle

Bodiam Castle remain intact. One of Britain's best known ruins, largely on account of its picturesque qualities, Bodiam sits sedately in the middle of a tree-lined moat, which reflects the stone towers and battlements when it is not thick with water-lilies. Richard II gave permission in 1385 for Sir Edward Dalyngrigge, a warrior of advanced years, to fortify his 'manor house of Bodyham, near the sea' as part of the south coast defence system against French invasion. In fact, Sir Edward demolished his manor house and raised this full-scale military castle instead, with drawbridges, portcullises and machicolations, but with built-in domestic comfort and convenience as

Benedictine monastery on the site of the Battle of Hastings, the high altar occupying the spot where King Harold fell. Little of it remains now. What one king founded in 1067, another suppressed in 1538. It was then granted to Sir Anthony Browne, Henry VIII's Master of the Horse, who demolished the church and cloisters and built a house out of the abbot's quarters. A monk is supposed to have laid a curse of fire on the family, fulfilled when Cowdray House (q.v.) was burnt down in the eighteenth century. The abbey has passed through many ownerships since the Dissolution, and has been much altered and restored, part becoming a school for girls. But there are still interesting remains at this historic site, including a fine gatehouse and the dormitory block, a tall gabled building with an undercroft.

English Heritage

2 BAYHAM ABBEY
Off B2169 4 miles (6.5 km) SE of Tunbridge Wells

[TQ6536] **★★**

Pevsner called it 'the most impressive ruin of Sussex', and it stands now as a picturesque ornament on the former estate of the Camden earls, near Tunbridge Wells. But it was originally an abbey of the Premonstratensian order, built early in the thirteenth century in a meadow beside the River Teise, which forms the modern boundary at this point between Sussex and Kent. The abbey was one of the early victims of the Dissolution, Cardinal Wolsey appropriating its wealth to finance his colleges at Oxford and Ipswich.

English Heritage

3 BODIAM CASTLE
Close to village, 3½ miles (6 km) SE of Hawkhurst

[TQ7825] **★★★** *Tel: 058 083 436*

The age of chivalry can never be dead, one may feel, while the outer walls of

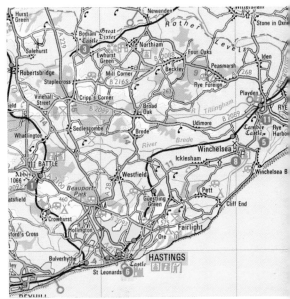

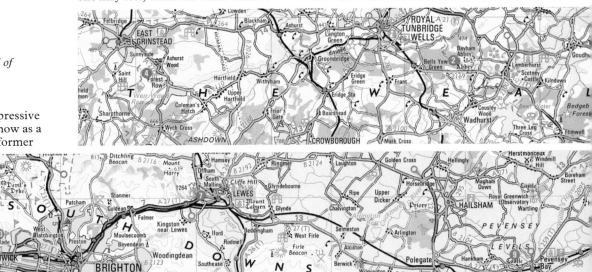

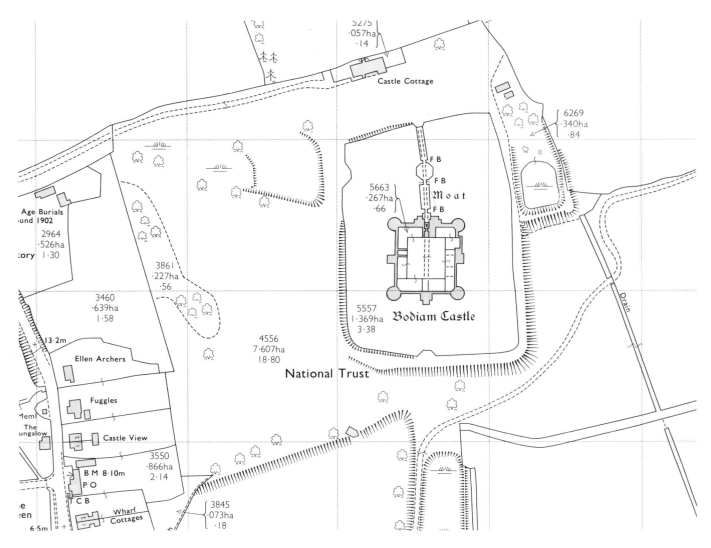

well, including more than 30 wall fireplaces – a fairly recent innovation – replacing the customary central floor-hearths, and plenteous garderobes draining into the moat which also supplied the drinking water! The castle was never attacked, in fact, until the Civil War, when its innards were reduced to the hollow shell we find when we cross the modern causeway over the moat and discover, beyond the romantic and complete façade, a scene of devastation.

National Trust

4 BRAMBLETYE

Off A22, ½ mile (0.8 km) NW of Forest Row

[TQ 4135]   +

Sir Henry Compton built the house in 1631. It was of Jacobean symmetry, with

Bayham Abbey

four-storey ogee-capped angle towers flanking the two-storey centre, with its porch and mullioned and transomed windows. It also had a fine gatehouse. In 1683 the house belonged to Sir James Richards, who came under suspicion as a traitor, involved in the Rye House conspiracy, when a store of arms was found here, and he disappeared while out hunting, having no doubt been forewarned. It was believed he fled to Spain, never to return, and his house was thus redundant.

Private

5 CAMBER CASTLE
E of A259, 1 mile (1.5 km) S of Rye

[TQ 9218] ⊜ *No access* ⊜

One of the artillery forts built by Stefan von Haschenperg for Henry VIII, to defend the south coast against the French. This one was a rebuilding of an

older castle on the site, at the estuary of the River Rother. The central circular tower belonged to the earlier building. The outer wall was provided with four semi-circular bastions and a gatehouse, stone outside and brick inside. By the Civil War, the sea had receded and the castle no longer had any value. It was dismantled anyway. At present there is no public access. It can be seen at a distance from the road between Rye and Winchelsea.

AM

6 HASTINGS CASTLE
West Hill, on sea front

[TQ 8209] +

The Bayeux Tapestry shows Hastings Castle being built – men (native labourers) are shovelling stones to raise the motte. This was a timber castle raised by William of Normandy before

the Battle of Hastings. It was replaced by the first stone structure a few years later, but nothing of significance remains from that either. The curtain wall, gatehouse and fragments of towers we can see now date from the twelfth and thirteenth centuries, as did the keep built by Henry II, which collapsed into the sea. The castle commanded a fine view, from its clifftop site, of the town and beach below.

Hastings Corporation

7 LEWES CASTLE
Close to town centre

[TQ 4110] ★★★

Unusual – indeed, rare – in having *two* mottes, the first stone castle was built of flint by about 1100. Both mottes (built of chalk blocks) had shell keeps, but nothing remains of the one on the more northerly mound. The ruins of the other

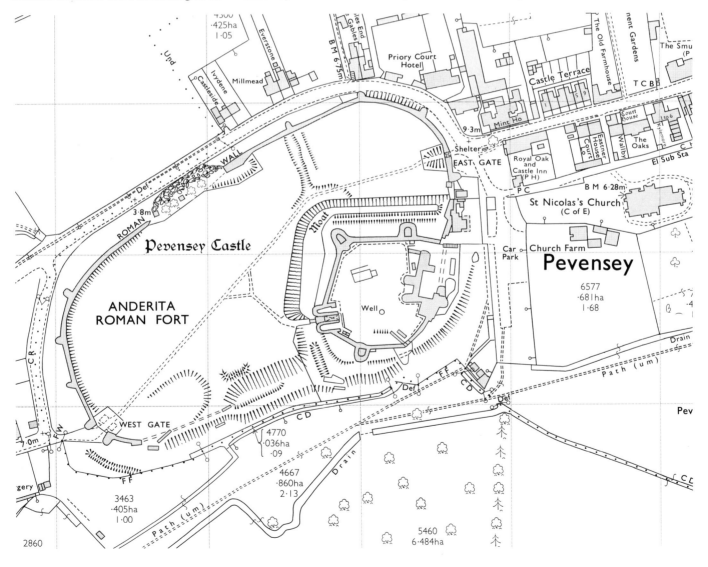

show an oval-shaped shell with two turrets added in the thirteenth century. There are also sections of curtain walling and fragments of towers, but the most substantial survival is the fourteenth-century barbican, partly restored, which formerly had four cylindrical turrets faced with knapped flints, and still shows two of them flanking a Gothic entrance arch, with arrow slits, machicolations and battlements above, as well as portcullis grooves. The castle was already deserted in the fourteenth century, and gradually fell into decay, helped along by local people taking its material.

Sussex Archaeological Society

8 NEW WINCHELSEA CHURCH
St Thomas Street, town centre

[*TQ 9017*]   +

'New' Winchelsea was built when the old town was threatened with inundation by the sea, which finally happened in the thirteenth century; but the regularly planned new town also suffered, both from silting up and from the French, and the church of St Thomas, though still in use, is reduced in size and partly in ruins.

Church of England

9 PEVENSEY CASTLE
Minor road off A27, in village

[*TQ 6404*]   ★

The Romans originally fortified this place, which they called Anderita, in the third century, on what was then an island in the marshy Pevensey Levels. The fort enclosed over 8 acres (3 ha), and the outer wall, to cope with the soft ground which was lapped by the sea at high tide, was raised on a bed of clay and flints 15 feet (4.5 m) wide with oak beams set on top in cement. The wall itself was of flint and rubble, faced with dressed stone and with courses of Roman tile, and was nearly 30 feet (9 m) high. It has withstood repeated bombardment, but remains largely intact. No wonder William of Normandy occupied it immediately when he landed 60,000 men in Pevensey Bay, and built a castle within it, using the Roman walls as the curtain walls of the outer bailey. The domestic arrangements of the Norman castle took second place to its defensive needs, and in terms of comforts, Pevensey was fairly primitive. A moat was created to protect the inner castle further, and D-shaped towers in the curtain wall imitated the Roman bastions. Among abortive besiegers of Pevensey Castle were King Stephen, Simon de Montfort and the allies of Richard II. The occupant of the castle on the latter occasion was Lady Jane Pelham, who managed to get a letter out to her absent husband, remarking almost nonchalantly: 'If it like you to know my fare, I am here laid by in manner of a siege . . . so that I may not out nor no victuals get me, but with much hard.' The castle had fallen into neglect by the Civil War period, but in the Second World War it was fitted with gun emplacements to guard the coast against Hitler's expected invasion.

English Heritage

The Norman inner bailey of Pevensey Castle

10 PORTSLADE MANOR
Close to parish church, W of Brighton

[*TQ 2506*]   *By permission*

At the western fringes of Brighton, the village churchyard at Portslade shares with the grounds of the adjacent convent the fragmentary remains of a mid-twelfth-century manor house, built of flint, and much robbed for local building, but showing a single-light window in one wall. It was one of the earliest manor houses built when the lords of manors felt it safe to come out of their fortifications. The ruins were considerably more extensive up to the early nineteenth century, but the stone of the real ruin was plundered for the purpose of building a sham one not far away.

St Mary's Convent

11 RYE PRIORY
On Conduit Hill, close to town centre

[*TQ 9220*]   +

On Conduit Hill lie the sparse remains of a chapel of a priory founded for Austin friars, moved to this location late in the fourteenth century to bring it in from the cold, as it were. It was formerly on East Cliff, outside the town walls, where it was also exposed to French attack. It is believed that the windows of the earlier building were taken out and transferred to the new one. The priory was finally destroyed, not by the French, but by Henry VIII, in 1539.

AM

---

15 Essex

See map on page 51

1 BALKERNE GATE, COLCHESTER
W side of town centre

[*TL 9925*]   +

The most impressive remaining part of the city walls of Camulodunum, colonized under the Roman emperor Claudius in AD 49 and sacked by the British queen Boudicca in 61. We might easily imagine the ghastly scenes these stones could describe if we could but induce sounds or images from them as from a record or video tape! But the walls and gate were built long after the British

revolt, for Tacitus tells us that destroying the Roman town seemed easy to the Iceni, for it had no walls. The Balkerne Gate was built on the road to London, and was over 100 feet (30 m) in length, with two wide openings for wagons and horses and two narrower ones for pedestrians. But after the Roman withdrawal, the London road was re-routed and the gateway partly blocked up, and it was further destroyed in the Civil War siege of the city and its consequences.

Colchester Corporation

2 HADLEIGH CASTLE

¾ *mile (1.2 km) S of A13 through village, 5 miles (8 km) W of Southend-on-Sea*

[TQ 8186]   +

To those who know the castle near Southend only in the dramatic paintings

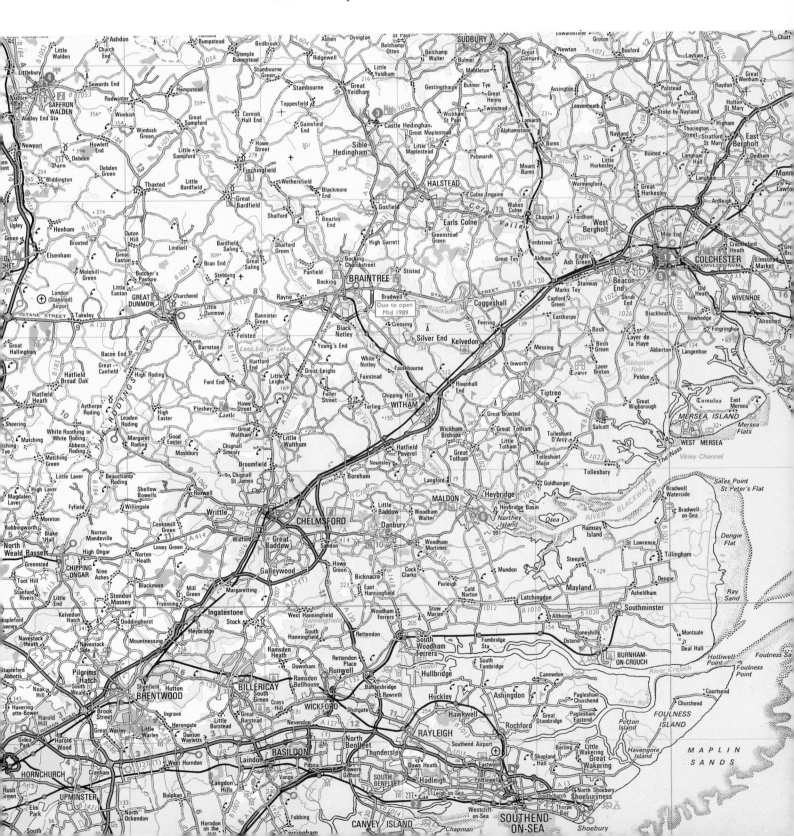

The keep of Hedingham Castle

and sketches of John Constable, a visit to this ruin may prove to be a let-down, for the artist elevated the broken towers and surrounded them with scudding clouds and wheeling birds in an evocative expression of melancholy feeling. The present castle was built by Edward III to guard the Thames estuary, but there was an earlier castle, built by Hubert de Burgh, and the plan of this was largely retained, though it was out of date from the military point of view. It had no keep, but relied for defence on its curtain wall and four circular towers.

English Heritage

3 HEDINGHAM CASTLE
N side of Castle Hedingham village, 7 miles (11 km) SW of Sudbury

[TL 7835] ★★★

This castle, which is still in private ownership, was built around 1130 by Aubrey de Vere, ancestor of the earls of Oxford. It stands on the site of a prehistoric earthwork, and all the castle's outer defences have now gone, but the four-storey keep of dressed Barnack limestone, originally over 100 feet (30 m) high, is an impressive relic, its walls being 12 feet (3.7 m) thick at the base. Entered via an exterior staircase and a decorated Norman arch, it was provided with wall fireplaces, and is believed to be one of the first castles to have chimney flues, which were built into one of its buttresses. King Stephen's consort, Matilda of Boulogne, is said to have died here in 1152. The castle's present ruined state is, for once, nothing to do with Cromwell. The 17th Earl of Oxford, a drunkard and spendthrift, dismantled and disposed of the property at the end of the sixteenth century, and it was further damaged by a serious fire in 1918.

Private

4 SAFFRON WALDEN CASTLE
NW of town centre

[TL 5338] +

All that remains of the twelfth-century castle are the flint rubble walls of the great rectangular keep, perched on a natural hill. It was built by Geoffrey de Mandeville on the site of an Anglo-Saxon fort.

AM

5 ST BOTOLPH'S PRIORY, COLCHESTER
Near St Botolph's station

[TL 9924] +

Only the west front and the nave of the priory church remain from this foundation of about 1095, but the ruins are impressive enough. The church was large, and was built partly of Roman brick, with massive piers nearly 6 feet (2 m) in diameter. Austere in appearance now, it is important as the first English house of Augustinian canons.

English Heritage

6 ST GILES HOSPITAL, MALDON
Near town centre

[TL 8506] +

Scant remains of the chapel of a lazar house, or leper hospital, founded by Henry II about 1164 and, as a dependency of Beeleigh Abbey, suppressed at the Dissolution, by which time it was an almshouse. All defective bread, meat and fish in the town went to the master for the maintenance of the leprous inmates, which cannot have helped their recovery rate. The surviving fragments include Norman work with Roman brick.

7 VIRLEY CHURCH
Minor road off B1026, 1¾ miles (3 km) NE of Tolleshunt D'Arcy

[TL 9513] +

The thirteenth-century church of St Mary was brought to ruin by the earthquake which occurred on 23 April 1884 – the most serious recorded in Britain for some 400 years. Many buildings were damaged in this area between Colchester and the River Blackwater, including several churches,

but whereas most were repaired, like the one at Salcott across the stream, Virley's was left to rot.

---

16 Gloucestershire

See map on page 54

1 BELAS KNAP
Minor road between B4632 at Winchcombe and Charlton Abbots

[SP 0225] +

Some restoration has been carried out on this neolithic long barrow to make it safe for access. It is the best example in the country of a chambered tomb with a false entrance, made not, perhaps, to mislead

grave robbers, like those of the Egyptian pyramids, but evil spirits, as Jacquetta Hawkes suggested. Its date is about 3500 BC. Many human remains were found during excavations. Many of them had obviously received blows to the head, though these were not necessarily the causes of death. The entrances to the burial chambers were from the sides of the mound, and were originally sealed up, but are now open to allow access.

English Heritage

2 CHEDWORTH VILLA
Minor road off A429 at Fossebridge, 1 mile (1.5 km) N of Chedworth village

[SP 0513] *** *Tel: 024 289 256*

A gamekeeper digging for his ferret discovered the remains of this impressive

Chedworth Roman villa

5 HETTY PEGLER'S TUMP
Beside B4066, 3½ miles (5.5 km) NE of Dursley

[*SO 7900*]   +

It only just qualifies as a ruin, for it is a remarkably complete neolithic long barrow, near Nympsfield. Its curious popular name comes from the wife of a farmer who owned the land in the seventeenth century. A massive lintel marks the entrance to a passage built of dry-stone walling and slabs of stone, giving access to five burial chambers originally, but two of them have been sealed off. As well as the 20 burials discovered inside during nineteenth-century excavations, two human skeletons were found buried outside, along with the jawbones of wild boars. You will require a torch to appreciate the interior fully.

English Heritage

6 ST JOHN'S HOSPITAL, CIRENCESTER
Spitalgate, close to town centre

[*SP 0201*]   +

Founded by Henry I before 1135 for three poor men and three poor women, the almshouse was built in Spitalgate Lane and dedicated to St John the Evangelist. It was extended by the Bishop of Worcester in 1317, so probably suppressed as an ecclesiastical establishment at the Dissolution, although hospitals of royal foundation were sometimes spared. It was certainly refounded later, but I am not sure what brought it to its present ruinous state. What remains is the four-bay arcade of the medieval common hall, alongside the street pavement, with pointed arches supported on short columns with scalloped capitals.

Cirencester Corporation

---

17 Greater Manchester

See map on page 55

1 ARDERN HALL
Minor road off A6017 between Stockport and Denton

[*SJ 9193*]   +

This ruined house with a tower, near Bredbury, is said to have been built in

---

Roman villa in 1864. It was probably the headquarters of an agricultural estate deriving its wealth from wool, and seems to have been built originally in the second century AD and enlarged in the third. It was a two-storey house built of Cotswold stone and tiles, with baths and underfloor heating. A chi-rho symbol was found on one of the stones forming a cistern, or nymphaeum, suggesting that the family who lived here at one time may have been Christian converts. The ruins have been rather over-protected, low walls being rebuilt with capping tiles which make them look rather artificial. But the layout can be followed clearly, and there is also a museum on the site.

National Trust

3 GREYFRIARS PRIORY, GLOUCESTER
Greyfriars Walk, off Southgate Street

[*SO 8318*]   +

Remains of the church of a Franciscan friary founded about 1230 and suppressed in 1538. Franciscan remains are fairly scarce because, since the nature of their order demanded the friars' presence in the midst of poverty, their establishments were in overcrowded medieval towns, which re-used the available space after the Dissolution. In Gloucester, only the nave and north aisle of the church remain, facing the churchyard of St Mary de Crypt, and attached to the nineteenth-century Greyfriars House.

English Heritage

4 HAILES ABBEY
Minor road off B4632, 2 miles (3 km) NE of Winchcombe

[*SP 0530*]   ***   Tel: 0242 602398

It is one of my favourite ecclesiastical ruins, partly because it remains serene, and its Cotswold limestone glows like old gold in the sunlight, among meadows grazed by sheep. It was founded as a Cistercian house in 1246 by Richard, Earl of Cornwall, and built at a cost of 10,000 marks. It was consecrated in the presence of Henry III and Eleanor of Provence, with a retinue of bishops, lords and ladies, and 300 knights, but its subsequent fame rests on the gift from Richard's son Edmund of a crystal phial containing, it was said, blood from the body of Jesus. This holy relic brought continuous pilgrimage to Hailes, and considerable wealth, until it was exposed at the Dissolution as clarified honey coloured with saffron. The remains are not extensive – the easily-worked stone made the place an irresistible quarry for local builders.

English Heritage

1597. As well as stepped gables, it has a curious tripartite stepped window with trefoiled lights. It was in ruins before the turn of the present century.

2 BROADLEY STATION
Minor road W of A671 at Healey, near Rochdale

[SD 8815] +

The railway station at Broadley, just north of Rochdale, was a casualty of the Beeching axe in the 1960s, when the Rochdale-Bacup line was closed, but its ruins can still be found, overgrown and almost entirely hidden among the vegetation of Healey Dell.

3 RINGLEY CHURCH
In parish churchyard, off A667 1 mile (1.5 km) E of Kearsley

[SD 7605] +

In the same churchyard as the parish church, a solitary tower remains from the church of 1625, which the new church of 1850 replaced.

Church of England

18 Hampshire

See map on page 58

1 BASING HOUSE
Minor road off A30, ½ mile (0.8 km) S of village. E of Basingstoke

[SU 6652] ★★★

This magnificent mansion, built largely in the sixteenth century by Sir William Paulet, Marquis of Winchester, was originally a castle dating back to the Norman period. It was brought to ruin by Cromwell, who himself led the final assault on the fortified Royalist house taking 300 prisoners, including the architect Inigo Jones. It was looted by Parliamentary troops and then destroyed by fire. Cromwell then decreed that 'whoever will come for brick or stone shall freely have the same for his pains'. Queen Elizabeth had twice been a guest of the Paulets here, and it is said that her second visit cost his lordship so much that he had to demolish part of the house to pay for it.

Hampshire County Council

Part of the palace at Bishop's Waltham

2 BEAULIEU ABBEY

*Off B3054 just NE of village, 6 miles
(10 km) NE of Lymington*

[*SU 3802*]   ★

A somewhat complicated site, the
present church is the former monks'
refectory of a large Cistercian abbey, and
the present home of the Montagu family
is the former gatehouse, much altered.
The original abbey church has almost
entirely gone except for the foundations,
Henry VIII having used the stone for
some of his south-coast castles. It was
among the country's largest Cistercian
churches. There are interesting remains
of the monastic buildings, though they
have partly been made to serve the
commercial purposes of a stately home –
the lay brothers' quarters now form a
restaurant. The abbey was founded by
King John in 1204 and its church was
consecrated in the presence of Henry III.

Lord Montagu of Beaulieu

3 BISHOP'S WALTHAM PALACE

*Close to village centre on A333, 7 miles
(11 km) N of Fareham*

[*SU 5517*]   ★★★   *Tel: 04893 2460*

This historic residence of the bishops of
Winchester was begun around 1136 by
Henry de Blois, brother of King
Stephen, and developed over the
centuries into a splendid palace in a 100-
acre (40-ha) park. Henry II held a
council of war here in 1182 before his
Crusade, and Richard I was entertained
after his coronation in Winchester
Cathedral. William of Wykeham carried
out major rebuilding of the palace and he
died there in 1404. The Civil War was
responsible for the palace's ruination. It
was besieged by Cromwell's troops, and
the then bishop escaped hidden, it is
said, in a cartload of dung. The remains
of the buildings, arranged round a
courtyard and surrounded by a moat, are
extensive, and show building of various
materials and periods.

English Heritage

4 THE GRANGE, NORTHINGTON

*Off B3046, ½ mile (0.8 km) S of village and
6½ miles (10.5 km) NE of Winchester*

[*SU 5636*]   + *(exterior)*

It is debatable whether this house should
be described as a ruin or not at present,
because although the interior is gutted,
one can only see the outside, and that is
perfect, having been restored in part.
The house was built by William Wilkins
in 1809–16 for Henry Drummond
around an earlier house on the site, and
was one of the earliest neo-classical
mansions in the country. The Prince of
Wales (later George IV) rented it for a
few years, and Thomas Carlyle stayed
here and admired the house. It was
threatened with demolition in the 1960s,
but has been saved as what Pevsner
called a 'national architectural
monument'.

English Heritage

5 HOLYROOD CHURCH, SOUTHAMPTON

*Near city centre, junction of High Street
and Bernard Street*

[*SU 4211*]   +

The fourteenth-century church, partly
rebuilt in the nineteenth century, was
bombed during the Second World War,
when, ironically, the parts that survived
best – the chancel and tower – were the
medieval and not the Victorian building
work. The ruin has been preserved as a
memorial to merchant seamen who lost
their lives in the war.

Church of England

6 HOLY TRINITY CHURCH, BASINGSTOKE

Chapel Hill, near the railway station

[*SU 6352*]   +

The brick remains of a guild chapel

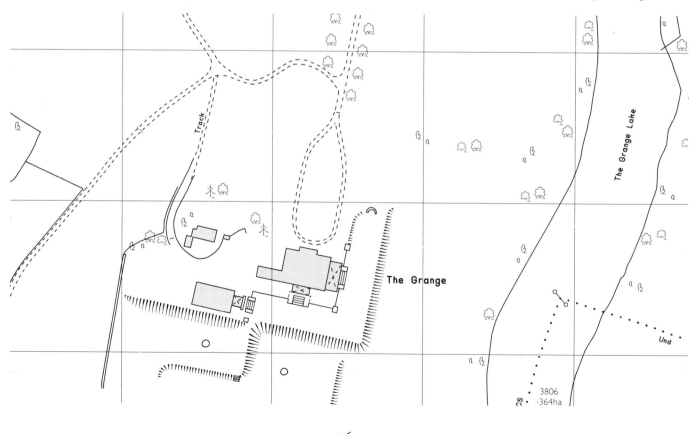

Netley Abbey

stand in an ancient cemetery north of the town centre. It was built by Lord Sandys in 1524, and was attached to the earlier flint chapel of the Holy Ghost, of which only a fragment remains.

7 NETLEY ABBEY
Minor roads from A3025 or B3397, 3 miles (5 km) SE of Southampton

[SU 4508] ★★★ *Tel: 0703 453076*

Almost within reach of Southampton's groping tentacles now, it was originally in the kind of wild and isolated spot beloved of the Cistercians, who colonized it from Beaulieu around 1238. Henry III assumed patronage of the abbey in 1251, and it was thus liberally endowed. The Cistercians had by then abandoned their earlier austerity and become self-indulgent, at least by the standards of Bernard of Clairvaux, and their buildings here took on aspects of Gothic art that their founder would have deplored, its Early English church being of surpassing majesty. It provided hospitality for mariners, and was actually praised by Henry VIII's commissioners as being 'To the Kinges Subjects and Strangers travelinge the same Sees great Reliefe and Comforte'. But, ironically, it had fallen on hard times long before, and was reduced to such poverty that its library contained only one book. Sir William Paulet converted it into a residence of brick, with its great hall in the nave of the church, and later a local builder proposed to demolish the whole complex for the sake of the building material, until he was killed by the stone tracery of the church's west window falling on him. Among the glories of the present remains, part ecclesiastical stone and part domestic brick, is the east window of the abbey church, and despite its proximity to Southampton, Netley is still a tranquil place of beauty.

English Heritage

8 ODIHAM CASTLE
Walk along canal towpath reached by lane from A32 N of village

[SU 7251] +

Also known as King John's Castle, it is actually at North Warnborough, near the

Odiham Castle

tow-path of the Basingstoke Canal which was cut through the castle's outer defences. Nothing remains but part of the octagonal keep, built by King John around 1210 at a cost of about £1000, and from here he set out to sign Magna Carta, in something of a bad temper, it is said. The Dauphin himself headed a French expeditionary force which, called in to aid the barons, besieged the castle in 1216. In the following century, King David of Scotland was imprisoned here for many years after the Battle of Neville's Cross.

Hampshire County Council

9 OLD BISHOP'S PALACE, WINCHESTER
In cathedral close, city centre

[*SU 4829*] ★★

One can find this ruin referred to by various names, including Wolvesey Castle and Wolvesey Palace. The 'Wolvesey' tag is misleading, as the ruin is in the cathedral close at Winchester.

The name Wolvesey is said to come from an annual tribute of 300 wolves' heads which had to be paid here by the Welsh to the king in ancient times. The 'old bishop' was Henry de Blois – he of Bishop's Waltham – who built in the twelfth century what was really a well-fortified palace, able to withstand a siege by David of Scotland. How often we find the medieval lords spiritual outdoing the lords temporal in their elaborate military defences! Although partly dismantled by Henry II, it was Cromwell who finally brought the palace to ruin, and the new Bishop's Palace close by was built in 1684.

English Heritage

10 PORTCHESTER CASTLE
Portsmouth Harbour, by minor road S from A27 from town

[*SU 6204*]   +

The Romans built the first fortress here in the third century AD, and it was continually re-fortified through the centuries until the seventeenth, when it was abandoned, but, as late as the nineteenth century, prisoners taken during the Napoleonic wars were kept here. Legend has it that the Emperor Vespasian landed here when he first visited Britain, and many English kings stayed in it up to Richard II's time. The chief architectural remains are the square enclosing walls of the Roman fort, 20 feet (6 m) high with some of its round bastions still in place, and the Norman castle, built in the north west corner by Henry I and protected on two sides by a moat. In this time also, an Augustinian priory was founded in the south east corner of the Roman fort, but it did not remain there for many years, presumably because a military fortress was an uncongenial place for the religious. The church is intact, but there are few signs of the conventual buildings. The eastern side of the castle is lapped by the waters of Portsmouth Harbour.

English Heritage

11 ROYAL GARRISON CHURCH, PORTSMOUTH
Approached via Penny Street, off High Street

[SZ 6399] ★★★

Originally the chapel of the hospital or almshouse founded by Bishop Peter des Roches in 1224, and dedicated to St John Baptist and St Nicholas. The establishment was surrendered at the Dissolution and then became an armoury and subsequently the residence of the military governor of Portsmouth. In the nineteenth century all the buildings except the church were demolished. Later, the church was given a thorough restoration and made the Garrison Church, but in 1940 the nave was reduced to ruin in a German bombing raid, the chancel surviving intact. There have been calls for this thirteenth-century church to be again restored, but at present the arcaded nave, which once housed the aged and infirm, remains roofless and empty.

English Heritage

12 SILCHESTER
Short distance E of village centre, off A340 between Reading and Basingstoke

[SU 6462] +

One of the most remarkable but desolate Roman remains in Britain, it consists of the virtually complete outer wall of the former town and tribal capital, Calleva Atrebatum, enclosing now nothing but farm, church and arable fields. The Romans took over the site in the first century AD, and built the enclosing wall of flint and limestone in the next century, over 20 feet (6 m) thick and nearly 2 miles (3 km) in circumference. Nineteenth-century excavation discovered Roman coins, mosaics and other relics, as well as the complete plan of the former town, with its forum, streets and houses, baths and temples. Exactly when and why this once thriving centre of population became a ghost-town is still a mystery, but it was doubtless destroyed so thoroughly by Saxon raids that it was never rebuilt.

English Heritage

13 TITCHFIELD ABBEY
Minor road off A27, N of village near Fareham

[SU 5406] ★★★ Tel: 0329 43016

Peter de Roches, Bishop of Winchester, founded at Titchfield in 1232 an abbey for Premonstratensian canons. It was said to have one of the finest of monastic libraries and was famous for the fish it served to its guests from its own large fishponds. When the abbey was suppressed, 305 years later, Thomas Wriothesley, Earl of Southampton, converted it into a mansion for himself, called Place House. But the family line ran out and the house passed through various hands until it, too, was demolished in 1781. The Wriothesley family's correspondence and records disappeared, too. They might well have given us valuable information about Shakespeare, for Henry, the third earl, was his patron, and probably his host here occasionally. The most impressive part of the ruins is the Tudor gatehouse (formerly the nave of the abbey church), externally almost complete, with towers and battlements, but there are also medieval and other sixteenth-century remains.

English Heritage

Goodrich Castle

19 Hereford and Worcester

See maps on pages 62 and 63

1 ABBERLEY CHURCH
Village centre, off B4202 near Stourport-on-Severn

[SO 7567] +

The old Norman church in the village centre is open to the sky except for its chancel, and stands in an attractive public garden. It was dedicated to St Michael.

2 CLIFFORD CASTLE
Behind village street, off B4350 N of Hay-on-Wye

[SO 2445] ⊖ No access ⊖

On private land, but can be seen clearly from the road through the village, as it is raised on a motte and stands high above the houses in front of it. It is a large sandstone castle of the Welsh borderland chain of defences. Built above the River Wye (which forms the border at this point) in the thirteenth century, it was held by the Clifford and then the Mortimer lords of the Marches.

Private

3 CRASWALL PRIORY
In village, minor road off B4350, 5 miles (8 km) SE of Hay-on-Wye

[SO 2737]   +

A small alien priory of the Grandmontine rule was founded here, remote in a valley of the Black Mountains, about 1225, but it was already foundering before Henry VIII came to the throne, and nature has been allowed to complete the job of destruction. Walls of the priory church and some of the other buildings remain among the undergrowth.

AM

4 EDVIN LOACH CHURCH
Minor road off B4203, 2½ miles (4 km) N of Bromyard

[SO 6658]   +

The sparse ruins of a Romanesque church stand close to the Victorian village church built to replace it. Herringbone masonry and an early Norman south doorway are the only things to see – the pathetic remains of a place of worship which served the local community for nearly 800 years.

English Heritage

5 EVESHAM ABBEY
Close to town centre

[SP 0344]   +

Nothing remains above ground but the intact and detached bell-tower of the abbey church of this Benedictine monastery, founded and refounded during a turbulent history which began around 700 AD with its foundation by Egwin, Bishop of Worcester. The monastery was destroyed by Danish raiders and rebuilt, and the church collapsed in the tenth century and was again rebuilt. Suppressed in 1539, the abbey church was demolished because there were, unusually, already two parish churches within the abbey precincts. Fragments of the chapter house, gateway and almonry remain.

AM

The chapel at Lower Brockhampton

6 GOODRICH CASTLE
In village, off A40 between Ross-on-Wye and Monmouth

[SO 5719]   ★

The red sandstone fortress of Goodrich was one of the great Welsh border strongholds of Edward I's reign, rising from its foundations of solid rock where a castle of timber had existed since the Conquest. Edward's uncle, William de Valence, Earl of Pembroke, built it high above the Wye Valley, with an eye to domestic comfort as well as military strategy. It became the property of the Talbot Earls of Shrewsbury later, but, by the time of the Civil War, was held for the king by Sir Henry Lingen and, despite the breaching of its walls, held out until the king's capitulation in 1646, when it was rendered uninhabitable. The ruin is still imposing, and among its interesting remains are a big square keep of grey stone contrasting with the distinct red colour of the rest, and built earlier; an early wall fireplace with corbelled hood in the great hall; and a slender column rising through two floors to form a screen with two Gothic arches in the solar.

English Heritage

7 KILPECK CASTLE
In village, off A465, 7 miles (11 km) SW of Hereford

[SO 4430]   +

Fragmentary remains of a twelfth-century shell-keep on a large motte. The

motte to join the bailey walls. The keep, however, had three buttress projections, one of which housed a newel staircase, and beside another is a garderobe projection. The two-storey keep was built in the late twelfth century.

English Heritage

10 LOWER BROCKHAMPTON CHAPEL

2 miles (3 km) E of Bromyard, farm road off A44

[SO 6855]   +

This tiny, bare rectangle of a ruin stands in a farmyard adjacent to the picturesque moated and half-timbered manor house which many visitors come to see, often unaware of the chapel's existence. It was here long before the present manor house. Only the gabled east wall remains to any height, with a primitive Gothic window and Perpendicular tracery, and the ruin is otherwise devoid of ornament or furnishing, except for a simple stone font. You can reach it via a long narrow track through the grounds of Brockhampton Park, from the A44 near Bromyard. Ask permission to cross the farmyard.

National Trust

11 LYONSHALL CASTLE

Near village, off A44, 2 miles (3 km) E of Kington

[SO 3356]   +

Nothing much to be seen except the remnants of a thirteenth-century circular stone keep, which stood on a platform within a moated enclosure. The castle was held by the Carey and then the Devereux lords of the manor.

12 RICHARDS CASTLE

W of village church, off B4361, 3½ miles (5.5 km) S of Ludlow

[SO 4870]   +

Only bits of the inner bailey wall remain on the overgrown motte, with fragments of the octagonal keep, but there was a castle here before the Conquest, and it may have been the one called Auretone in the Domesday Book. The remnants we see now are of a Norman building, held at one period by the Mortimers. Its name came from Richard FitzOsbern, the Norman lord who built it.

AM

castle had three outer baileys as well as the inner one containing the keep.

AM

8 LIMEBROOK PRIORY

1 mile (1.5 km) SE of Lingen, on minor road between Knighton and Mortimer's Cross

[SO 3766]   +

Scant – indeed, almost non-existent – remains of a priory for Augustinian canonesses, founded in the late twelfth century and suppressed in 1539. The

stone remains are of one uncertain building, apparently of the thirteenth century.

9 LONGTOWN CASTLE

Near village centre, on minor road 4½ miles (7 km) W of Pontrilas

[SO 3229]   +

The circular sandstone keep still looks fairly impressive, for one of the smaller castles, on its 35-foot (11 m) high motte overlooking the River Monmow, but there is little else left except a substantial section of walling running down the

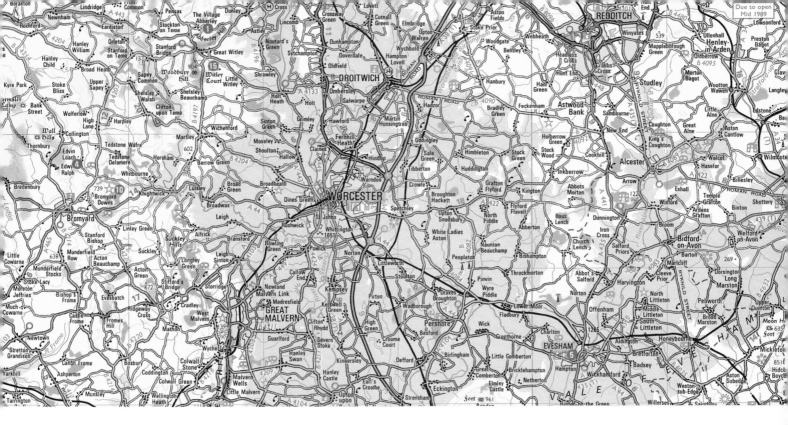

13 SNODHILL CASTLE
In village, on minor road off B4348, 6 miles (10 km) E of Hay-on-Wye

[SO 3240]   +

Fragments of a polygonal keep on a motte, and the bailey walls of a fourteenth-century castle with extensive earthworks.

14 WIGMORE CASTLE
In village on A4110 between Leintwardine and Mortimer's Cross

[SO 4069]   +

Badly overgrown, the stone remains are of a sizeable castle already complete by the time of Domesday Book (1087), where it is said to have been built by William FitzOsbern, Earl of Hereford. The Mortimers held it from the eleventh until the fifteenth century, and Edward IV and Richard III held it after their Mortimer forebears, but it was neglected by the sixteenth century and in ruins by 1732. There are remains of the walls and towers of the inner defences and of an oval shell-keep.

Private

15 WITLEY COURT
Track from A433 near Little Witley 8 miles (13 km) NW of Worcester

[SO 7664]   ★★★

Easily the most impressive ruin in the county, upstaging even Goodrich Castle, and perhaps the most spectacular domestic ruin in Britain, Witley Court

Witley Court

was a stupendous country mansion which was gutted by fire in 1937. What a blaze that must have been! The house's origins go back to the Jacobean period, but Thomas Foley, son of a Stourbridge ironmaster, rebuilt it in 1683, and then in the mid-nineteenth century it was again extended by Lord Ward, Earl of Dudley, with Samuel Dawkes as his architect. Exterior features of the magnificent shell include a splendid Ionic portico, with balustrade above, overlooking the landscaped gardens with the superb Perseus fountain by James Forsyth. William IV's widow, Queen Adelaide, lived in this house for a time. Plans are afoot to restore the fountain to working order. What an outstanding historic site Witley Court will then be!

English Heritage

Ayot St Lawrence's old church

20 Hertfordshire

See map on page 66

1 AYOT ST LAWRENCE CHURCH
Centre of village, 2½ miles (4 km) W of Welwyn

[TL 1916]   +

No victim of Henry VIII or Cromwell, this village church was brought to ruin in the eighteenth century by the lord of the manor, Sir Lionel Lyde, who intended to build a new church in classical style within sight of his new house. When he began, without eccclesiastical consent, to demolish the old village church, which had stood here for 500 years, the bishop intervened and prevented further despoliation, but the damage was done, and the church has stood in ruins at the village centre ever since, with ivy increasingly enveloping its flint walls and battlemented tower. Not open, but visible from the churchyard wall in the village street.

Church of England

2 BERKHAMSTED CASTLE
Minor road from town centre, just beyond railway

[SP 9908]   ★

Not mightily impressive, and difficult to feel romantic about, despite its long and eventful history, but extensive enough for the railway to have been constructed through its outer defences in 1838, so that regular travellers in and out of

The Roman theatre at Verulamium (St Albans)

Euston are as familiar as the keenest olethrophile with its flint walls. Robert of Mortain, William the Conqueror's half-brother, built it originally, but its subsequent owners have been a motley assortment of saints and sinners – Thomas Becket, Richard, Earl of Cornwall, Edward II's lover Piers Gaveston, and the Black Prince. It was besieged and captured by Louis of France in the thirteenth century, but in the next, King John of France was kept in lenient confinement here. It was 'much in ruins' by John Leland's time, and Elizabeth I's Keeper of the Jewels, Sir Edward Cary, demolished it, using the materials to build Berkhamsted Place nearby.

English Heritage

3 LAYSTON CHURCH
Minor road off A10, ½ mile (0.8 km) NE of Buntingford

[TL 3630] +

Only an irreverent congregation of starlings hears the ghostly preaching of its incumbents nowadays, for the village was deserted long ago, and the tree-lined path once used by the villagers to go to their worship is now a muddy track leading to nowhere. The church dedicated to St Bartholomew was replaced by the church of Buntingford on the main road, to which the population of Layston gradually migrated, leaving the old church isolated and derelict. The fifteenth-century tower still stands to its full height, complete with the characteristic mini-spire of the county known as the 'Hertfordshire spike'. Was Layston the medieval village known as Ichetone? No one seems to know.

Church of England

4 OLD GORHAMBURY HOUSE
Off A4147, just W of St Albans

[TL 1107] +

When Elizabeth I visited the new house of her Lord Keeper of the Great Seal, Sir Nicholas Bacon, she remarked, 'My Lord, what a little house you have gotten.' It is even littler now – only a porch and a few sections of wall remain. The house where the great Sir Francis Bacon grew up, to become Baron Verulam and Lord Chancellor, philosopher and playwright, was demolished when a new house was built in the eighteenth century.

English Heritage

5 VERULAMIUM
W fringes of St Albans; theatre close to A4147 on same drive as Gorhambury (above)

[TL 1307] + *(Verulamium)*
Theatre: privately owned ★

The Roman municipium beside the River Ver arose on the site of the tribal capital, or *oppidum*, of the Catuvellauni, which was referred to by Sir Mortimer Wheeler, who excavated the site, as a 'prehistoric metropolis'. The Roman town which superseded it is a place of blood and tears. The Iceni under Boudicca stormed the place and massacred men, women and children

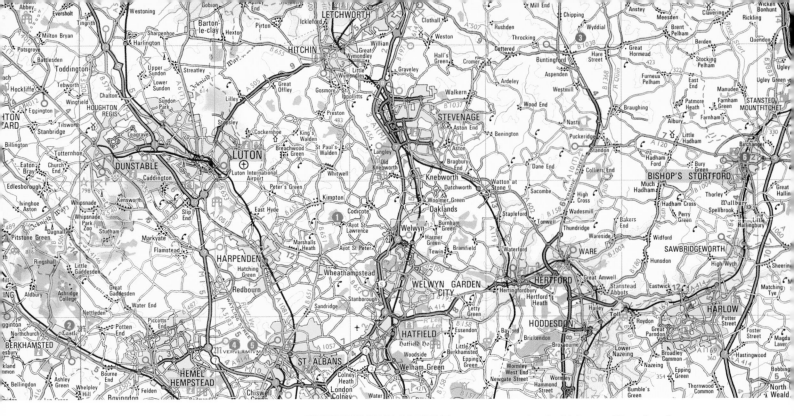

without discrimination, and later the first English martyr, Alban, was executed here for harbouring a Christian priest. The ruins are fairly widespread, including town walls and hypocaust, but most notable is the open-air theatre, a rarity in Britain, and possibly the scene of blood sports as well as religious ceremonies.

Verulamium: City of St Albans

The chapter house of Howden Minster

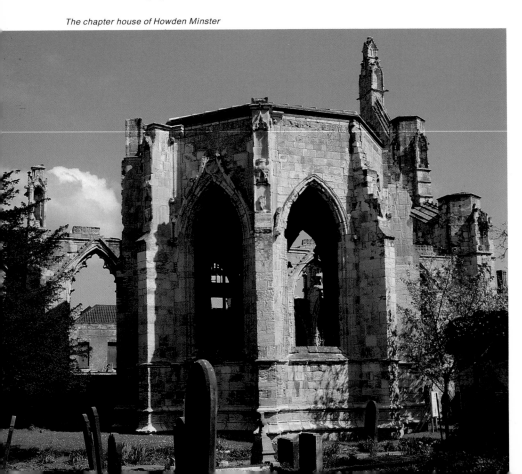

6 WAYTEMORE CASTLE
Bridge Street, Bishop's Stortford

[*TL 4921*]   +

Very little remains to be seen of this mainly twelfth-century castle which was used latterly as a local gaol for Bishop's Stortford. It had a rectangular tower or keep on the motte, and the bases of flint walls of an outer defensive shell survive. The castle was held for many centuries by the bishops of London, but was already in decay by the sixteenth century, and the motte itself was said later to be 'much undermined and destroyed by rabbits'.

AM

21 Humberside

See map on page 67

1 HOWDEN MINSTER
In the town off junction 37, M62, 2½ miles (4 km) N of Goole

[*SE 7428*]   +

The collegiate church of St Peter is a large and impressive church still very much in use, but its chancel, choir and chapter house are in ruins, and these parts are equally impressive, with fine ornament and gargoyles. After the Dissolution the building was too large to be kept up as the parish church, and from the early seventeenth century only the nave was used, with lead removed from the chancel roof to repair that of the nave. Then in 1696 a thunderstorm wreaked havoc on the chancel, and in 1750 the roof of the neglected chapter house collapsed. This was a fine octagonal Perpendicular work built by Bishop Skirlaw late in the fourteenth century. Bishop Skirlaw's intact crossing tower dominates the town and flat surrounding country. At the time of writing this ruin is undergoing preparation to allow public access.

English Heritage

Wressle Castle

2 LAXTON CHURCH
In village on minor road 3 miles (5 km) NE of Goole

[SE 7925]   +

The chancel of the medieval church remains in the churchyard of its Victorian replacement.

Church of England

3 THORNTON ABBEY
Minor road off A1077 at Thornton Curtis, 5 miles (8 km) SE of Barton-upon-Humber

[TA 1119]   ***   Tel: 0469 40357

It began as an Augustinian priory in 1139, and was elevated to abbey status when it became wealthy and influential. Because it provided hospitality to Henry VIII and Jane Seymour during a journey from the north back to London, it was treated leniently at the Dissolution, but was suppressed in the reign of Elizabeth. A great deal of its stone was plundered, and few of its walls remain standing to any height. The most impressive part of the early buildings is the octagonal chapter house. The huge gatehouse was a fourteenth-century addition, licence to crenellate being granted in 1382, apparently to defend the abbey against piratical raids from the Humber. A wide defensive ditch further protects the approach, crossed by a stone bridge, and gives the abbey the appearance of a medieval castle at first, except for the ecclesiastical sculpture remaining on the gatehouse façade.

English Heritage

4 WEST RAVENDALE CHAPEL
Minor road W off B1203 at East Ravendale, 8 miles (13 km) SW of Grimsby

[TF 2299]   +

A tiny overgrown chapel ruin on a hilltop a few miles south-west of Grimsby is all that remains of an alien priory founded about 1202 and already deserted early in the fifteenth century. The chapel was an external one.

5 WRESSLE CASTLE
In village, on minor road off A63, 6 miles (10 km) E of Selby

[SE 7031]    *No access*

Sir Thomas Percy built this castle beside the River Derwent around 1380 – more of a fortified manor house really, built round a courtyard, the moat being perhaps more fashionable than military, for who would threaten the great Percys in this region? The remains are substantial, built in fine pale ashlar stonework, and consist of two bulky towers with turrets and the range between them. The castle was brought to its present state in the Civil War, and now stands on farmland. It is easily seen from the road through the village.

Private

Appuldurcombe House

22 Isle of Wight

See map on page 70

1 APPULDURCOMBE HOUSE
Along drive from minor road off B3327 just W of Wroxall

[SZ 5479] ★

The park in which this ruin stands was landscaped by Capability Brown for Sir Richard Worsley, who made various other improvements to the house his family had built over a long period from 1701, bringing stone from Portland and craftsmen from London. The Worsleys had been lords of the manor for centuries, and the new mansion was occupied by them for nearly 100 years, housing Sir Richard's vast collection of paintings and Greek marbles, and providing a bed for his wife's lovers. But eventually the Worsleys departed; the house was sold; the art collection dispersed; and over the next century and a half Appuldurcombe was used as a hotel, as a temporary home for the monks whose Quarr Abbey (q.v.) was being rebuilt, and as a billet for troops in both world wars. It was a landmine which sealed its fate. The windows of this ruin have been glazed and it has been partially re-roofed and although it

Steps up to the keep at Carisbrooke

The gatehouse at Carisbrooke Castle

has been threatened with demolition more than once, it fortunately still survives – a stylish and ghostly mansion.

English Heritage

2 BRADING VILLA
Minor road SW of village off A3055

[SZ 5986] ★★

The Isle of Wight was brought under Roman rule by Vespasian. It was called Vectis then. Brading has the best of the island's Roman villas, actually on a farm at Yarbridge, west of the village. It was a large country house, doubtless the administrative headquarters of an agricultural estate, and was built round three sides of a courtyard, with fine mosaic floors.

AM

3 CARISBROOKE CASTLE
¼ mile (0.4 km) S of church, W of Newport

[SZ 4887] ★

Although it is not the most extensive of medieval military ruins, some of its building being Elizabethan and still intact, few castles have a longer history as a defensive site, a Roman fort having stood here and before that, it is believed, a British camp. After the Roman withdrawal, the Saxons probably raised the huge artificial mound, or motte, on

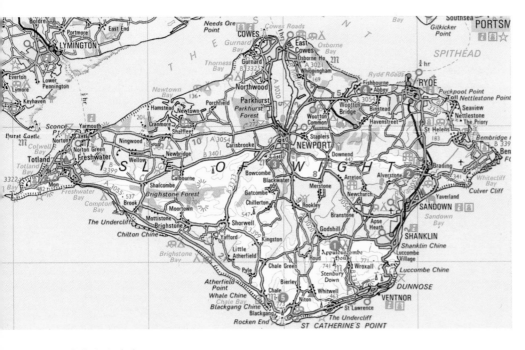

St Catherine's Oratory

which the shell-keep was subsequently built. The present castle was begun in the twelfth century by Baldwin de Redvers. It came to the Crown at the end of the thirteenth century, but was owned by Edward II's lover Piers Gaveston for a time, and was afterwards in the tenancy of the lords of the island until the Civil War. The castle withstood attacks by the French, but its defences were reinforced in Elizabeth's time by her favourite military architect, Federigo Giambelli, the queen herself giving £4000 towards the cost, at a time when the danger of attack was from Spain. Charles I was a prisoner here, and made two abortive attempts to escape. The Parliamentary forces used the castle as a state prison, so its more modern buildings were kept in good order, and came into use as the island governor's residence until the Second World War, then the house was converted into the Isle of Wight Museum. The gatehouse is particularly fine; built around 1335, it was improved late in the fifteenth century by the addition of the parapets and machicolations. As well as the moat, the castle was protected by three portcullises. There is a deep well here, operated by a donkey on a tread-wheel.

English Heritage

4 QUARR ABBEY
Minor road N of A3054, 1½ miles (2.5 km) W of Ryde

[SZ 5692]   +

Very little remains other than the precinct walls of this Cistercian monastery founded in 1132 and dissolved in 1536. The church was completely demolished, and other buildings and masonry are all incorporated in later buildings. The monks owned the limestone quarries from which the abbey was built. The whitish stone was much used in Roman and medieval buildings (e.g. Portchester Castle, q.v.), but the quarries were already exhausted by the fourteenth century, and the modern Benedictine abbey ½ mile (0.8 km) away is built of brick.

Quarr Abbey

5 ST CATHERINE'S ORATORY
Walk from car park on A3055 at Blackgang, S tip of island

[SZ 4977]   +

There was a medieval chapel on this hilltop near the island's southernmost point in the fourteenth century, and this octagonal buttressed stone tower, rocket-like in appearance, was probably the west tower of the chapel, but its eight 'windows' or openings at the top make it clear that it was intended as a beacon lighthouse. One version says that it was built as an act of penance after illegal dealings with a wrecked wine ship. Whatever its origin, ecclesiastical lighthouse-keepers kept its beacon burning to warn shipping of the rocky coastline below, probably until the Dissolution. You must walk $\frac{1}{2}$ mile (0.8 km) up the hill from the main road to examine it closely.

English Heritage

23 Kent

See map below and on page 74

1 CANTERBURY CASTLE
Lane off Castle Street, near city centre

[TR 1457] ★★★

Only the massive rectangular keep remains, just inside the southern extremity of the city walls, and probably built soon after the Conquest, of flint, sandstone and stone brought across the Channel from Normandy. Except for a short period in the thirteenth century, it seems to have been permanently in royal ownership, but it was progressively reduced, and in 1817 the upper part of the keep was demolished, when it was in use as a coal store for the local gas company. It had been used as the county gaol for a long period before that.

Canterbury Corporation

2 CHILHAM CASTLE
In village off A252, 6 miles (10 km) SW of Canterbury

[TR 0653] ⊖ *No access* ⊖

Henry II built this octagonal keep of flint, which has one projection for three

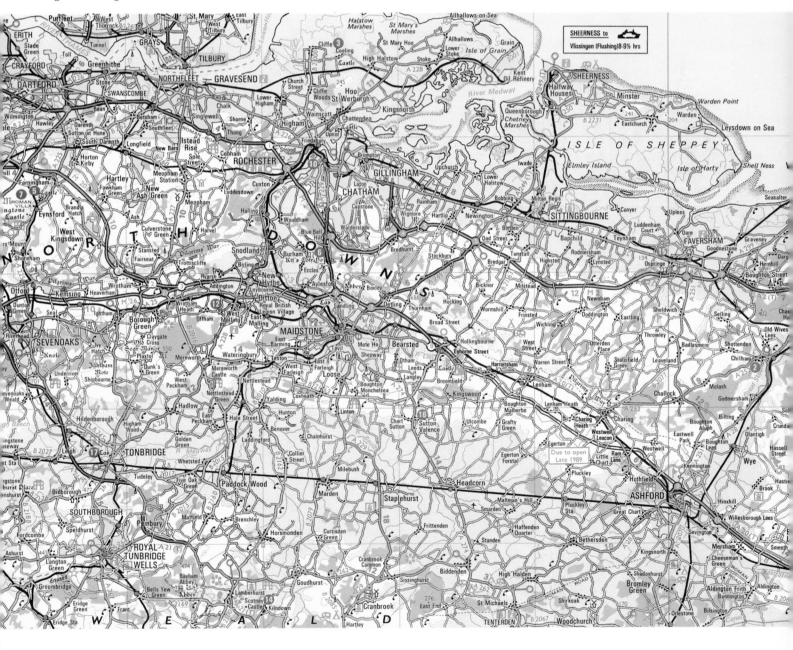

71

garderobes and another as a stair-turret. The rest of the castle was demolished as a quarry for building stone, except for a forebuilding which incorporates a Norman hall. The keep is not open to the public, but can be seen from the grounds

Private

3 COOLING CASTLE
Minor road off N end of B2000 at Cliffe, N of Rochester

[TQ 7576] ⊖ *No access* ⊖

Seen from the road through the village, the intact gatehouse is more impressive than the remnants of this fourteenth-century castle built by John de Cobham, who claimed patriotism as his motivation in a tablet on the gatehouse:

Knouwyth that beeth and schal be
That I am mad in help of the cuntre
In knowying of whyche thyng
Thys is chartre and wytnessyng.

The castle was hardly sited with strategic flair, however, and would scarcely have stood up to determined attack from the French. The Lollard rebel Sir John Oldcastle held it in the thirteenth century through his marriage with Joan de la Pole, and corresponded with Hussite leaders in Europe from here.

Private

4 DUBRIS LIGHTHOUSE
Within walls of Dover Castle, NE of town centre

[TR 3241] ★

Standing in the outer bailey of Dover Castle, at the west end of the castle's Saxon church of St Mary, is a Roman lighthouse, or *pharos*, built in the fort of Dubris in the first century AD to guide ships across the Channel. It originally stood about 80 feet (24 m) high, but the top part was rebuilt in the Middle Ages, to a lower level. Octagonal outside, the tower is a hollow square inside, and had a beacon at the top which would still be clearly visible to shipping in the Channel today if it were re-lit.

English Heritage

5 EYNSFORD CASTLE
In village on A225 between Dartford and Sevenoaks

[TQ 5465] +

The twelfth-century undercroft of a hall-house, built of flint and Roman tiles, stands within an almost complete curtain wall of coursed flint rubble built late in the preceding century. It originally enclosed timber buildings, and was itself surrounded by a moat. The gatehouse was built at the same time as the hall, and was reached via a timber bridge across the moat. The castle was held at that time by William de Eynsford, who was excommunicated after Becket's martyrdom, as one of the primate's enemies, and he was shunned to such an extent, it is said, that he left the castle and it was never inhabited again.

English Heritage

6 KIT'S COTY HOUSE
Off A229, 3 miles (5 km) N of Maidstone

[TQ 7460] +

This megalith near Aylesford is one of the country's best-known prehistoric tomb remains, evidently named after a local shepherd named Christopher who used it for shelter from the elements. ('Coty' means a little house, like 'cot' or 'cote'.) The huge upright slabs support another across them, and were probably at the entrance of a neolithic long barrow originally covered by a mound of earth.

English Heritage

7 LULLINGSTONE VILLA
Off A225, ½ mile (0.8 km) SW of Eynsford

[TQ 5365] ★

Re-opened in April 1990 after a two-year closure, this is one of the country's best remains of Roman villas, well known both for its fine mosaics and for its incorporation of a small Christian chapel in the fourth century. The villa was discovered in the eighteenth century, but was not properly excavated until after the Second World War, when it was found that the site had been more or less continuously occupied from the first century to the fourth, when the house was burnt down. The remains show a transition from pagan to Christian occupation, with a small temple, mosaics depicting pagan myths, and the chapel where a chi-rho symbol was found.

English Heritage

8 RECULVER TOWERS
In Roman fort on shore, ½ mile (0.8 km) E of village, N of A299 and E of Herne Bay

[TR 2269] ★★★ *Tel: 02273 66444*

Reculver is the site of the Roman fort of Regulbium, on the clifftops east of Herne Bay. Part of the fort's precincts has been destroyed by erosion, and only earthworks remain of the Saxon Shore fort guarding the entrance to the Wantsum Channel, but within it are the twelfth-century twin towers flanking the gabled entrance to a church founded in 669 by Egbert, King of Kent. The church, except for these towers comprising the west front, was demolished in 1809 or thereabouts at the instigation of the vicar's mother, but Trinity House secured the preservation of the towers, lighting beacons in them for many years as an aid to shipping.

English Heritage

9 RICHBOROUGH FORT
Minor road off A257, 1½ miles (2.5 km) N of Sandwich

[TR 3260] ★

This was the cradle of the Claudian invasion of Britain, begun in AD 43 under the General Aulus Plautius, who brought military elephants across the Channel as well as his stores and legions, and built the fort of Rutupiae as his first stronghold, though it consisted then only of earthworks and timber buildings. The sea has now receded, but the stone walls of the later fort remain, built as one of the defences of the Saxon Shore. The walls still stand 25 feet (8 m) high in places, and had projecting turrets and corner bastions. We know that a great triumphal arch was built on a prepared foundation about AD 85, doubtless in honour of the Emperor Claudius and his conquest of Britain, but the overwhelming local monuments now, alas, are the unsympathetic cooling towers of the Richborough power station.

English Heritage

10 ROCHESTER CASTLE
Close to city centre

[TQ 7468] ★

Little remains of this once-important fortification, apart from its keep, but when a keep has the qualities of this one, who needs more? It still stands to its original height of 125 feet (38 m), and is the tallest keep in England – a massive square brute of a tower with walls of Kentish ragstone, 12 feet (4 m) thick. It was built around 1130 by William of Corbeuil, Henry I's Archbishop of Canterbury, to guard the approach to the town and the London–Dover road from the River Medway. From the outside it looks formidable, but when you enter it the immediate impression is of an awesome, damp and dungeon-like void. The cavernous and echoing honeycomb of arcades and galleries gives the imagination an outsize task in peopling the keep with medieval lords, knights and ladies feasting and revelling in the great hall, with a roaring fire and minstrels playing. It evokes rather a sinister feeling of menace and decay. But its architectural detail is of Norman purity, the castle having been in neglect long before the Civil War and untouched by later styles. The keep stands in a public park which was the castle's former bailey.

English Heritage

11 ST AUGUSTINE'S ABBEY, CANTERBURY
Monastery Street, E of Cathedral Close

[TR 1557] ★

The first English Benedictine abbey, founded to the east of the city by Augustine in 598, was to have a fine church in which Augustine was to be buried at his death. Pope Gregory had warned Augustine against vanity, and this building seems like self-exaltation with hindsight. He died before the church was finished, but was duly buried in it, outside the city walls, as the Romans had been traditionally buried. Only the foundations of that church remain, and of the later buildings, the ruins are not among the most exciting visually, though some of the walls are full of Roman bricks. Building went on here until 1538, when the abbot surrendered the property to the king, who made parts of it into a palace for Anne of Cleves, the 'Flanders Mare' of whom Henry VIII said, 'I like her not'. In the nineteenth century a missionary college was superimposed on the old buildings, absorbing more of the monastic remains.

English Heritage

12 ST LEONARD'S TOWER
Minor road off A228 at West Malling

[TQ 6757] +

Generally regarded as one of the best examples of an early Norman keep, this tower at West Malling, 60 feet (18 m) high, is all that remains of a fortified house built, apparently, by Gundulph, Bishop of Rochester, around 1100. It has four storeys, and a stair-turret in one corner.

English Heritage

The interior of Rochester Castle

13 ST RADEGUND'S ABBEY
Minor road W off A256 at Buckland, Dover

[TR 2741] +

Not much remains of the Premonstratensian abbey founded 2 miles (3 km) from Dover about 1192. At the end of the sixteenth century, the buildings, deserted after the Dissolution, were converted into a house by Simon Edolph, part of the abbey church forming a gatehouse! Some of the remains were used as farm buildings. The abbey was also known by the name Bradsole.

AM

14 SCOTNEY CASTLE
Off A21, 1½ miles (2.5 km) SE of Lamberhurst

[TQ 6935] ★★★ Tel: 0892 890651

It is certainly one of the most picturesque ruins in Britain, though precious little remains of the fortified manor house built under licence by Roger Ashburnham at the end of the fourteenth century. Apart from one surviving circular tower, formerly a battlemented angle-tower with machicolations, what we see now is mainly a seventeenth-century manor house which was never completed, and the remains were artfully treated to form

Scotney Castle

the centrepiece of a magnificent artificial landscape when a new Gothic Revival house was built nearby for Edward Hussey in 1837. The ruins of mellow grey stone and red brick, framed by trees and shrubs and reflected in the still waters of the moat, make a seductive scene of English tranquillity.

National Trust

15 STONE-NEXT-FAVERSHAM CHURCH
Just off N side of A2, 1¾ miles (2.8 km) W of Faversham

[TQ 9961]   +

Only a few bits of flint and ragstone, on farmland just north of the Roman Watling Street, remain to show where the village church stood, but excavation in the 1960s showed that the chancel was built on the site of a pagan mausoleum, of Romano-British origin. The visible remnants now are of a pre-Conquest church which fell into ruin in the Tudor period, but Roman coins and pieces of painted walls, as well as the skeleton of a child, were found beneath the Saxon remains.

English Heritage

16 SUTTON VALENCE CASTLE
In village near church, off A274, 6 miles (10 km) SE of Maidstone

[TQ 8149]   +

The overgrown remains of a small square keep, built in the twelfth century and already abandoned by the thirteenth. Built of Kentish ragstone, with 8-foot (2.5 m) thick walls, there is little to be seen now.

AM

17 TONBRIDGE CASTLE
Close to town centre

[TQ 5846]   ★★★

You might think that its builder was a very insecure fellow, for the castle was erected to guard a crossing of the Medway, but on its town side had a massive twin-towered gatehouse with arrow-slits, machicolations, portcullis grooves and double gateway, not to mention a moat! The gatehouse, however, came later, being built by Gilbert de Clare (who also built Caerphilly Castle, q.v.) in about 1275, and its domestic arrangements were good enough for Edward I to be entertained here. The castle was here at least as early as 1088, for it is mentioned in *The Anglo-*

Saxon Chronicle as being stormed in that year by William Rufus. Most of the stonework apart from the gatehouse dates from the early twelfth century. The castle was brought to ruin in the Civil War.

Tonbridge Urban District Council

18 WESTENHANGER CASTLE

Off minor road N of A20, near Folkestone racecourse, 3 miles (5 km) NW of Hythe

[TR 1237] ⊖ *No access* ⊖

The remains of a fourteenth-century fortified house are adjacent to an early eighteenth-century farmhouse built from its stone, standing close to the Folkestone racecourse. The original house was said to contain 126 rooms, and was built on the site of an earlier castle reputed to have been the home of Henry II's mistress Rosamond Clifford, known as 'Fair Rosamond'. Parts of the walls and towers of the fourteenth-century ranges

enclosing a courtyard remain.

Private

24 Lancashire

See map below

1 CLITHEROE CASTLE

Castle Street in town, A671 8 miles (13 km) NW of Burnley

[SD 7441] +

A small Norman keep, standing on a limestone crag, is sometimes said to be the smallest in the country, though I think that could easily be disproved. At any rate, it was owned by the de Lacy family and then by the Earls and Dukes of Lancaster before passing to the Crown in the person of Henry IV. The tower's interior was, to say the least, austere, and

the rest of the castle was mostly destroyed in the Civil War. The keep now stands in a park at the centre of the town.

Clitheroe Borough Council

2 GREENHALGH CASTLE

Off B6430 at S end of Garstang

[SD 4945] +

Fragments of a stone tower, of rectangular shape, at Garstang, are all that remains of a castle owned by Thomas Stanley, Earl of Derby, who was licensed to crenellate in 1490.

3 ST PATRICK'S CHAPEL

N of Heysham parish church, W of Lancaster

[SD 4061] +

Overlooking Morecambe Bay at Heysham are the rude stone walls of a chapel of the late eighth or early ninth

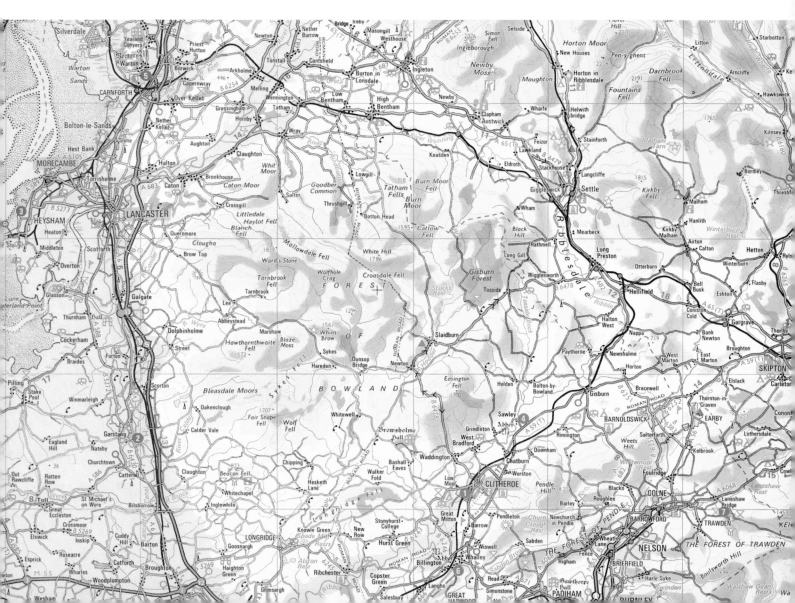

century, so called because the Apostle of Ireland is supposed to have landed here during his travels, though that was hundreds of years earlier, if true. It has a doorway with one curved stone as its arch, with unusual grooved moulding, and equally rare in Britain are rock-cut graves found near it. There are also fragmentary remains of other monastic buildings, probably founded in the time of King Alfred, and destroyed by Angle invaders.

Whalley Abbey

4 SAWLEY ABBEY
In village, off A59 NE of Clitheroe

[SD 7746] ★

Known locally as Salley Abbey, the remains are of a twelfth-century Cistercian monastery, never a wealthy foundation, and what is left shows an abbey church with a nave so short that its length is exceeded by its width. There are foundations of the monastic buildings. It had already been suppressed and vacated when the Pilgrimage of Grace occurred, but monastic life at Sawley was actually resumed for a short time, in vain hope of a reversal of the king's policy.

English Heritage

5 WARTON RECTORY
In village, off A6 N of Carnforth

[SD 4972] ★

Behind the modern vicarage are the ruins of an early fourteenth-century rectory or hall-house, with a complete gable and window at the high table end, and doorways to pantry, buttery and kitchen beyond the screens passage at the other.

English Heritage

6 WHALLEY ABBEY
In village, off A59 6 miles (10 km) NE of Blackburn

[SD 7336] +

The ruins of this Cistercian establishment are fairly scant, and its church virtually non-existent, but once it exercised power over large parts of Lancashire, and ruled with a rod of iron. It was founded in 1296 as a replacement for an earlier foundation on the Wirral which was regularly flooded when the Mersey rose with the spring tides. Never devotees of the frugal vegetarian diet recommended by their founder, the abbots were famed for their prodigal hospitality. No wonder the last, John Paslow, joined the Pilgrimage of Grace to try and preserve his way of life. But he was hanged here, in front of his own gatehouse, one of his prosecutors being the Assheton lord of the manor who acquired the property and built himself a house from the ruins. The mansion remains, and is used as a conference centre and retreat house by Blackburn Diocese.

English Heritage

7 WYCOLLER HALL
Near Trawden, 2½ miles (4 km) E of Colne, on minor road off A6068.

[SD 9339] +

The ruined stone manor house of this Pennine hamlet near Colne is said to have been the model for Ferndean Manor in Charlotte Brontë's *Jane Eyre* (1847). Half a dozen miles (10 km) across the moor from Haworth, it was a sixteenth–seventeenth-century house, for long the home of the Cunliffes, one of whom Charlotte may have taken as her model for Rochester.

Lancashire County Council

25 Leicestershire

See maps on pages 78 and 79

1 ASHBY CASTLE
In Ashby de la Zouch, on A453 Tamworth road

[SK 3616] ★★★ Tel: 0530 413343

William Lord Hastings, head of a great Leicestershire family, and Lord Chamberlain to Richard III, built this stone castle in the late fifteenth century, strengthening what was originally a fortified manor house by adding a high curtain wall and a huge tower-house, four storeys high, with no windows on the ground floor. It was all to no avail. When Lord Hastings' erstwhile friend

The Hastings Tower, Ashby Castle

Richard of Gloucester accused him of treason, there was not even a trial. Hastings' head was chopped off without ceremony on Tower Green. The Hastings properties were restored to the family after Bosworth, and Ashby became the home of Lord William's descendants, the earls of Huntingdon, but Cromwell's men ordered the demolition of the castle in the Civil War and it has stood here in ruins ever since, though the Hastings Tower still stands to a height of 90 feet (27 m), with an ornately carved fireplace still visible on the upper floor.

English Heritage

2 BRADGATE HOUSE
In Bradgate Park, on foot from Newtown Linford or Cropston, 5 miles (8 km) NW of Leicester

[SK 5310] ★★★

According to legend, Bradgate – once the home of Lady Jane Grey – was reduced to ruin in 1694, when the Countess of Stamford, unable to stand the place any

longer, set fire to it one night and ran away by the light of the blaze. Although this is a romantic fiction, it contains elements of truth. There *was* a fire, though the damage was not extensive, and the Grey family *did* desert Bradgate, though not in the person of the countess. Nor is it surprising if the Greys grew weary of this house of sorrows. It was built at the end of the fifteenth century by the Marquis of Dorset, Thomas Grey. It was one of the earliest country houses in England, and one of the first buildings of brick in the county. The chapel, where members of the family lie buried, survives. Lady Jane was the eldest daughter of Henry Grey, the third marquis, and his wife Frances Brandon, grand-daughter of Henry VII. The future nine-days'-queen grew up here, learning Latin, Greek, French and Italian under the finest tutors of the day, unaware that she was being used as a pawn in the political ambitions of her scheming relatives. She was 16 when they chopped her head off in the Tower of London, and legend has it that the ancient oaks of Bradgate were pollarded

Bradgate House from the park

Bradgate House

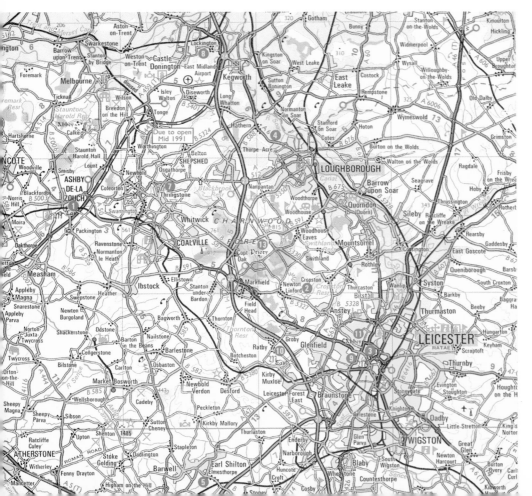

as a mark of mourning for her. Jane's sisters, Katherine, the 'lady of lamentations', and Mary, also died young. The ruin has a romantic quality of its own, apart from its tragic history, standing as it does in a completely unspoilt medieval hunting park, where a stream meanders between rock outcrops and a herd of deer roams freely among the oaks and bracken. Although the ruins are open only at certain times, they can be seen clearly from the outside at any reasonable time.

Bradgate Park Trust

3 CAVENDISH HOUSE
Entrance to Abbey Park, Abbey Lane, N of Leicester city centre

[SK 5805] +

Close to the ruins of Leicester Abbey (q.v.) is the ill-fated Cavendish House, so called because it came into the possession of William Cavendish, first Earl of Devonshire, in 1613. But it was built by Henry, Earl of Huntingdon, around 1565, from the materials of the abbey remains. In the Civil War, Charles I used it as his headquarters before the Battle of Naseby, and then it was burnt down by his own troops, less than a century after its erection. The attractive remaining walls show mullioned and transomed windows.

City of Leicester

The forlorn remains of Grace Dieu

4 DISHLEY CHURCH
Just off A6 at Dishley Grange, 1¾ miles (2.8 km) NW of Loughborough

[SK 5121] +

The forlorn overgrown ruins of a church which once served a village removed by Garendon Abbey. The ruin is in the grounds of Dishley Grange, the home of the great eighteenth-century agricultural pioneer Robert Bakewell, who was buried in the church. It was much favoured by pigeons when I last saw it.

Private

5 ELMESTHORPE CHURCH
B581, ¾ mile (1 km) S of Earl Shilton

[SP 4696] +

The chancel of the church, rebuilt in the nineteenth century, remains in use, but the roofless nave became a ruin after Richard III's officers used it as a billet before the Battle of Bosworth, and it was employed later as a cattle pen, until the deserted medieval village began to be revived.

Church of England

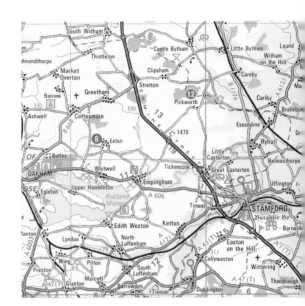

6 EXTON OLD HALL
In park beside village, 5 miles (8 km) E of Oakham

[SK 9211] ⊖ *No access* ⊖

The ruins of the house which belonged to the Noel family, Earls of Gainsborough, stand near the new hall and the village church, within Exton Park. The house was burnt down in 1810. Built early in the seventeenth century, by the Harington lords of the manor, it was a fine house with Dutch gables, balustrades and a profusion of windows. The new house which replaced it eventually became a school. The whole group can be seen from the church of this fine limestone village, formerly in Rutland.

Private

7 GRACE DIEU
Beside A512, 5 miles (8 km) E of Ashby de la Zouche

[SK 4318] ⊖ *No access* ⊖

This scant ruin in a field beside the Loughborough–Ashby de la Zouch road was the birthplace of Francis Beaumont, the poet and dramatist, and collaborator with John Fletcher in Elizabethan plays such as *The Maid's Tragedy* (1619). The house was originally a thirteenth-century Augustinian nunnery, founded by Roesia de Verdun, and was converted into a dwelling after the Dissolution by Sir John Beaumont, Master of the Rolls. But the Beaumont family left Grace Dieu in the seventeenth century, and the subsequent owners, the Phillips, abandoned it to nature. The 'ivied ruins of forlorn Grace Dieu', as Wordsworth called them, are in private ownership and

Hemington Church

not directly accessible, falling masonry being one danger and the resident bull another. Clearly visible from the road, however.

Private

8 HEMINGTON CHURCH
In village, minor road off A453 at Castle Donington

[SK 4527] ⊖ No access ⊖

Little enough of it remains now, standing all forlorn on waste ground, but it once had a thirteenth-century west tower and broach spire, characteristic of the area. It was already disused by the end of the sixteenth century, probably because it had belonged to Leicester Abbey and was neglected after the Dissolution. There is a public footpath beside it.

9 JEWRY WALL, LEICESTER
By Vaughan College and St Nicholas church, short distance W of city centre

[SK 5804] +

This massive section of arched Roman masonry, with the Saxon church of St Nicholas towering over it, was part of the palaestra, or exercise hall, attached to the baths at the city of Ratae Coritanorum, according to one interpretation; or part of the basilica, or town hall, according to another. At any rate, it was built around AD 130, and now has the excavated Roman baths in front of it. The popular name may be a corruption of 'Jurat', from the aldermen of the medieval borough, though Celia Fiennes thought it was the place where Jews burnt their sacrificial offerings.

English Heritage

10 KIRBY MUXLOE CASTLE
In village, minor road off B5380 W of Leicester

[SK 5204] ★★★ Tel: 0533 386886

Ashby (q.v.) was the Hastings' stone castle; this was their brick one. But Lord William's summary execution by Richard III brought building at Kirby Muxloe to a fairly abrupt halt, as his widow could not afford to continue, and the castle gradually fell into ruin. The regular plan of this late castle in the new material even extended to the moat, which is almost square. Circular gun-ports are among the earliest in Britain. The chief survivals are the gatehouse and the south-west angle tower of three storeys with an adjoining battlemented turret 70 feet (21 m) high.

English Heritage

All that is left of Pickworth's old church

Kirby Muxloe Castle

11 LEICESTER ABBEY

Abbey Park, N of city centre

[SK 5806]   +

Founded on the west bank of the Soar in 1143 by Robert le Bossu, Earl of Leicester, it was consecrated as the Abbey of St Mary Pratis (St Mary of the Meadows), and became one of the country's largest and wealthiest monastic houses for Augustinian canons. The once rich and mighty Cardinal Wolsey came here to die, on his journey from York to London to answer a charge of treason:

An old man, broken with the storms of
    state,
Is come to lay his weary bones among ye;
Give him a little earth for charity!

He lingered for three days, and they gave him a tomb in the Lady Chapel, but the abbey was so ruthlessly destroyed at the Dissolution that neither the tomb nor the abbey's plan can be discovered with any confidence, the remains consisting only of a conjectural layout marked by low stone walls.

City of Leicester

12 PICKWORTH CHURCH

Short distance W of crossroads, minor road off A1, 5 miles (8 km) NW of Stamford

[SK 9913]   ⊖ *No access* ⊖

A solitary Gothic arch is all that remains above ground level of the medieval village of Pickworth. It stands on bumpy former farmland which could never be ploughed because the stone foundations of houses lay beneath the soil. The arch was the doorway of the village church, which once had a spire visible for miles around. But Pickworth was a casualty of the Wars of the Roses, for it was recorded in 1491 as having no parishioners, and over the centuries its church and houses were demolished and its stones taken away for other buildings. The poet John Clare came here in 1817, to work as a lime-burner, and wrote an *Elegy on the ruins at Pickworth*, which were known locally as 'the old foundations'. The forlorn arch can be seen clearly from the road, among the new building which has been going on recently.

Private

13 ULVERSCROFT PRIORY

Lane off minor road between A50 and B5330, 1¾ miles (2.8 km) NE of Markfield

[SK 5012]   *On application*

It was a priory for Austin canons, founded in the twelfth century in the wild forest country of Charnwood, and so was enclosed by a wall and moat. Suppressed in 1539, after being reprieved in the first round of dissolution, parts of the priory church, including its west tower, survive as parts of a farmhouse built from its ruins. It makes a picturesque ruin in what is still romantic countryside.

Private

26 Lincolnshire

See maps below

1 CALCEBY CHURCH
Minor road W from A16 at Ulceby Cross, 4 miles (6.5 km) W of Alford

[*TF 3875*] ⊖ *No access* ⊖

These sparse and flimsy-looking remains are what is left of St Andrew's church, where the villagers of Calceby came to worship before they deserted the place, possibly as a result of the Black Death's devastation in the fourteenth century. The pale masonry of the north wall of the nave and tower, with its Norman arch just barely defying the elements, stands in a field on farmland 2 miles (3 km) north-west of Ulceby Cross, and can be seen clearly from the road. Cattle use it as a sunshade.

Private

2 CROWLAND ABBEY
In village, off A1073 NE of Peterborough

[*TF 2410*] +

The origin of its name is obscure. Sometimes referred to as Croixland, the land of the cross; sometimes as the land of mud, from the Latin *crudum terram*; its modern name means, obviously enough, the land of crows. Whatever its name meant originally, it was a disaster-prone Benedictine foundation, despite the fact that it grew into a renowned centre of learning and the wealthiest monastic foundation in Lincolnshire. According to legend, Hereward the Wake was buried here. It was repeatedly destroyed – by fire, by Danish raiders, and even, in 1118, by earthquake. Its economy suffered hugely from the Black Death, and the Dissolution ended its monastic existence, although ruin did not finally overtake it until 1720, when the nave of the church collapsed. The church's north aisle remains intact, and in use as the parish church. The west end of the ruined nave – Early English below and Perpendicular above – shows clearly how magnificent the final rebuilding of the abbey church was, with tiers of stone figures flanking and surmounting the window over the doorway. Some of the statues have been removed. One of them, believed to represent Christ, is on the famous triangular stone bridge in the village centre.

Church of England

3 LINCOLN CASTLE
Short distance W of cathedral

[*SK 9771*] +

Like Lewes in Sussex (q.v.), Lincoln Castle has two mottes, for what reason we are not sure. The castle was begun in 1068 within a Roman enclosure, and modern buildings here are still in use, but there are ruinous parts, especially the curtain wall and towers. The site covered 5 acres (2 ha) and 166 houses were demolished to make way for it. The so-called Lucy Tower was a shell-keep on the larger of the two mottes. For a long time executed criminals from the eighteenth-century prison were buried in the keep, as well as children who died in the prison. The smaller motte carries a nineteenth-century observatory tower built from the base of a medieval remnant.

City of Lincoln

4 OLD BISHOP'S PALACE, LINCOLN
Cathedral precinct

[*SK 9871*] ★★★

The present ruins are the remains of a building begun in the thirteenth century, but there was a palace here before then.

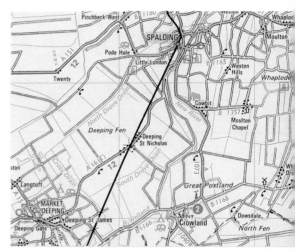

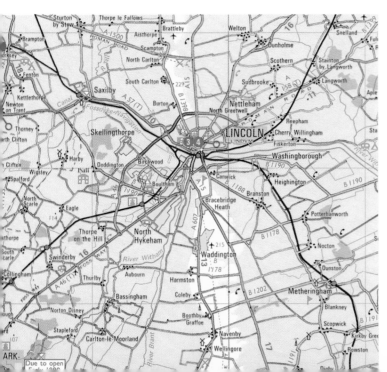

Calceby church

The palace was erected on a steep slope south of the cathedral. Building was still going on here in the fifteenth century, but by the seventeenth the palace was in ruins, and has remained so except for the conversion of one part into a chapel.

Little of substance remains, but the ruins show the extent of a medieval bishop's palace which was certainly one of the largest built, with a great hall 105 feet (32 m) long.

English Heritage

5 OLD BOLINGBROKE CASTLE
In village between A155 and B1195 SE of Horncastle

[TF 3464]   +

Henry Bolingbroke, later Henry IV, was

Redundant bishops at Crowland Abbey

born in this castle in 1367. It was built by Ranulph de Blundeville, Earl of Chester (builder of Beeston Castle in Cheshire and Chartley Castle in Staffordshire, q.q.v.), around 1220, but very little remains other than the excavated bases of walls and towers. It was already in decay by the Civil War, and the royalist garrison surrendered after a siege of a few days, the castle then being demolished, leaving only the gatehouse standing to any height, and this collapsed early in the nineteenth century.

English Heritage

6 TATTERSHALL COLLEGE
In village, off A153, 7 miles (11 km) S of Horncastle

[TF 2157]   +

Behind the houses on one side of the market place are the scant remains of the grammar school and almshouse, founded in 1438 by Lord Treasurer Ralph Cromwell. The school was for the church choristers. The carpenter's contract for the almshouse survives, with detailed specifications. He was paid £16 in weekly instalments for his work, building a hospital with separate cells and a chapel for twelve poor men.

English Heritage

7 TORKSEY CASTLE
In field behind village, A1133, 9 miles (14.5 km) NW of Lincoln

[SK 8378]   +

Not a castle at all, but an Elizabethan mansion, three storeys high and built of stone at the bottom and brick at the top. Only one façade remains standing, with four octagonal towers and a variety of windows. The house was built by Sir Robert Jermyn and it was captured by royalist soldiers in the Civil War, which no doubt resulted in its ruin, but neither the plan of the house nor its history are very clear. It stands in a field on the banks of the Trent.

27 *London*

See top map on page 86

1 ELSING SPITAL
Beside St Alphage House, tower block in London Wall, City of London

[TQ 3281]   +

The fourteenth-century tower in London Wall is the only remnant of the medieval hospital founded in 1329 by William de Elsing and incorporated a few years later into an Augustinian priory. The tower belonged to the chapel of the priory, which was suppressed at the Dissolution. Elsing was a wealthy mercer who founded the almshouse for 100 men, who were to include old and disabled clergymen.

2 ROMAN GATE AND CITY WALL
St Alphage Gardens, off N side of London Wall, City of London

[TQ 3281]   +

The remains of the first-century west gate of a Roman fort lie in an underground car park beneath the highway known as London Wall. The entrance is opposite Noble Street. The fort was found, like other ancient remains in London, during the clearance of bomb damage after the Second World War. The fort was here before the city wall, which was built in the second century. A good section of that can also be seen nearby in the public garden that was formerly St Alphage's churchyard. The Roman work has some medieval rebuilding above it in stone and knapped flint.

City of London

3 ROSE THEATRE
S Bank of River Thames near Southwark Bridge

[TQ 3280]

The discovery of the remains of the Rose Theatre, opened in 1587 by Philip Henslowe, and threatened with having an office block built directly on it in 1989, drew distinguished members of the theatrical profession into lying down in front of bulldozers and treating the scant

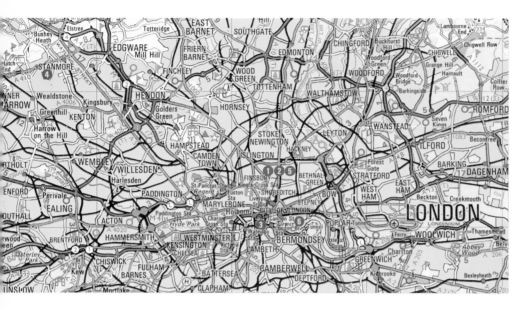

remains as if they were holy relics, because William Shakespeare may possibly have *acted* there. Still, a vigorous campaign did bring about a change of mind, and the office building has undergone a design change which will allow the remains to be preserved for public viewing, doubtless under the auspices of English Heritage. It is fondly believed that the first performance of *Henry VI* (1597) took place here, although the play of that title reported by Henslowe may not have been the one we know, and even if it was, little of it was Shakespeare's work. The Rose Theatre was demolished in 1605.

4 STANMORE CHURCH
In parish churchyard, Church Road, Stanmore (Harrow)

[TQ 1692]   +

The parish church of St John the Evangelist was consecrated in 1632 by William Laud, Bishop of London and by the following year Archbishop of Canterbury. In 1849 a new church was begun in the same churchyard, and the old one remains behind it, a picturesque ruin with a battlemented tower and a cloak of ivy. There is a Victorian mausoleum to the local Holland family in the roofless nave.

Church of England

5 TEMPLE OF MITHRAS
Terrace beside Temple Court, 11 Queen Victoria Street, short distance from Bank of England

[TQ 3281]   +

The remains of this Roman temple,

uncovered during redevelopment in 1954, have been moved from the original site and reconstructed in the adjacent forecourt of Temple Court. The temple was built in the first century AD, and had an aisled nave like later Christian churches, but was dedicated to Mithras, a sun-god of Persian origin venerated in the Roman Empire by merchants and soldiers. Whether this reconstruction is really to be regarded as a ruin is debatable, but I have included it because it is known that other parts of the basilica still lie unexcavated beneath the street called Walbrook to the east.

City of London

6 WARDROBE TOWER AND CITY WALL
Tower of London

[TQ 3380]   ***   Tel: 071 709 0765

Within the Tower of London, and close to the enormous Norman keep known as the White Tower, are the slight remains of this twelfth-century tower, which adjoins a section of the Roman city wall of Londinium and was built on the base of one of its bastions. The Roman wall ran northward from the Thames through what are now Waterloo Barracks and the Bowyer Tower. Built in the second century, it was constructed of Kentish ragstone with courses of Roman brick. The Wardrobe Tower was probably built towards the end of the twelfth century by Richard I, using the rubble of the Roman bastion which it replaced. It is believed to have been part of an enceint, or fortified enclosure.

English Heritage

28 Merseyside

See map below

1 BIRKENHEAD PRIORY
Priory Street in town, W bank of River Mersey

[SJ 3288]   +

Founded in the twelfth century by Hamon de Massey as a priory for Benedictine monks, it was built on a headland above the Mersey, on the Wirral peninsula, and was eventually granted a monopoly in ferrying travellers across the river. After the Dissolution, the chapter house was taken into use as a chapel. Not much remains of the priory church, rebuilt in the thirteenth century, but there are ruins of the monastic buildings, which became enveloped in shipyard surroundings in modern times.

Birkenhead Corporation

2 THURSTASTON CHURCH
In village churchyard, A540 W of Birkenhead

[SJ 2484]   +

A battlemented tower in the churchyard is a remnant of the rebuilding of the parish church in the first quarter of the nineteenth century, eventually displaced by the later church.

Church of England

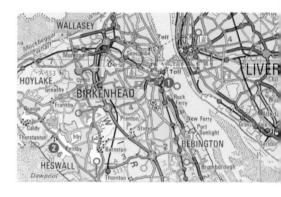

29 Norfolk

See maps on pages 90 and 91

Norfolk is a county second to none in its collection of ruined churches of all shapes and sizes, and those that follow are only a selection.

Baconsthorpe Castle

1 ANTINGHAM CHURCH
In village churchyard, just off A149, 2½ miles (4 km) NW of North Walsham

[TG 2532] +

The ancient church of St Margaret stands in ruins in the churchyard of the present parish church of St Mary, with overgrown fragments of nave and chancel as well as the remains of the tower.

Church of England

2 APPLETON CHURCH
Beside drive off B1440, near Sandringham

[TF 7027] +

A small fourteenth-century church with a twelfth-century round tower, left to decay when the medieval village was deserted. Built in brown stone, little remains but part of the tower and other fragments, covered in undergrowth.

Private

3 BACONSTHORPE CASTLE
Farm lane N of village, 3 miles (5 km) SW of Sheringham

[TG 1238] +

Walls, towers and gatehouse of a fifteenth-century fortified house, more correctly called Baconsthorpe Hall, built round a courtyard by the Heydon lord of the manor, within a rectangular moat crossed by a drawbridge. The place became a cloth factory in the seventeenth century, when the family's fortunes had declined, and much of the mansion was demolished and sold as building material after the Civil War. The gatehouse was only deserted in the 1920s.

English Heritage

4 BAWSEY CHURCH
Farm track off B1145, 2½ miles (4 km) E of King's Lynn

[TF 6620] +

There is some confusion as to whether this is the ruin of St James's church at Bawsey or St Michael's at Mintlyn. Both places are lost medieval villages which stood close to King's Lynn. I believe this ruin to be Bawsey's church. At any rate, its stone tower with fragments of round arches stands tall like a sentinel in a field,

Bawsey church

and is visible from the roads east of King's Lynn. Approachable on Church Farm track from B1145.

AM

5 BEESTON REGIS PRIORY
Beside A149 through village, E of Sheringham

[TG 1642]   +

There is nothing to see of the monastic buildings, partly consumed by modern development, but the cruciform church of this small Augustinian priory, founded about 1216 by Lady Margaret de Cressy, is a fairly substantial ruin near the coastal village church. The priory was suppressed in 1539.

6 BINHAM PRIORY
Short distance NW of village centre, 5 miles (8 km) SE of Wells-next-the-Sea

[TF 9839]   +

Binham was a Benedictine priory founded in the eleventh century, and the central part of the priory church (i.e. the nave) remains intact and in use as the parish church, with a huge Early English west window dominating the exterior view, built by Prior Richard de Parco early in the thirteenth century, and now unfortunately bricked up. The former aisles and east end of the church are ruined, but there is much of interest here, with some remains of other priory buildings.

English Heritage

7 BROOMHOLM PRIORY
At Bacton, on B1159 near coast NE of North Walsham

[TG 3433]   ⊖ *No access* ⊖

Reputedly a place of miracles, Broomholm (or Bromholm) was a Cluniac priory founded in 1113 by William de Glanville. It became a place of pilgrimage on account of the 'Holy Rood of Bromholm', asserted by the monk-historian Matthew Paris to be a piece of the true Cross brought from Constantinople. It seems that it had been hawked across Europe and only the Norfolk priors fell for the story. But it was soon being claimed that this doubtful relic was curing blindness and bringing the dead back to life, and believers naturally flocked here, the place earning mentions by Chaucer and Langland. Among the pilgrims was Henry III, and John Paston, whose family were patrons of the priory, was given a sumptuous burial in the church. But the priory went the way of all such establishments under a later Henry, and although parts of the ruins are impressive, you have to sort them out from concrete relics of a later age – fortifications built out of the ruins in the Second World War. The flint remains include the transept of the church, the gatehouse, chapter house and dormitory, but all are now, alas, parts of a farm and have silos and wooden buttresses for company. Visible from the gateway.

Private

Binham Priory

8 BURGH CASTLE

At end of minor road in Burgh village W of Great Yarmouth

[TG 4704]   +

Although popularly known by this name, it is actually the Roman fort of Gariannonum, defending the Saxon Shore, but left inland by the receding waters, behind the sand-bank where Great Yarmouth now stands. The mighty walls still stand to an impressive height on three sides of the former rectangular enclosure. No wonder the people who followed the Romans thought such structures must be the work of giants. The seaward wall has gone, and one or two of the huge projecting bastions have toppled outwards under their own weight, but the walls testify to both the engineering skill and the sense of purpose of the imperial occupiers of Britain in the third century. You have to walk ½ mile (1 km) to it from the nearest parking spot.

English Heritage

9 BURNHAM NORTON FRIARY

Beside minor road linking B1155 and B1355 just N of Burnham Market

[TF 8342]   +

Apart from the gatehouse, only slight remains can be seen of this house of Carmelite friars, founded in 1241. The priory was dissolved in 1539. The ruins are now closer to Burnham Market, standing east of the isolated church on the road between the two villages.

Norfolk County Council

10 CAISTER CASTLE

W of Caister-on-Sea, on minor road S from A1064

[TG 5012]   ★★★   Tel: 0493 720267

Nowadays, visitors come to see the motor museum rather than the ruins, but this was the moated castle built of brick in the fifteenth century by Sir John Fastolf, veteran of Harfleur and Agincourt, and the original of Shakespeare's Falstaff. It was also the

home for 140 years of the Paston family, of the famous *Paston Letters*, who inherited Sir John's properties in a disputed will. A letter from one member of the family to another warned that, unless urgent repairs were carried out at Caister, 'many of the walls will lie in the moat ere long . . .'. The best part of the ruins is the 90-foot (27-m) high round tower with machicolated parapet, and an attached stair-turret remaining even higher, which can be climbed by those with sufficient stamina.

Private

11 CASTLE ACRE PRIORY

W edge of village, off A1065 4 miles (6.5 km) N of Swaffham

[TF 8114]   ★★★   Tel: 07605 394

Prior Thomas Malling surrendered the priory to the king's commissioners in 1537, and during the following centuries the buildings passed through a series of ownerships – Howard, Gresham, Cecil, Coke – and were quarried by all the

masons in the neighbourhood for their flint and dressed stone. Nevertheless, the priory is still a substantial ruin, and the most important Cluniac remnant in the country, as well as being easily the most impressive ruin in East Anglia. It was founded around 1090 by one of the de Warenne Earls of Surrey, for a prior and 26 monks, and was richly endowed by Henry I and II. It possessed land locally and in Yorkshire, and five watermills were among its properties, but it was heavily taxed by Edward I and his successors for rendering financial tribute to its parent house across the Channel – Cluny in Burgundy. What the Cistercians saw as the virtue of architectural restraint did not impress the Cluniacs. They were noted for the grandeur of their church services, the *Opus Dei*, and the priory displays some splendid architectural detail, especially in the almost full height of the priory church's west front, with its orders of columns and rich wall arcading, and the arcaded south-west tower. The monastic buildings are chiefly of flint, the only locally-available building material.

English Heritage

12 CASTLE RISING
In village of same name, 3½ miles (5.5 km) NE of King's Lynn

[TF 6624] ★

The proportions of this castle's square keep, built within enormous earthworks which are probably Roman in origin,

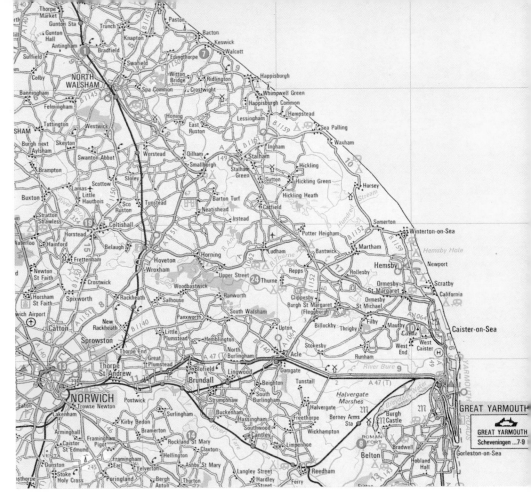

The Roman walls of Burgh Castle

Castle Acre Priory

make it appear from the outside, and especially in photographs, almost like a child's model fort rather than a real castle, but once you step inside the impression is quite different. There is no access to the ground floor from outside. A stone staircase leads directly to the upper floor of the cavernous and roofless interior. The castle was already derelict by Edward IV's reign, and the keep is virtually all that remains of a once-substantial fortress built in the twelfth century by the Earl of Arundel. Edward III's mother, Isabella – the 'She-wolf of France' – lived in retirement here after the execution of her lover Roger Mortimer, and was visited regularly by the king and by the Black Prince, who later owned the castle.

English Heritage

13 CITY WALLS, NORWICH
NE of cathedral, on bank of River Wensum

[TG 2409]   + (Cow Tower)

The remains of the walls still surround the medieval town on all sides except where it was protected by the river, and in some places stand to their full original height of 20 feet (6 m), with battlements and wall-walk more or less intact, and

Flint walls behind the façade at Castle Acre Priory

the remains of circular or semi-circular towers. The best of the latter is the so-called Cow Tower, at the wall's north-eastern corner by the river. It is 50 feet (15 m) high and was built of brick, with arrow-slits of stone, in the fourteenth century.

City of Norwich

14 CLAXTON CASTLE
Minor road W of village, off A146, 7½ miles (12 km) SE of Norwich

[TG 3303] ★★★

A long section of wall with the remains of several towers, built of brick, are all that is left of a fourteenth-century fortified house of which very little seems to be known, close to a modern house built on the site. The castle was moated, and was originally the property of Walter de Kerdiston.

Private

15 COXFORD PRIORY
In field beside minor road off A148, 5 miles (8 km) W of Fakenham

[TF 8429] ⊜ *No access* ⊜

One tall arch remains standing of the priory church, otherwise only chunks of masonry. The arch is easily visible from the road between the village and Broomsthorpe. It was an Augustinian house refounded here about 1215 and suppressed in 1536.

Private

16 CREAKE ABBEY
Off B1355, ¾ mile (1.2 km) N of North Creake

[TF 8539] +

Founded as a priory for Augustinian canons in 1206, it was promoted to abbey status in 1231. In 1506 the entire community was wiped out in a plague epidemic. The most impressive remains are of the abbey church's transepts and chancel, complete with Gothic arches, on farmland 1 mile (1.5 km) north of North Creake.

English Heritage

17 EGMERE CHURCH
In field beside minor road from B1105 at Little Walsingham to B1355 at North Creake

[TF 8937] +

Built early in the fourteenth century, the church was then at the centre of a little community which may have been a

Inside Castle Rising

victim of the Black Death, or of economic depression, or both. Now, the forlorn church tower and fragments of the nave walls stand isolated in a field. The modern hamlet, such as it is, is ¾ mile (1.2 km) to the east.

Private

18 GODWICK CHURCH
Farm track from minor road linking Whissonsett and Tittleshall, 5 miles (8 km) S of Fakenham

[TF 9021] ★★

The tower of the old church stands up in a field, the only remnant of a village that

Creake Abbey

The deserted village church at Egmere

The church of the lost village of Godwick

became deserted, notwithstanding that, as late as 1585, Lord Chief Justice Coke built himself a manor house here. The church of flint and brick was already, in 1602, described as 'wholly ruinated and decayed', and the house has been totally obliterated in recent years.

English Heritage

19 GREAT HAUTBOIS CHURCH
Beside minor road NW from Coltishall to Little Hautbois

[TG 2620]   +

Unlike the churches of deserted medieval villages, in the north of the county, which usually consist of an isolated tower or fragments of masonry in fields, this one, by the River Bure at the western edge of the Broads, is reasonably complete, though roofless. It has an unornamental cylindrical tower which resembles a factory chimney. The village's name is pronounced 'Hobbis', and it was given a new church in 1864.

Church of England

20 HACKFORD CHURCH, REEPHAM
In parish churchyard at Reepham

[TG 1022]   +

The churchyard at Reepham once held three churches, all serving different parishes. Those of Reepham and Whitwell (St Mary's and St Michael's respectively) still stand, but nothing remains of Hackford's except one wall. This church fell into ruin after the Dissolution, in 1543, though not as a direct result – it was gutted by fire and eventually pulled down.

Church of England

21 MANNINGTON CHURCH
In grounds of Mannington Hall, 5 miles (8 km) NW of Aylsham

[TG 1432] ⊖ *No access* ⊖

The eccentric and misogynous Earl of Orford, of Mannington Hall, who was buried in this church, collected architectural and sculptural ornaments, some of which now adorn the church's ruinous nave and chancel. It has been in ruins a long time, there being no population large enough to support it in the present century. Its fragments are *just* visible in a garden beside the road.

Private

22 NORTH ELMHAM CATHEDRAL
N end of village, B1110 near church, 6 miles (10 km) N of East Dereham

[TF 9821]   +

This unlikely village on the River Wensum was the site of the Saxon cathedral of the North-folk until about 1075, when the see moved first to Thetford and finally to Norwich. The cathedral was then allowed to fall into ruin, and in the fourteenth century Bishop Henry le Despencer built a fortified manor house out of the remains, enclosing it within two moats – after his part in the cruel suppression of the Peasants' Revolt, he needed the security. Investigation in the nineteenth century revealed the true origin of the ruins, and only the excavated foundations and a few low flint walls are visible. The cathedral was probably built here originally in the seventh century, but it was completely destroyed by Danish raiders in the ninth, and then rebuilt.

English Heritage

23 PUDDING NORTON CHURCH
In field beside B1146, 1 mile (1.5 km) S of Fakenham

[TF 9227]   ⊜ *No access* ⊜

Fifteen families lived here in the fourteenth century, but sterile soil and the poverty of the tiny population had led to desertion of the village by 1401, and only the jagged tower of flint and stone, and fragments of walls, remain of St Margaret's church, at the edge of a field, as a kind of memorial to the medieval villagers who struggled against the odds to eke a living out of this barren land to the south of Fakenham. Can be seen clearly from the road.

Private

24 ST BENET'S ABBEY
By River Bure, minor road and track from A1062, 2 miles (3 km) E of Horning

[TG 3815]   +

Beside the River Bure, and difficult to reach by land, are the scant remains of a pre-Conquest Benedictine foundation which attracted several artists of the Norwich school in the nineteenth century, largely on account of the windmill which had been erected in the ruins of its gatehouse, to drain the marshes. Now the windmill is a ruin as well. The abbey was not suppressed by Henry VIII, and the then abbot having

become Bishop of Norwich, the present Bishop is still technically Abbot of St Benet's as well.

AM

25 SALTHOUSE CHAPEL
In village churchyard, off A149, 1¾ miles (2.8 km) E of Cley-next-the-Sea

[TG 0743]   +

The ruin stands in the churchyard of the present parish church of St Nicholas. It was a small chapel with, according to Pevsner, a piscina and an altar, but I do not know its origin or history.

Church of England

26 THETFORD PRIORY
In town near railway station

[TL 8683]   +

Thetford is a little treasure-house for the really enthusiastic ruin-hunter, but alas, only one of its several ruins is of any extent or substance. The town had twenty parish churches in the fourteenth century, but the Dissolution brought its religious activity to heel. There are fragmentary remains of three churches and a nunnery, as well as the castle mound, but the most important ruins in the town are those of the Cluniac Priory of Our Lady, founded in 1103 by Roger Bigod, Earl of Norfolk, and established on this site in 1107. Henry I laid the foundation stone in that year. There are considerable remains of the priory church and less impressive ones of the monastic buildings.

English Heritage

27 WALSINGHAM FRIARY
In Little Walsingham, W of B1105

[TF 9336]   ⊜ *No access* ⊜

The church of this Franciscan friary, founded in 1347, has been totally demolished, but the ruins of the monastic buildings are interesting and impressive. They can only be glimpsed, however, from a gateway on the road through the village, being rather aggressively inaccessible.

Private

28 WALSINGHAM PRIORY
In Little Walsingham, E of B1105

[TF 9336]   ★★★   *Tel: 032 872 259*

The modern house on the site is called Walsingham Abbey, but there are many instances (Bolton Abbey, North Yorkshire; Newstead Abbey,

Nottinghamshire) where the Romantic movement elevated priories to abbey status for the sake of a good address, and Walsingham was really a priory for Augustinian canons, founded about 1160, which was famous for its Shrine of Our Lady, drawing great numbers of pilgrims who included Richard I, Erasmus of Rotterdam, and the less likely figure of Henry VIII, who is supposed to have walked barefoot from Barsham Manor to the priory he promptly dissolved when he fell out with the Church. The chief remaining part of the priory is the church's east wall with its large window.

Walsingham Estate Office

29 WEETING CASTLE
Track N from B1106 in village, 6 miles (10 km) NW of Thetford

[TL 7789]   +

A fortified manor house, within an almost square moat, built of flint in the twelfth century and consisting apparently of a hall with a tower at one end. It was the seat of the de Plaiz family.

English Heritage

30 WEST ACRE PRIORY
In village, 2½ miles (4 km) W of Castle Acre

[TF 7814]   ⊜ *No access* ⊜

This was a large priory for Augustinian canons, founded around 1100, but its ruins are not nearly so extensive or impressive as those of its neighbour, Castle Acre (q.v.). Parts of the church tower and chapter house remain to some height, as well as the gatehouse, all of flint, and can be seen from the road nearby.

Private

31 WEST RAYNHAM CHURCH
Path behind public house in village, 5 miles (8 km) SW of Fakenham

[TF 8725]   ⊜ *No access* ⊜

The remaining wall and other fragments of St Margaret's church, built of flint and brick with stone dressings, are in an old churchyard behind the village pub, and almost totally hidden among trees and undergrowth. The church was still complete early in the seventeenth century, and it seems that the village as it existed then was a victim of Lord Townshend's ruthless development of his park and the view from the mansion.

The Saxon cathedral at North Elmham

32 WEYBOURNE CHURCH
N side of A149 in village, 2¾ miles (4.5 km) W of Sheringham

[TG 1143] +

Part of the village church near Sheringham is in ruins. It was originally the church of an Augustinian priory, founded in the thirteenth century, and the surviving part was dedicated as the parish church of All Saints. Excavation has revealed other parts of the priory buildings.

Church of England

33 WIGGENHALL ST PETER CHURCH
Minor road through village, S from A47 at King's Lynn

[TF 6013] +

All the other Wiggenhalls, near King's Lynn, have their churches intact, but St Peter's has long been a ruin. It stands right beside the east bank of the Great Ouse, and its walls are Perpendicular in both senses, rising to their full original height, but it has no roof.

Church of England

34 WYMONDHAM ABBEY
SW side of town

[TG 1101] +

Founded as a priory by William d'Albini, Earl of Arundel, in 1107, it became a Benedictine abbey in 1449. Most of the abbey church is intact, and in use. It is peculiar in having a tower at each end, owing to long medieval disputes between the parish interests and those of the priory. After the Dissolution, the chancel was destroyed, but the rest was saved by the townspeople, who purchased it as

97

their parish church, which it had in fact been all along, as well as the monks' church. The abbot who had surrendered the monastery, Elisha Ferrers, became vicar of the parish. Apart from the ruins of the chancel, only a fragment of the chapter house remains.

Church of England

30
Northamptonshire

See map on page 99

1 BARNWELL OLD CASTLE
N end of village, off A605 S of Oundle

[TL 0485] ★★★

Peterborough Abbey owned this castle at the time of the Dissolution, and it was then purchased by Sir Edward Montagu, who built a mansion in the outer ward, now the home of the Duke of Gloucester. The ruin is of a thirteenth-century castle built (evidently without permission) by Berengar le Moine, and comprising a quadrangular enclosure with a twin-towered gatehouse at one corner and circular towers at the others, with various attached turrets on those at the eastern end.

Private

Wiggenhall St Peter church

Kirby Hall

2 HOLDENBY HOUSE

In village, minor road between A50 and A428, 6 miles (10 km) NW of Northampton

[SP 6967] ⊖ *No access* ⊖

Sir Christopher Hatton, whom we meet again at Kirby Hall (q.v.), built himself a great house at Holdenby at about the same time, completing it in 1583. In 1651 it was largely demolished, and the remaining part incorporated in a new house in the nineteenth century. In the grounds of this house stand two fine ornamental arches of Hatton's original mansion. They were the entrance to one of the courtyards of the house where the dashing young Hatton entertained Queen Elizabeth, and where James I and Charles I spent some time.

Private

3 KIRBY HALL

Reached by minor road off A43 or A6116, 4 miles (6.5 km) NE of Corby

[SP 9292] ★★★ *Tel: 0536 203230*

What a superb mansion this must have been in its prime, for even in ruins it is magnificent. It was begun by Sir Humphrey Stafford in 1570, the first stone being laid by the master mason's young son, John Thorpe. But Sir Humphrey died as soon as his house was finished, and the estate was purchased by Sir Christopher Hatton, one of Queen Elizabeth's favourites, to whom she gave

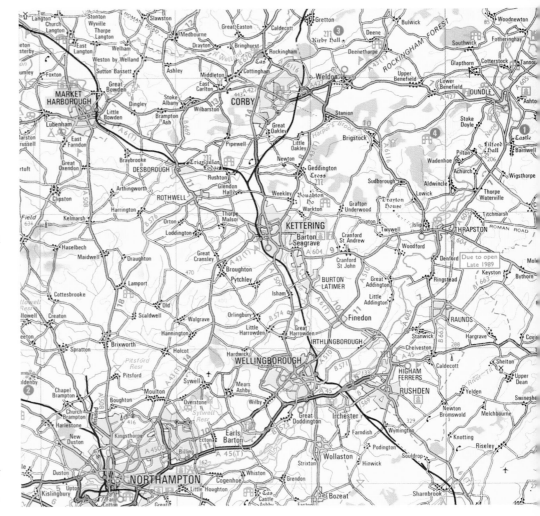

Lyveden New Bield

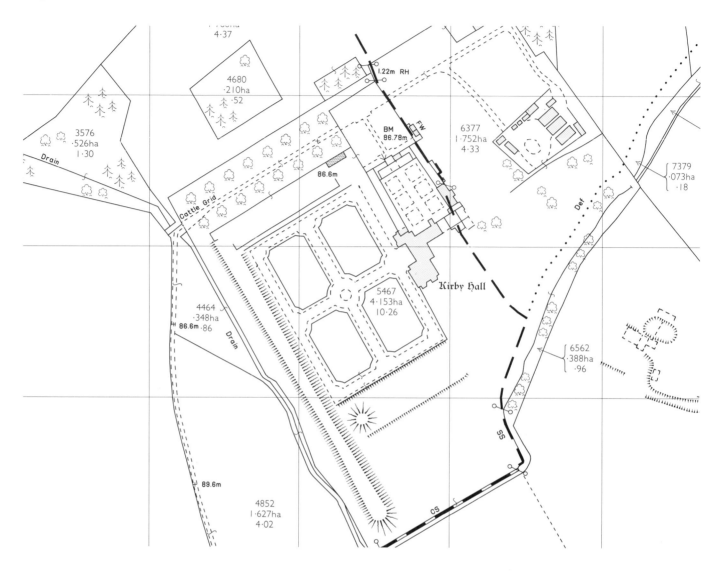

Corfe Castle. He became her Lord Chancellor in 1587, but fell ill when Raleigh replaced him in the queen's affections. Some say he died of a broken heart. Kirby Hall was lived in until 1820, and then fell into neglect. Its ruins are spectacular, with fine renaissance details added by Inigo Jones to the buildings arranged round a square courtyard. Lawns set off the mellow limestone brought from the quarries at Weldon, 2 miles (3 km) away.

English Heritage

4 LYVEDEN NEW BIELD

2½ miles (4 km) E of Brigstock. Footpath signed from minor road off A6116 from Brigstock to Oundle

[SP 9885] ★

Northamptonshire is not rich in ruins, and strictly speaking, this one is not a ruin at all. It was begun by Sir Thomas Tresham, a Catholic whose taste for religious symbolism had already led him to build the famous Triangular Lodge at Rushton as an allegory of the Trinity. Here the house was to symbolize the Passion, with the ground plan in the form of a cross and the three-storey building incorporating mystical numbers and appropriate inscriptions. But Sir Thomas died in 1605 after years of harassment and imprisonment for his faith, and his son, implicated in the Gunpowder Plot, forfeited all the family's estates. So the house was never completed, and it stands here still, *sans* roof and windows, like an unfinished symphony in stone. To reach it, you must walk ½ mile (0.8 km) along a track, crossing two fields, from a minor road between Oundle and Brigstock. It is well worth the effort.

National Trust

31 Northumberland

See maps on pages 102 and 103

1 BEADNELL KILNS

By harbour of village, minor road S from B1340 SE of Seahouses

[NU 2328] +

The remains of a group of round eighteenth-century limekilns stand beside the harbour of this fishing village which was redeveloped for the transport of lime in the 1790s.

National Trust

2 BERWICK-ON-TWEED CASTLE

W of town centre near railway station

[NT 9953] +

A section of the curtain wall, with three

round bastions, remains from the castle begun in the twelfth century, part of the fortified town, of which a ruined sixteenth-century gun-tower also remains, by the River Tweed. The rest of the castle was demolished in the nineteenth century to make way for Berwick's railway station.

English Heritage

3 CHIBBURN PRECEPTORY

Minor road E off A1068, ¾ mile (1.2 km) NE of Widdrington, between Ashington and Amble

[NZ 2697]   +

This preceptory of the Knights of St John of Jersualem (the Knights Hospitallers), north-east of Widdrington, seems to have been founded about 1313. A moat surrounded the chapel, courtyard and living accommodation. Not much of them remains, and though listed as an Ancient Monument, the ruins seem in imminent danger of being totally consumed by vegetation.

AM

The latrine block at Housesteads fort, Hadrian's Wall

4 DODDINGTON TOWER

In village on B6525, 2½ miles (4 km) N of Wooler

[NT 9932]   +

Northumberland is pre-eminently the county of peel-towers and bastel-houses, the fortified homes which were built here (long after the rest of England had left its castles and fortified manors for the comforts of country houses and town mansions) because of raids across the border by Scottish moss-troopers. Many of them remain intact and inhabited. This L-shaped tower in the middle of Doddington is the ruin of a bastel-house, distinguished from a peel by being the more ambitious home – though that is not saying much – of a family of greater wealth. This one was built in 1584 for the Grey family, and was intact until the late nineteenth century. It was a three-storey house of thick stone walls.

5 DUNSTANBURGH CASTLE

[NU 2622]   ★

By the time Edward I granted a licence

to his nephew Thomas, Earl of Lancaster, to fortify this castle, in 1316, the work was already complete, for it was the king against whom Lancaster needed to defend himself! The castle rose on a 100-foot (30 m) cliff above the North Sea, but it was a refuge rather than a fortress, its gatehouse being virtually the only line of defence. Although protected on two sides by the sea, only a ditch defended it from the open country to the west. When the castle came into John of Gaunt's ownership, he strengthened its defences considerably, but it eventually surrendered under siege by 10,000 men of Edward IV's army, and then slowly fell into ruin, being sold at last by James I. You must walk to the ruin from Craster, 1 mile (1.5 km) away, or Embleton, 1½ miles (2.5 km).

English Heritage

6 EDLINGHAM CASTLE

In village off B6341, 6 miles (10 km) SW of Alnwick

[NU 1109]   +

A late fourteenth-century tower house with a walled courtyard or bailey,

Hadrian's Wall looking east from Housesteads

Edlingham's tower is square with corner buttresses, and of three storeys. The ruin is entered at first-floor level, where the hall is rib-vaulted and has clerestory windows and a fine hooded fireplace with heads carved in the corbels.

English Heritage

7 ETAL CASTLE

In village on B6354, 10 miles (16 km) SW of Berwick-on-Tweed

[NT 9239]   +

Not among the most attractive or exciting of castle ruins, standing rather delapidated at one end of the village street, it is nevertheless characteristic of the smaller border strongholds, having a

Lindisfarne Priory, Holy Island

four-storey tower, gatehouse and parts of an enclosure wall with an angle tower. There was one room to each floor of the great tower, and fireplaces remain on the first and second floors. The castle was built of squarish blocks of pink sandstone in the fourteenth century, and was captured by the Scots before Flodden.

English Heritage

8 FARNE PRIORY
On Inner Farne, Farne Islands, off coast near Bamburgh

[NU 2135]   ***   Tel: 0665 721099

Fragments of a chapel remain on the island of Inner Farne where St Cuthbert built a cell around 651, having – according to Bede – driven out the evil spirits which had made everyone before Cuthbert afraid to live there. The chapel was the first chapel of a small Benedictine priory established in 1255, which had only two monks in permanent residence. A new chapel was built in 1370, dedicated to St Cuthbert, and this one was restored in the nineteenth century, the old chapel having fallen into ruin after the Dissolution. There is a stone tower of about 1500, called Prior Castell's Tower, which also contained a chapel. The island is part of a nature reserve.

National Trust

9 HADRIAN'S WALL
B6318, A69 and B6264 follow line of wall most of the way from E to W

Wall   +
Forts ★
[NZ 3065–NY 2363]

The Romans' northern imperial frontier under Hadrian ran from Wallsend on the Tyne to Bowness-on-Solway, so that its remains now traverse Tyne and Wear and Cumbria as well as Northumberland, but this county possesses its most dramatic stretches as well as its best remaining forts and milecastles. Built in ten years in the second century AD, with stone quarried along the route, the wall was 73 miles (118 km) long and generally about 10 feet (3 m) wide and 15 feet (4.5 m) high, with a great parallel ditch on the northern side and a military supply route on the southern. There were gates at intervals along it for the passage of traders and livestock. There were two turrets between each pair of milecastles, and 17 forts. The best remains of forts are at Chesters, near Humshaugh, and

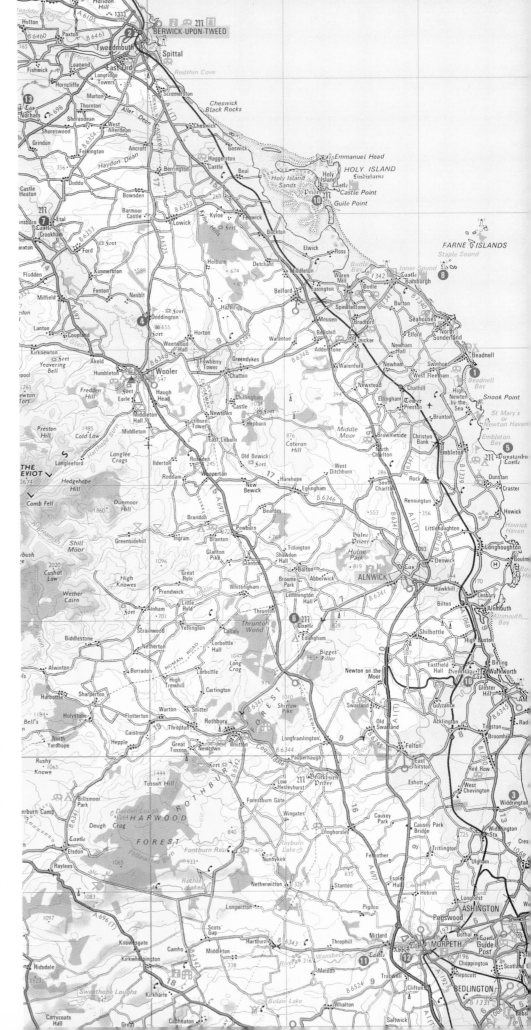

Housesteads, in a stretch owned by the National Trust – the first including a fine bath-house, and the second a well-preserved latrine. The finest view of the wall itself is looking east from near the inn known as Twice Brewed, on the B6318, where the wall snakes across the bleak landscape with characteristic Roman contempt for difficult terrain.

English Heritage

10 LINDISFARNE PRIORY
S end of Holy Island, accessible at low tide by minor road off A1, 8 miles (13 km) SE of Berwick-on-Tweed

[NU 1241]   ★

The Anglo-Saxons called the place Lindisfarne, and the Normans called it Holy Island, but it is only an island at high tide, and at low water you can walk or drive across to it on a surfaced causeway that was once a dangerous ridge of sand used by monks and pilgrims. It was accurately described 1200 years ago by the Venerable Bede. Celtic monks had founded the first monastery here, but that was destroyed by the Danes (the first English victim of Viking piracy), and the remains we see now are of the Benedictine priory of Norman foundation, occupied at first by a colony of monks from Whitby Abbey. St Cuthbert was bishop at the ancient monastery, and the Lindisfarne Gospels originated here, the famous illuminated manuscripts now in the British Museum, and one of the great works of art of the so-called Dark Ages. They were made in an atmosphere very different from that in which the later monks lived, who gorged themselves on venison, goose, pork, strong ale and wine from their various estates, and dressed in fine silk vestments. Nevertheless, this attractive ruin represents one of the holiest spots in English Christianity, and the red sandstone remains are reminiscent of the great Romanesque cathedral at Durham.

English Heritage

11 MITFORD CASTLE
Just SW of village on minor road off B6343, 1¾ miles (2.8 km) W of Morpeth

[NZ 1785]   ⊜ *No access* ⊜

Both the thirteenth-century castle of the Bertram family and the manor house built by the Mitfords to replace it in the seventeenth century are now in ruins. The castle, on the south bank of the Wansbeck, had what is probably the only five-sided keep in England, standing on a natural mound inside a shell-keep. It can be seen from the road. It was already neglected by the early fourteenth-century, and was in ruins by Leland's time.

AM

12 NEWMINSTER ABBEY
1 mile (1.5 km) W of Morpeth, off B6343

[NZ 1985]   ⊜ *No access* ⊜

The Cistercian abbey founded in 1137 near Morpeth was the first daughter of Fountains, and it became one of the largest monasteries in the far north of England, itself spawning several other houses. But although there are plenty of fragments, little of substance remains of what have been called the 'strangely neglected ruins of one of the most notable monastic houses in Northumberland'. The abbey was suppressed in 1537.

Private

13 NORHAM CASTLE
E end of village on B6470, 7½ miles (12 km) SW of Berwick-on-Tweed

[NT 9047]   ★★★   Tel: 028982 329

Best known as a misty, almost floating impression in the limpid landscapes painted by Turner over a period of 40 years, Norham, perched on a cliff above the Tweed, is in fact one of the mightiest of the border fortresses, begun in the twelfth century and maintained by the bishops of Durham, who made Norham a borough within the County Palatine of Durham, the town being long regarded as the most dangerous place in England. The great sandstone keep, part of the curtain wall, and the inner and outer gateways remain from the earliest castle in stone, but building went on here over a period of 400 years, with constant repairs and strengthening operations being carried out after Scottish attacks, Norham taking the brunt of Caledonian bombardment. It was protected by two moats on the landward side, and a fine barbican was added to the west gate in the fourteenth century. The castle was in use until the mid-sixteenth century – much later than the majority of castles – but peace with Scotland made it redundant at last, and it gradually fell into ruin through neglect, having endured centuries of war.

English Heritage

14 PRUDHOE CASTLE
N side of town, near railway station, off A695, 9 miles (14 km) W of Newcastle-on-Tyne

[NZ 0963]   ★★★   Tel: 0661 33459

Prudhoe was one of the Percy strongholds from the late fourteenth century, but it was begun in the twelfth century, on the site of an earlier motte castle, by the d'Umfraville family. Its ruins are extensive and, for those devoted to military architecture, impressive. Curtain wall and earthworks remain, along with the gatehouse, barbican and rectangular keep, on a natural spur on the south bank of the Tyne. The gatehouse had a chapel on the first floor, with what is often said to have been the country's earliest oriel window, though I believe thirteenth-century examples are known. In the courtyard is a Georgian house, with exhibits on the castle's history and, reputedly, a ghost.

English Heritage

15 THIRLWALL CASTLE
At Greenhead, by Hadrian's Wall, minor road off B6318, 9 miles (14 km) NE of Brampton

[NY 6666]   +

A tower-house, supposedly of the mid-fourteenth century, stands in ruins close to Hadrian's Wall near Greenhead, and was built mostly from the Romans' materials. Its walls are over 9 feet (3 m) thick in parts.

16 WARKWORTH CASTLE
In village, A1068, 6 miles (10 km) SE of Alnwick

[NU 2405]   ★

Edward II granted this castle in 1332 to Henry Percy, Lord Alnwick, later Earl of Northumberland and Marshal of England, and it remained the seat of the mighty Percys for six centuries afterwards, their lion symbol being carved on many of its stones, one of them facing the village street. The castle suffered attacks from the Scots and during the Percy rebellion against Henry IV, when it was forced to surrender. The ruin looks remarkably complete from a distance, its outstanding fifteenth-century keep having not only military might, but also architectural style and symmetry – a square building with bevelled corners and a polygonal turret on each face. It had its own kitchen and domestic chapel, and a square light-well in the centre, rising through the whole

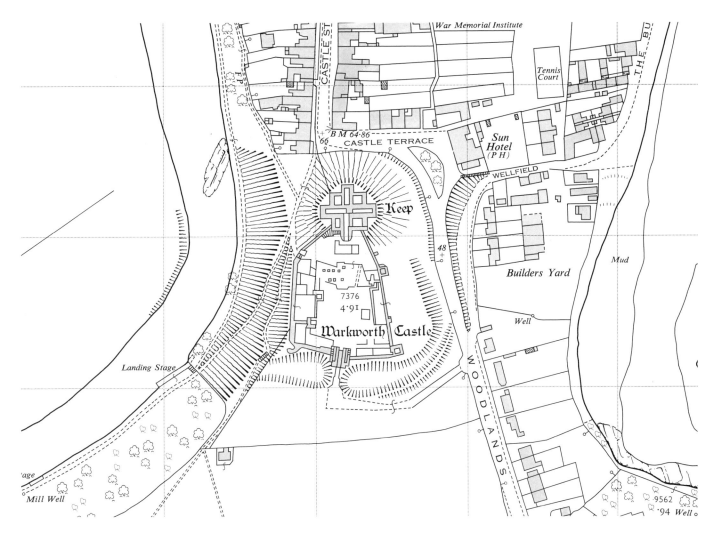

height of the tower, with a rainwater cistern which was used to flush the garderobe shafts. But much of the castle is considerably older than that, a stone keep with curtain wall having been built in the mid-twelfth century by a son of King David I of Scotland. The Grey Mare's Tail Tower is of the thirteenth century and has long fantailed arrow-slits.

English Heritage

---

32 *North Yorkshire*

See maps on pages 106 and 111

1 BARDEN TOWER
Beside B6160, 2½ miles (4 km) NW of Bolton Abbey

[SE 0557] ***

Occupying a fine position above the meadows of Wharfedale, this ruin was a tower house of the early Tudor period, built by an ancestor of Lady Anne Clifford, who restored it in 1658, before it again fell into ruin. It may have *begun* as a sort of gamekeepers' lodge for Barden Forest, but it grew into a stone three-storey house with domestic chapel.

AM

2 BOLTON CASTLE
In Castle Bolton village, off A684, 5 miles (8 km) W of Leyburn

[SE 0391] *** Tel: 0969 23408

A thuggish-looking fortified manor house, overlooking Wensleydale, it was built in the fourteenth century by Richard Scrope, Lord Chancellor to Richard II. Four great square towers were joined by three-storey ranges which enclosed a courtyard, and not only was the sole entrance guarded by a gatehouse with double portcullis, but all the doorways from the courtyard into the buildings were also provided with portcullises, and the family's quarters were completely isolated from those of the lord's retainers. Clearly there were not many people Lord Scrope felt he could trust. One turret contained a basement dungeon with a trap-door over it. In 1568 Mary, Queen of Scots was imprisoned in this house for six months before moving on to Tutbury (q.v.) in Staffordshire. The castle was besieged during the Civil War, and surrendered to Cromwell's troops only after holding out for a year. The ruin is mostly still standing to its original height, and looks more powerful and menacing than many a place which experts distinguish as a *real* castle!

Private

3 BOLTON HALL
Off A684 at Wensley, near Leyburn

[SE 0889] ⊖ *No access* ⊖

The seventeenth-century mansion built in Wensleydale by the Duke of Bolton

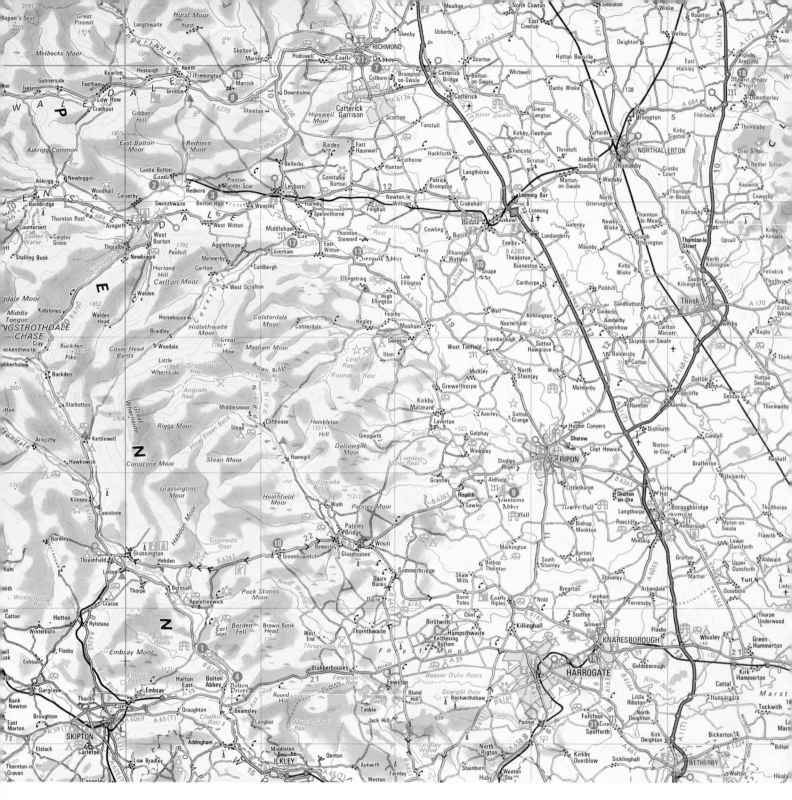

was destroyed by fire in 1902. The roofless shell remains standing, with a five-bay front.

Private

4 BOLTON PRIORY

Footpath from Bolton Abbey village, on B6160 NW of Ilkley

[SE 0754]   +

There is scarcely a more beautifully situated ruin in the land, and it has attracted artists such as Turner and Landseer, poets such as Wordsworth, and writers of the calibre of Ruskin. Set among the hills and meadows of Wharfedale, it was originally founded by Alicia de Romille in 1154, or at any rate transferred to this site from Embsay, where her parents had founded a priory earlier. The new priory was of the Augustinian order, and was established for a prior and 15 canons, who provided hospitality here, and supervised their trade in wool, iron and lead. Prior Richard Moone began the building of a new tower at the west end of the church in 1520, but it was left unfinished when he surrendered the property to the Crown nearly 20 years later, and Henry VIII sold it to the Earl of Cumberland for £2490. 1s. 1d. The nave of the church was kept up as the local parish church. The remains stand in the grounds of Bolton Hall, a nineteenth-century mansion of the Dukes of Devonshire. Although the village is called Bolton Abbey, the ruin never was an abbey. It is

Barden Tower, in Wharfedale

perhaps worth pointing out for the benefit of strangers to Yorkshire that Bolton Priory is not in the same locality as Bolton Castle.

Church of England

5 BYLAND ABBEY
On minor road near Wass, 2 miles (3 km) W of Ampleforth

[SE 5478] ★

Byland is one of the important and beautiful Cistercian ruins for which North Yorkshire has long been famed. Colonized by monks from Furness Abbey (q.v.) in 1178, after abortive attempts at settlement elsewhere, the abbey church shows clearly the extent to which by this time the Cistercians had abandoned the plain and simple architecture so passionately advocated by St Bernard of Clairvaux, in opposition to the self-indulgent ornament of other orders: 'We are more tempted to read in the marble than in our service books and to spend the whole day in wondering at these things than in meditating the law of God. For God's sake, if men are not ashamed of these follies, why at least do they not shrink from the expense?'

Byland Abbey

Follies or not, the remains of the large thirteenth-century abbey church at Byland are highly seductive, and include colourful and elaborate tiled floors and the lofty west end with the lower semi-circle of its former huge rose window. Although badly ruined, the monastic buildings can be followed clearly, and the wooded valley surroundings make it easier here than in some other places to imagine the white-cowled monks going about their daily business in solitude, although, as an antidote to romance, we ought to remember that they had enormous practical problems to overcome in draining this marshy site before they could build on it.

English Heritage

6 CLIFFORD'S TOWER, YORK
Tower Street, S of city centre

[SE 6051] ★

William the Conqueror erected castles very soon after the Conquest on either side of the Ouse at York, on artificial mounds. These were timber castles, and in the thirteenth century they were replaced by stone ones. The castle on the river's west bank has entirely disappeared. The rare and striking quatrefoil keep of pale limestone on the east bank is called Clifford's Tower from Roger de Clifford, one of the barons involved in the rebellion against Edward II. It was built by Henry III, his architect or 'ingeniator' being Henry de Reyns. The tower is reached by 55 steps straight up the side of the motte. Nothing much can be made of the inside, though there are fireplaces and garderobes, but from the top you can see how well the castle commanded the city.

English Heritage

7 EASBY ABBEY
Off B6271, 1½ miles (2.5 km) SE of Richmond

[NZ 1800] ★★

Founded about 1154 for Premonstratensian canons, the remains of Easby are substantial and picturesque, and ought to be as well known as the more famous Cistercian ruins of Yorkshire. They stand beside the River Swale near Richmond, with wooded slopes rising behind them. Little of the abbey church is left, but the monastic remains are fairly extensive and notoriously unusual in layout, due in part to the sloping ground and the drainage requirements. The canons

resisted suppression in 1536, and many of them were hanged.

English Heritage

8 ELLERTON PRIORY
B6270 E of Grinton, 6½ miles (10.5 km) SW of Richmond

[SE 0797] +

It was established in 1227 for Cistercian nuns, and was never a wealthy foundation. The ruins are extremely sparse – merely fragments of the tower and nave walls.

AM

9 FOUNTAINS ABBEY
Minor road off B6265, 3 miles (5 km) SW of Ripon

[SE 2768] ★

The aristocrat of British ruins suffers today from its very popularity, the crowds of visitors drowning its impact as a Cistercian monastery tucked away in what was called, at the time of its foundation, a 'lonely and forbidding spot . . . fit rather to be the lair of wild beasts than the home of human beings'. This kind of situation was just what the austere Cistercians always sought – a low-lying riverside site in remote

Arcade of the western porch of Fountains Abbey church

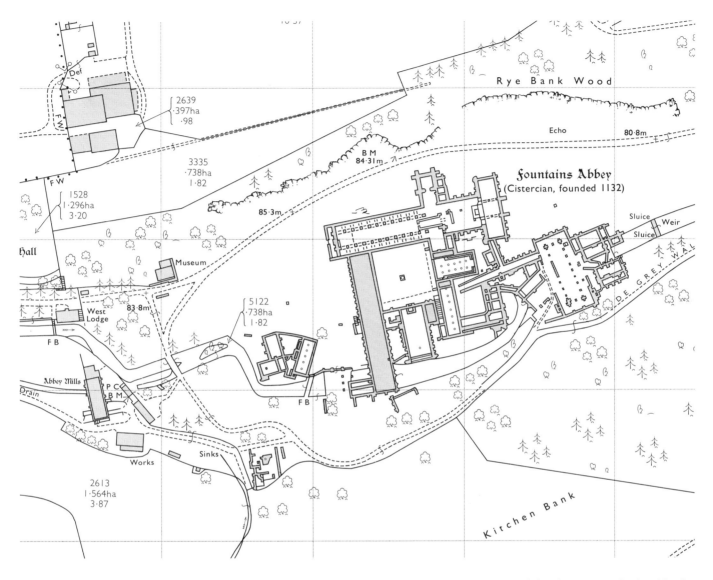

country. But in the eighteenth century, William Aislabie incorporated the ruins into the romantic landscape of his Studley Royal Park, and now, far from being a hidden and peaceful spot, Fountains is a huge tourist attraction, so its spirit is entirely lost. Nevertheless, its majestic remains are among the most beautiful of all ruins in Britain. The abbey was founded in 1132 in this valley of the River Skell, and was dedicated to St Mary of the Springs – *Santa Maria de Fontanis*. It was built of the pale local sandstone in the simple style enjoined on the Cistercian order by its founder, St Bernard of Clairvaux. But Fountains was enriched by gifts from princes and popes, and within 400 years it came to be the richest Cistercian foundation in England, with extensive farming, mining and quarrying interests which helped to bring new prosperity to a region which had never recovered from William of

Normandy's 'harrying of the North'. The abbey's wealth brought inevitable corruption to the purity of the Cistercian spirit, and fresh building took on hints of architectural lavishness, particularly in the Chapel of Nine Altars, one of the masterpieces of the period, and Abbot Huby's tower, built in contravention of the order's ban on towers and steeples as symbols of vanity. All this provided Henry VIII's henchman Thomas Cromwell with ample excuse, along with trumped-up charges (of theft, sacrilege and the keeping of whores) against the abbot, to grab the abbey's treasures for the Crown. The monastic remains are unusually extensive, and show clearly the common Cistercian layout of buildings extending south from the church. There is a 300-foot (90-m) *cellarium* or undercroft beneath the monks' dormitory, and the elaborate tunnelling and drainage system by which the monks

re-routed the river to supply the abbey's water-works can still be seen.

National Trust

10 GREENHOW HILL
B6265, 3 miles (5 km) W of Pateley Bridge

[*SE 1164*] (*village*)   +

The melancholy of industrial decline hangs over this area. On the bleak Pennine moors around this former lead mining village are to be found the ruins of terraced cottages, smelting mills and engine houses mostly abandoned in the late nineteenth century when the ores were worked out.

11 HARWOOD DALE CHURCH
Village on minor road off A171, 6½ miles (10.5 km) NW of Scarborough

[*SE 9596*]   +

The ruin of the former St Margaret's

Fountains Abbey

church is 1 mile (1.5 km) north-west of its 1862 replacement in this isolated moorland village. It was built by Sir Thomas Posthumus Hoby in 1634.

12 HELMSLEY CASTLE
Close to town centre

[SE 6183]   ★

The one remaining medieval building of any substance, the ruined keep or great tower can be seen thrusting upward from the countryside all around, but the most impressive things about Helmsley are its surrounding earthworks – deep double concentric ditches surround the castle, with a rampart between them, the inner ditch having been cut down into the rock. The castle was built, or begun, around 1200, and the ditches were probably added half a century later. The castle was well defended in other respects, too, yet its history is uneventful until the Civil War, when it was besieged by Fairfax, and then slighted.

English Heritage

13 JERVAULX ABBEY
Footpath from A6018, 3 miles (5 km) SE of Middleham

[SE 1785]   ★

To my mind, this, with Fountains and Rievaulx, forms Yorkshire's holy trinity. I have seen it criticized as untidy, but this is precisely its virtue, surely. Privately owned, it has never been subjected to the cosmetic treatment that state-owned ruins all show nowadays. Broken columns and carved stones lie about on the grass and the walls are overgrown, so that you feel a greater sense of communication with the past than in most ruins, and see Jervaulx much as the Romantics discovered the beauty of ruins in the eighteenth century. It was a Cistercian foundation of the latter half of the twelfth century (i.e. somewhat later than Rievaulx and Fountains), and was built here in the valley of the River Ure (hence its name, pronounced 'yervo'). It became famous for the cheese it produced from ewes' milk, and for the fine horses it bred. But when the threat of suppression came, the abbot, Adam Sedbar, was forced by the local populace, against his will, to join the Pilgrimage of Grace, and was taken to London and hanged at Tyburn. The king's demolition gang moved in and did a thorough job at Jervaulx, but what

The gatehouse at Kirkham Priory

Jervaulx Abbey

remains is fascinating, and the place itself is a peaceful oasis, set among green fields and parkland.

Private

14 KIRKHAM PRIORY
Beside minor road off A64, 5 miles (8 km) SW of Malton

[SE 7365] ★

Founded about 1125 by Walter l'Espec, a wealthy landowner who gave the land for Rievaulx (q.v.) to the Cistercians later on, Kirkham was a house of Augustinian canons. The earliest buildings began to be replaced in a major rebuilding programme in the thirteenth century, but it was never completed because the money ran out. This ruin is fairly fragmentary, but some of the fragments are of outstanding interest, especially the façade of the gatehouse, which has a wide Gothic arch flanked by figures of St George and the dragon, David and Goliath, and heraldic shields. There is

also a fine arcaded *lavatorium*, where the canons washed before meals. The ruin stands in a delightful spot beside the River Derwent.

English Heritage

15 KNARESBOROUGH CASTLE
Close to town centre

[SE 3456] ★

High above the town and the River Nidd, the ruins are of a fourteenth-century tower house built by Edward II, within an earlier enclosure wall with flanking towers. It passed through many hands from the time of its Norman foundation, including those of Piers Gaveston and John of Gaunt, but was mainly a royal possession. This was the castle where the four murderers of Thomas Becket hid, and where Richard II was held before his fatal move to Pontefract. It was thoroughly dismantled by Cromwell.

AM

16 MARRICK SMELT MILLS
Minor road off A6108, 5½ miles (9 km) W of Richmond

[SE 0799] +

The Pennine moors above Swaledale are dotted with the ruins of mine shafts, engine-houses and smelting mills for the lead mined in the area up to the end of the nineteenth century. The upper and lower mills here, near Reeth, are examples of the type.

17 MIDDLEHAM CASTLE
S edge of village, off A6108, S of Leyburn

[SE 1287] ★

It was built and enlarged over a very long period beginning around 1170, when a Norman baron replaced the earlier motte-and-bailey castle with a big stone keep to guard the road between Richmond and Skipton. Its value as a military fortress was very limited, but it was a baronial seat of the Neville family, and young Richard, Duke of Gloucester, came to the household for his schooling and met Anne Neville, daughter of Warwick the Kingmaker. When he married her, hot on the heels of her first husband's funeral, Richard acquired the castle as well, and was a responsible and respected northern landlord far removed from Shakespeare's villainous Richard Crookback, at least until he was informed of Edward IV's death by a messenger from Lord Hastings of Ashby. The grey ruins, which were uninhabitable long before the Civil War, dominate the village of Middleham, and the stables once probably housed horses from Jervaulx Abbey (q.v.), just down the road.

English Heritage

18 MOUNT GRACE PRIORY
Off A19, just NW of Osmotherley

[SE 4598] ★

Founded in 1398 by Thomas de Holand, Duke of Surrey, it is the best remaining example of a Carthusian priory, or charterhouse. The Carthusians were extreme in their austerity, embracing a rule of silence and strict isolation, eating only coarse bread and vegetables, and wearing black cassocks over hair shirts. They lived in individual cells in seclusion, meeting only at church services and on special feast days. There were 24 cells at Mount Grace, arranged round two cloisters with the priory church between them. Each cell had a hatch in the wall with an elbow bend in it, where a servitor placed the monks' meals without setting eyes on them. Parts of the buildings were converted into a house after the Dissolution, and this remains occupied beside the ruin, but what is left, particularly the limestone church with its crossing tower, is evocative of the period in its unworldly prosperity.

English Heritage

19 MULGRAVE CASTLE
Minor road off A174 at Lythe, 3 miles (5 km) NW of Whitby

[NZ 8412]　★★★

The medieval castle's ruins are in the grounds of the eighteenth-century house of the same name built by the Duchess of Buckingham. Relatively little is known of the history of the old castle, but it was built in the thirteenth century and consisted of a rectangular keep with semi-circular angle-turrets, surrounded by a curtain wall with gatehouse and towers.

Private

Middleham Castle

Mount Grace Priory

Rievaulx Abbey

Swale. Its most famous features are Scolland's Hall, one of the earliest surviving two-storey hall-houses, and its great tower or keep, built in the twelfth century and still standing to its full height of 100 feet (30 m), with walls 10 feet (3 m) or more thick. Yet there was no obvious need for such a fortress here, and the castle has played no significant role in the history of England.

English Heritage

22 RIEVAULX ABBEY
In village off B1257, 2½ miles (4 km) W of Helmsley

[SE 5784] ★

North Yorkshire is indeed thrice blessed to have such exquisite ecclesiastical remains as Fountains, Jervaulx and Rievaulx within its boundaries. The poet William Cowper was tempted to make his home in the village of Rievaulx, so that he could gaze at these ruins for the rest of his life. The abbey's remains are among the most precious treasures of our heritage, the soaring piers and majestic arches rising from the valley floor in such awe-inspiring splendour that we can easily forget the nature of the early Cistercians, who colonized this land – given to them in 1131 by the lord of the manor of Helmsley, Walter l'Espec – and established the first major settlement of their order in the north of England. The first abbot had been secretary to Bernard of Clairvaux, and the nave of the abbey church is pure Cistercian. The site – described as a place of 'horror and waste solitude' – was so restricted that the alignment of the church was made north-south instead of the traditional east-west, but within 30 years of its foundation the abbey accommodated 140 monks and 500 lay brethren: poor and illiterate folk whom the abbey sheltered in return for their labour on the buildings and in the fields. But increasing wealth led to corruption of pure principles, and as the monks abandoned their former austerity, so the numbers of the faithful decreased. Scottish raids dealt heavy blows to Rievaulx, and one of its fourteenth-century abbots died from the Black Death. By the time of the abbey's suppression only 22 monks were left. Some of the abbey's stone was plundered for building houses in the village, and it is only the isolation of Rievaulx that has preserved so much of it in a condition that makes it, architecturally, perhaps the most beautiful ruin in England. Its appreciation by the Romantic movement led to the creation of Rievaulx Terrace

20 PICKERING CASTLE
Short distance N of town centre

[SE 7984] ★

Although there are extensive remains and the castle has a long history, the ruins are singularly unexciting, being neither monumentally overpowering nor architecturally fascinating. Begun in the mid-twelfth century, the castle eventually consisted of a shell-keep on top of a mound, and an inner and outer curtain wall with one or two towers, enclosing two baileys. Nothing remains to any great height, the castle having fallen into decay in the seventeenth century.

English Heritage

21 RICHMOND CASTLE
Short distance S of town centre

[NZ 1700] ★

The details read like a boys' adventure story. It was begun very soon after the Conquest by Alan the Red, son of Ode, Count of Penthievre, whose two younger sons continued the castle after Alan's death, and whose great-nephew married the Duke of Brittany's daughter. There is a 'Gold Hole Tower', so called because it was reputed to have treasure buried under it (though it actually contained latrines), and a Robin Hood's Tower. Richmond was one of the country's earliest stone castles, occupying a triangular enclosure above the River

Scarborough Castle above the harbour

(National Trust) high above the valley floor, from which a fine bird's-eye view can be enjoyed.

English Heritage

23 ROSEDALE KILNS
Track S of Rosedale Abbey village, on minor road through Rosedale, 8 miles (13 km) NW of Pickering

[*SE 7294*] +

Nineteenth-century kilns built to calcine the iron ore mined here, 1 mile (1.5 km) south of the village of Rosedale Abbey, to save the costs of transporting unrefined ironstone to the furnaces. Before the branch railway was built, the ore was carried by packhorses to the railway at Pickering. Other remains of the iron-mining industry can be seen higher up Rosedale.

24 ST LEONARD'S HOSPITAL, YORK
Museum Street, short distance from Minster

[*SE 6052*] ★★★

It was one of the greatest of the English medieval hospitals or almshouses, founded or refounded by King Stephen in 1155 and coming under the patronage

Slingsby Castle

of the canons of York Minster. By the late fourteenth century it accommodated 224 inmates and had three chapels, and was allowed to take wood from the royal forest for fuel and building purposes. But, as an ecclesiastical establishment, this charitable foundation was suppressed at the Dissolution. The ruins are scanty, consisting of the walls of a chapel, a long passage and the vaulted undercroft.

City of York

25 ST MARY'S ABBEY, YORK
In Museum Gardens, Museum Street

[SE 5952] +

The ruins of St Mary's, though scant, are fascinating and often spectacular. The abbey was a Benedictine foundation of William Rufus in 1088, and soon became the wealthiest monastery of that order in the north of England. Its remains now stand in the Yorkshire Museum Gardens, fragments of the domestic buildings being in the basement of the museum itself. Above ground level, there are very fine remains of the thirteenth-century Decorated abbey church, with ornate carving, particularly part of the transept and the north wall of the nave, and sections of

walls with blank arcading, their pale stone looking almost pure white in strong sunlight, as if this were a bleached ancient Greek temple rather than a northern English church. The lusciousness of the architectural detail hints at the desertion of pure and simple monastic principles that led the prior and some of his monks to leave and found Fountains Abbey, but the beauty of these ruins must make us grateful today for the fact that the austerity enjoined on their brethren by the medieval saints was not always followed.

City of York

26 SAND HUTTON CHURCH
In village off A64, 7½ miles (12 km) NE of York

[SE 6958] +

In the parish churchyard of St Mary stand the remains of the Norman church dedicated to St Leonard.

Church of England

27 SCARBOROUGH CASTLE
On headland in town

[TA 0589] ★

It spreads itself expansively over the headland, with a clear view of the coast

to both north and south. The promontory is such an obvious strategic site that it was occupied by Iron Age, Roman and Viking people before the medieval stone castle was begun by William le Gros, Earl of Albemarle, in the late 1130s, the earliest part being the curtain wall overlooking the harbour. The castle as it stood in 1155 was seized by Henry II, and then remained a royal castle for over 400 years, undergoing much improvement and modernization, and covering 19 acres (8 ha) of land. The shattered twelfth-century keep was ruined by siege during the Civil War, and some damage was done by shelling from German ships in the First World War. The only entrance to the castle is still by the triangular barbican built around 1240.

English Heritage

28 SHERIFF HUTTON CASTLE
In village on minor road off A64, 10 miles (16 km) N of York

[SE 6566] *On application*

Built by Lord Neville of Raby in 1382, it belonged to Richard III at one time. It consisted of four towers linked by ranges enclosing a courtyard, and was a fortified manor house rather than a castle, but it was strong enough to be used as a prison

The former church of Wharram Percy

for Anthony Woodville, Lord Rivers, before his execution at Pontefract, and just possibly for the sons of Edward IV, the princes allegedly murdered later by Richard III in the Tower of London. Leland was still able to call the castle 'princely' half a century after Bosworth, but it was falling into ruin by the early seventeenth century. Its broken towers draw the eye from miles around, but its courtyard is now a farmyard.

Private

29 SLINGSBY CASTLE
In village off B1257, 6 miles (10 km) W of Malton

[SE 6975] ⊜ *No access* ⊜

Too unsafe to allow public access at present, this 'castle' of pale limestone is tucked away at the back of the village, fenced off and overgrown and, in the summer months, hidden by trees. But even in this neglected condition, it is an impressive domestic ruin, clothed in ivy and supporting birds' nests in its crumbling stonework. It was not a castle, but a seventeenth-century house of two storeys with corner turrets and plenty of windows. It was begun, but apparently never completed, for the dwarf soldier and philosopher Sir Charles Cavendish, on the site of what was originally, I believe, Wyville Castle, the fortified manor house of the Earl of Huntingdon. The ruin has served as a sort of cattle-shed in its time.

AM

30 SNAPE CASTLE
W end of village on minor road off B6268, 2½ miles (4 km) S of Bedale

[SE 2684] ⊜ *No access* ⊜

The castle is only partly in ruins, the sub-divided and inhabited part being the work of Thomas Cecil, Lord Burghley. The older ruined castle was a courtyard castle built by the great Neville family, and Catherine Parr, widow of John Neville, Lord Latimer, lived here before leaving to become Henry VIII's last wife at Hampton Court.

AM

31 SPOFFORTH CASTLE
In village, off A661 4 miles (6.5 km) SE of Harrogate

[SE 3651] ★

The shattered walls of this fortified manor house stretch the imagination; there is not a lot to help visualize the daily lives of its medieval occupants. But this is reputed to be the birthplace of Sir Henry Percy, Shakespeare's 'Hotspur', the celebrated warrior 'who turns his head against the lion's jaws', in the Bard's memorable phrase. It was his ancestor, Henry de Percy, who built the place in 1308, against a natural buttress of rock, with his great hall raised over an aisled undercroft. Its defences were not mighty – there was access to both floors from the ground. The Percy barons were fearless warriors who had ruled these parts since the Conquest. Their chief seat was Alnwick Castle in Northumberland, and Spofforth was already falling into decay by the end of the fifteenth century, and was finally dismantled early in the seventeenth.

English Heritage

32 WHARRAM PERCY
On foot from minor road off B1248 near Wharram-le-Street, 6 miles (10 km) SE of Malton

[SE 8564] +

The ruined St Martin's church of Wharram Percy is practically all that remains above ground of the country's most carefully studied lost medieval village. It lies in a dip in the Yorkshire Wolds and can only be reached on foot (¼ mile – 0.5 km) from the B1248 near Wharram-le-Street. The walk, however, is very pleasant in fine weather. Excavation of the site began in 1952, and is continuing. It has revealed that there was a Saxon settlement here, which grew into a well-populated village over the centuries, but became deserted by the beginning of the sixteenth century. The church continued to be used until 1870 by a neighbouring village which did not have its own church until then, and it remained intact until after the Second World War, but then the lead was stripped from its roof by thieves, the roof collapsed in 1954, and in 1960 part of the tower fell. Despite the long period of research the reason for the village's desertion is not known with certainty, but it was probably demolished to create sheep pastures for the feudal landlord, who stood to make more money from wool than from arable farming.

English Heritage

33 WHITBY ABBEY
Above town, on E side of River Esk

[NZ 9011] ★

There is nothing to be seen of the monastic buildings of the Celtic abbey founded in 657 by St Hilda and destroyed by the Danes in the ninth century, nor of the great Benedictine abbey which succeeded it, founded about 1067. But the ruins of the abbey church make one of the most spectacular and moving sights in England, standing partly to their full original height on a starkly exposed headland above the red-roofed town and harbour. The church is mainly of the Early English style, and was begun early in the thirteenth century. The monastery was suppressed in 1539, but the elements have done more damage to the church than its subsequent owners. The nave collapsed in 1762, the south transept in the following year, and the crossing tower in 1830. Nevertheless, the remains look remarkably solid, and feature moulded arches, carved capitals, and lancet windows in a tall gable. The ruin is all the more awesome for being on a hilltop, usually the province of military men rather than monks.

English Heritage

33 Nottinghamshire

See map on page 118

1 COLSTON BASSETT CHURCH
Lane off minor road ½ mile (0.8 km) NW of village, 10 miles (16 km) SE of Nottingham

[SK 6933] +

Aristocratic vandalism, of which there are plenty of examples in this book, put paid to this church in 1892, when the lord of the manor dismantled it in the course of building a new one in the village, which had migrated eastward. St Mary's was an imposing village church at one time.

Church of England

2 MATTERSEY PRIORY
1 mile (1.5 km) E of village on B6045, 4 miles (6.5 km) NE of Blyth

[SK 7089] +

Fragmentary remains of a twelfth-century priory of the Gilbertine order, burnt down in 1279 and partly rebuilt. Sections of walls of the church and some of the buildings round the cloister remain. The site near the River Idle is said to have been an island at the time of

4 NEWSTEAD ABBEY
In public park, off A611 at Annesley Woodhouse, S of Kirkby-in-Ashfield

[SK 5353]   *

The 'melancholy mansion of my fathers', as Lord Byron called this place, had never been an abbey. It was originally an Augustinian priory, founded by Henry II, and it came into the hands of the Byron family after the Dissolution, Sir John Byron dismantling all of it except the church's imposing west front and building himself a mansion on the site with the cheaply-acquired stone. It was the romantic poet himself who posthumously promoted the former priory to 'abbey' status. The mansion itself was in a badly neglected condition when Byron inherited it, and although he did his best to maintain it, the expense proved too much for him, and it was eventually sold. The house remains intact beside the ruined façade of the priory church, which still looks impressive with its huge central window beneath a gable with a statue of the Virgin. The famous monument to Byron's dog Bosun remains where the high altar of the church used to be. The grounds are now maintained as a park.

Nottingham City Council

5 RUFFORD ABBEY
In Rufford Park, off A614, 2 miles (3 km) S of Ollerton

[SK 6464]   +

The name is that of an imposing mansion reputedly built by Bess of Hardwick on the site of a Cistercian abbey which the Earl of Shrewsbury acquired after the Dissolution. It was the home of Arabella Stuart, who died in the Tower of London. The mansion passed through various hands and was much altered over the centuries, notably by Salvin, until it fell into neglect and ruin. Only fragments of the abbey remain, and only the exterior of the great house, once favoured by royalty as a hunting lodge, can be seen at present.

Nottinghamshire County Council

34 Oxfordshire

See map on page 119

1 BIX BOTTOM CHURCH
Beside lane N from minor roads off A423

---

the priory's foundation. The priory was suppressed in 1538.

English Heritage

3 NEWARK CASTLE
Short distance from town centre

[SK 7954]   +

The castle was raised in the twelfth century on a cliff above the River Devon, a tributary of the nearby Trent, and King John died here in 1216. It was already in 'great decay' by the late sixteenth century, but it was defended for the king in the Civil War, being finally surrendered by Lord Bellasis in May 1646, and then slighted. Not much of it remains except a gateway and the waterfront curtain wall and towers, which have later additions. The view from the river is arguably the best.

AM

at Bix or B480 at Middle Assendon, 3¾ miles (6 km) NW of Henley-on-Thames

[SU 7286] +

The tiny church of St James stands choked by vegetation, its flat gravestones lying beneath the grass and nettles, beside a narrow lane beyond Valley Farm, to the north of the village. It was abandoned when the new village church had been built, in 1875, the population having migrated southward. Some old maps call the site of the ruined church Bix Gibwen. Could it be part of the lost medieval village called Bispedone?

2 GREYS COURT
Off minor road from A423 at Henley-on-Thames, 2 miles (3 km) W

[SU 7283] *** Tel: 049 17 529

The de Grey family built here a fortified manor house of brick and flint in the fourteenth century, and its sparse ruins, clothed in vegetation, remain in the grounds of the subsequent Tudor mansion built by the Knollys family. Some of the material of the old house was used for the new one, and parts of it were incorporated whole, including the kitchen. The brickwork of the original house was among the earliest in the county. There is not much left of the ruined house, but Greys Court itself is an interesting place, and has a deep well

operated by donkey wheel, like that at Carisbrooke Castle, Isle of Wight (q.v.).

National Trust

3 MINSTER LOVELL HALL
In village, on B4047, 2½ miles (4 km) W of Witney

[SP 3211] ★

There is not a great deal of it left, but this was once a vast and splendid mansion, the fortified baronial home of the Lovell family from the fifteenth century. Standing in a wooded landscape by the River Windrush, the house was built by William Lovell, the 7th Baron, and was palatial in extent, raised round three sides of a courtyard, with great hall, solar and chapel in one range, kitchens, buttery and stables in another, and family and guest rooms in the third. In 1465 the property passed to William's grandson Francis, the 9th Baron, and friend since childhood of Richard of Gloucester, with whom he had been schooled at Middleham Castle. He eventually became Richard III's Lord Chancellor. After the Battle of Bosworth, Lord Lovell went into hiding, but later emerged as a supporter of Lambert Simnel's rebellion against Henry VII, raising an army in the north, but again escaped with his life after the ensuing battle at Stoke in Nottinghamshire, and

was apparently never seen again – not alive, at any rate. Legend has it that he made his way back to Minster Lovell and was hidden in a cellar by a loyal servant who fed him daily for months, sharing the secret with no one. But the servant either died or was taken away, and Lord Lovell was buried alive. His ghost is said to haunt the place. An absurd tale, you may think, but when the house was dismantled by Thomas Coke, Earl of Leicester, in the eighteenth century, workmen were said to have discovered a vault which they opened and glimpsed, a second before it crumbled into dust on exposure to the air, the corpse of a man seated at a table.

English Heritage

4 WAYLAND'S SMITHY
Ridgeway footpath from B4000, 8 miles (13 km) E of Swindon

[SU 2885] +

Standing beside the prehistoric trading route known now as the Ridgeway, it is a neolithic burial chamber probably 1000 years older than the earliest parts of Stonehenge. Its name is a reflection of the awe-struck Anglo-Saxon view of such massive works. They connected it with Wayland or Volund, the smith of Viking myth, and equivalent of the Greek Hephaestus and the Roman

Minster Lovell Hall

Wayland's Smithy

Vulcan. The legend grew that any horse left at the entrance to the 'cave' with a coin would be found magically shod when the owner came back. But the ruin is actually a gallery grave, which contained at one period eight corpses from which the heads had been severed. Reached by foot ($\frac{1}{3}$ mile – 0.5 km) from a signposted road off the B4000.

English Heritage

35 Shropshire

See map on page 122

1 ACTON BURNELL CASTLE
In village, on minor road between A49 and A458, 7 miles (11 km) S of Shrewsbury

[SJ 5301]   +

Really a fortified manor house, it has some significance in the history of England. Built at the end of the thirteenth century of red sandstone from the quarries at Grinshill, not far away, it was among the earliest of such fortified houses in the country, contemporary with Stokesay (q.v.). It was the home of Robert Burnell, Bishop of Bath and Wells and Edward I's Lord Chancellor. In the park close by are two stone gables, more than 150 feet (46 m) apart, which are presumed to be the end walls of the 'great barn' in which the king held a properly constituted Parliament in 1283, and enacted the Statute of Acton Burnell by which all debtors were to lose their property if they failed to discharge their debts within an agreed period. This Parliament also condemned Daffyd ap Gruffydd, the captured leader of the Welsh resistance, to be hanged, beheaded and quartered, the head being exhibited on the end of a lance at the Tower of London. The Commons may have sat in the barn and the Lords in the house, though it cannot have been finished at that time. The roofless ruin of the 'castle' is attractive and interesting, its battlemented walls and angle-towers remarkably intact.

English Heritage

2 ALBERBURY CASTLE
In village, off B4393, 8 miles (13 km) W of Shrewsbury

[SJ 3514]   +

The ivy-clad ruins of a stone tower and a

Acton Burnell Castle

section of wall are all that remain of a small thirteenth-century castle built as part of the defences of the Welsh Marches.

3 BRIDGNORTH CASTLE
In town park, W of River Severn

[SO 7192]   +

Nothing much remains except an enormous chunk of the twelfth-century tower or keep, which stands or rather leans in a public park, tilting hair-raisingly out of the vertical, at a greater angle than that of Pisa's famous leaning tower. This was a result of undermining by Parliamentarian troops in 1646. The castle was built by Robert de Belesme on a ridge of rock above the Severn, and was a royal castle for most of its existence.

4 BUILDWAS ABBEY
Just off A4169 near junction with B4380, 3 miles (5 km) N of Much Wenlock

[SJ 6404]   ★

Never a large or wealthy abbey, the remains of this Savignac, later Cistercian, foundation are nevertheless a must for the connoisseur of ruins. They

stand beside the Severn at the head of the famous Ironbridge Gorge, with the cooling towers of a power station for company, and there is little of the conventual buildings to be seen. But never mind that – just look at the church. It is impressive in its simplicity and its completeness, with Norman arcading on thick round piers unaltered through more than 800 years. Before the Dissolution the abbey was working the local iron ore deposits, and the cloisters echoed to the sounds of the monks hammering at their anvils. One of the abbots was murdered by a renegade monk, and another captured by Welsh raiders.

English Heritage

5 CLUN CASTLE
In village, on A488 between Bishop's Castle and Knighton

[SO 2980]   +

Easily the county's best castle ruin after Ludlow (q.v.), the choicest view of it is from the north-west, where its high motte and keep soar above the junction of the river Unk with the Clun (Celtic names to conjure with). The rectangular

keep was built in the twelfth century – unusually, on the sloping north side of the motte, rather than on top, with its foot in the ditch. The reason for this is not clear. The round towers were later additions. The castle was built by the FitzAlans, one of the most powerful of the Shropshire defenders of the Welsh Marches. It is in preparation for public viewing at the time of writing.

English Heritage

6 COALBROOKDALE FURNACE
In Ironbridge Gorge Museum, Coalbrookdale, off A4169 S of Telford

[SJ 6604]   ★

Although now enclosed and protected within the Ironbridge Museum complex, this brick furnace is perhaps the most important industrial ruin in Britain. Here in 1709 Abraham Darby successfully smelted iron using coke as his fuel, and so effectively set the Industrial Revolution in motion. The Coalbrookdale iron works were soon involved with Newcomen's and Watt's steam engines, with Trevithick's locomotive, and with Brunel's steam ships. But within a century the local

industry had collapsed under competition from elsewhere, soup kitchens becoming more numerous than blast furnaces, and Coalbrookdale declining almost into an industrial ghost town. This treasured relic is the cradle, nevertheless, of Britain's modern iron and steel industries.

Ironbridge Gorge Museum

7 HAUGHMOND ABBEY
Off B5062, 3½ miles (5.5 km) NE of Shrewsbury

[SJ 5415]   ★★★   Tel: 074377 661

Founded about 1130 as a priory for Austin canons, it was quickly elevated to abbey status and became a large establishment with various dependencies. In this case, unlike Buildwas, the monastic remains are more substantial than those of the church, the triple-arched entrance to the chapter house being particularly fine, the transitional doorway flanked by symmetrical windows, all with shafts, foliage capitals and decorated hoodmoulds. The infirmary building is also impressive, and the lavatorium and refectory are not to be ignored. The abbey church was demolished immediately after the Dissolution by Sir Rowland Hill, a local bigshot and subsequently Lord Mayor of London.

English Heritage

8 HOPTON CASTLE
In Hopton Castle village, on B4385, 9½ miles (15 km) W of Ludlow

[SO 3677]   +

The shattered stone keep of Hopton Castle stands on a low mound beside a tributary of the River Clun. It is of uncertain date, but possibly thirteenth-century, though the castle had been established in the century before that. In the Civil War, this castle was captured by the Royalists, and 29 of its Parliamentary defenders were clubbed to death.

AM

9 LILLESHALL ABBEY
Minor road from A518, 1 mile (1.5 km) S of village, NE of Telford

[SJ 7314]   ★★

This abbey was founded as an Arrouaisian house, but soon became Augustinian, and was a prosperous establishment tucked away by a stream at the edge of a wood. There are a few remains of the monastic buildings, but

The round chapel at Ludlow Castle

those of the church are more impressive, with a fine doorway into it from the cloister, and an exceptionally splendid west door with shafts and moulding, carved capitals and dogtooth ornament, as well as other details mostly Transitional and Early English. The abbey was ruined more thoroughly in the Civil War than at the Dissolution.

English Heritage

10 LUDLOW CASTLE
Close to town centre

[SO 5074]   ★

One of the first English castles to be built of stone, it began to rise in about 1085, the stronghold of one of the Conqueror's Marcher lords, Roger de Lacy. The Lacys were followed by the Mortimers, and Ludlow became in due course the

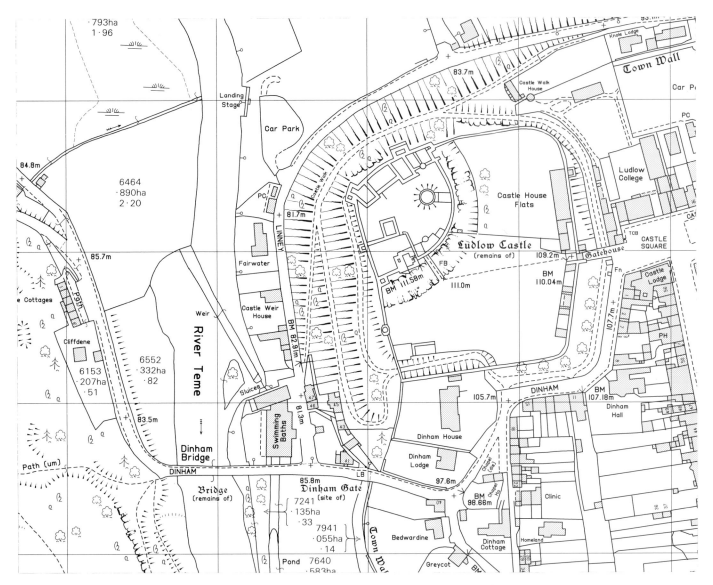

palace from which the English princes of Wales ruled their domain. Prince Edward, the short-lived Edward V, lived here from the age of three until he made his ill-fated journey to the Tower of London. The young prince regularly attended morning Mass in the castle's unique chapel, with its circular nave, which stands detached in the inner bailey or courtyard. Henry VII's eldest son, Arthur, came here with his Spanish bride, Catherine of Aragon, for their honeymoon, but the 15-year-old heir to the throne died of consumption within a few months and left his bride, as well as the crown, to his brother Henry. It was possibly an event that changed the course of English history. Sir Philip Sidney and his sister Mary also spent much of their childhood here, their father being Lord President of the Marches. In 1634, Milton's masque *Comus* was staged in the castle's great hall, and the ruins are the scene for part of Ludlow's annual summer festival nowadays, when open-air performances of Shakespeare are given.

Private

11 MORETON CORBET CASTLE
In village, off B5063, 8 miles (13 km) NE of Shrewsbury

[SJ 5623]   +

This fine gabled Elizabethan mansion, rich in mullioned and transomed windows and ornamental carving on its stonework, was burnt to a shell by Cromwell's troops when it was defended by the Royalist Corbet family in 1644. It had been built, mainly by Sir Richard Corbet towards the end of the sixteenth century, of red sandstone faced with pale ashlar from the quarries at Grinshill, a few miles away. The Corbets were powerful Marcher lords from the Conqueror's time, and a fragment of the castle keep which this mansion replaced remains behind the house. In building the new 'castle', they demolished the village to make way for their private park, and earthworks of the former village are still traceable.

English Heritage

12 MYDDLE CASTLE
S end of village, off A528, 7 miles (11 km) N of Shrewsbury

[SJ 4623]   ⊖ *No access* ⊖

Of the moated castle built in 1307 by Lord Lestrange of Knockin (yes, really!), only one circular turret remains. Parts were destroyed by earth tremors in 1688,

Moreton Corbet Castle

according to Myddle's eighteenth-century historian, Richard Gough, but it had already become fairly ruinous by Leland's time, after neglect by its last owner, the squire Humphrey Kynaston, who had taken to highway robbery after falling deeply into debt.

Private

13 RUYTON CASTLE
In Ruyton-XI-Towns, on B4397, 8½ miles (13.5 km) NW of Shrewsbury

[SJ 3922] +

Close to the church are the fragmentary remains of a small and square stone tower built by Edmund, Earl of Arundel, in the fourteenth century.

14 ST CHAD'S CHURCH, SHREWSBURY
Princess Street, close to town centre

[SJ 4912] +

Although it looks at first glance like an intact little chapel, it is actually the remnant of a substantial church with a history reaching back to Anglo-Saxon origins. In 1788 Thomas Telford, then the county's Surveyor of Public Works, was called in by the church wardens to report on a leaking roof. He told them that the roof was the least of their problems. The whole building was subsiding, and if they did not do something very urgently, it would collapse about their ears. Three days later, two chimney-sweeps were walking past early in the morning when the church bell began marking the hour, and the church disappeared with a thunderous roar in a great cloud of dust, leaving only this south chancel chapel standing. Only the outside can be seen.

15 SHRAWARDINE CASTLE
In village on minor road off A5, 6 miles (10 km) W of Shrewsbury

[SJ 4015] +

Precious few remains can be seen today of the former royal castle close to the Severn, kept up by Henry II, Richard I and King John. It was severely damaged in attacks by the Welsh under Llewellyn the Great, but survived until the Civil War, when it was demolished after being captured by Parliamentary forces in June 1645. Only a few chunks of masonry stand on the motte, the remains having been thoroughly quarried.

16 SHREWSBURY ABBEY
Abbey Foregate, just E of English Bridge over River Severn

[SJ 4912] +

Surely one of the more bizarre among British ruins, the frater pulpit of the former Benedictine abbey stands in a little garden on the opposite side of the road from Holy Cross church, the surviving west end of the former abbey church, and still in use. The abbey was partly destroyed at the Dissolution, of course, but much of it still remained in 1815, when the civil engineer Thomas Telford was commissioned to re-align

Stokesay Castle

and improve the Holyhead road. Persuaded to take his new road through Shrewsbury, Telford drove it straight through the abbey ruins, and left this fine stone pulpit in its present isolation.

17 SNAILBEACH MINES
On minor road off A488, 10 miles (16 km) SW of Shrewsbury

[SJ 3702] +

On the eastern edges of the hills known as the Stiperstones, lead was mined in the Roman period from what was once one of the richest seams in Britain; silver and zinc were extracted too. Mining was revived centuries later, and nineteenth-century engine-sheds are still dotted about among the white spoil-heaps, the mines being finally abandoned in the first decade of the present century. Remaining pits and shafts make the area dangerous and exploration is inadvisable.

18 STOKESAY CASTLE
Track off A49, 6 miles (10 km) NW of Ludlow

[SO 4381] ★★★ Tel: 05882 2544

This is one of the best-preserved medieval fortified manor houses in Britain, and also one of the earliest,

The 'Old Work' at Viroconium (Wroxeter)

126

Wenlock Priory

having been built from around 1240 by the de Say family and continued by Lawrence de Ludlow, a wealthy wool merchant, who was granted a licence to crenellate in 1291, and whose successors lived here for three centuries. It seems to have been remarkably optimistic for a manor in the Welsh Marches, at a time when the Welsh kept the sort of welcome in the hillsides that made Englishmen sleep with their hands on their swords. But, ironically, it was the English who finally brought it to ruin, Cromwell's men doing only minimal damage to it when the occupants hastily surrendered without a struggle, but local farmers badly mistreating it later when it was sublet to them for storing grain in the cellar and making barrels in the hall. Since 1869 it has been well looked after by the Allcroft family, and presents a clear picture of the medieval domestic layout, with some roofs still intact and later additions including a half-timbered overhanging storey on the north tower and a pretty, if incongruous, Tudor gatehouse.

English Heritage

19 VIROCONIUM CORNOVIORUM

Near Wroxeter on B4380, 5 miles (8 km) SE of Shrewsbury

[*SJ 5608*] ★

The civic capital of the Cornovii tribe, who had been in these parts long before the Romans came, grew to become the fourth largest city of Roman Britain, but its wooden houses were destroyed by serious fires around AD155 and again in 287, and after the second conflagration the city was not rebuilt. It had been dedicated originally 'To the Emperor Caesar Trajanus Hadrianus Augustus, Father of his Country', having risen on the site of a legionary garrison on Watling Street where the modern village of Wroxeter now stands. It was the first-century headquarters of the XIV Gemina legion during the conquest of Wales. The city's most substantial remains are the walls of a gymnasium, called later the 'Old Work', and consisting of courses of local red stone and Roman brick.

English Heritage

Interlaced wall arcading in Wenlock Priory chapter house

20 WENLOCK PRIORY
*At Much Wenlock off B4376, 7½ miles
(12 km) NW of Bridgnorth*

[SJ 6200]   ★★★   Tel: 0952 727466

With Castle Acre in Norfolk (q.v.), this
is one of the only pair of important
remains of Cluniac priories in England,
and although much decayed, this ruin in
the market town of Much Wenlock is an
enchanting place. It was founded by the
Earl of Shrewsbury on the site of an
earlier nunnery, and built of local
limestone which has taken on a variety of
subtle hues. Friars came here from La
Charite-sur-Loire, but the priory was
subsequently penalized for its allegiance
to a foreign power, and in 1395 it severed
its French connections. At the
Dissolution its annual value was £400,
its wealth being derived from iron
working in this valley that became the
birthplace of the Industrial Revolution.
There are many interesting details
among the ruins, but easily the most
outstanding is the roofless twelfth-
century chapter house, entered via three
decorated Norman arches, and having
superb interlaced wall arcading, and
dragons on the lintel of a doorway.

English Heritage

21 WHITTINGTON CASTLE
*Beside B5009 through village, 2¾ miles
(4.5 km) NE of Oswestry*

[SJ 3231]   +

The ruin stands beside the main road,
and the road provides the best view of it,
aesthetically at least. The remains of a
twin-towered gatehouse stand behind a
pond, originally part of the castle's
elaborate water defences, and the
stonework reflected in it is attractive.
The castle dates from the early thirteenth
century, and was the work of Fulke
FitzWarine, one of whose descendants
may have given a certain cat-fancier
named Dick, who *may* have come from
this village whose name he bore, his first
job in London.

AM

36 Somerset

See maps on pages 130 and 131

1 BISHOP'S PALACE, WELLS
Close to town centre and cathedral

[ST 5545]   ★★★   Tel: 0749 78691

The palace is mainly a fortified mansion
of the fourteenth century, and is mostly
intact, but it incorporates the ruin of the
thirteenth-century great hall of Bishop
Burnell, with one spectacular wall,
containing huge Gothic windows, still
standing to the battlements, and one or
two detached turrets. The hall was 115
feet (35 m) long, with screens passage
and kitchen at one end, the kitchen
fireplaces are still there. The hall was
gradually dismantled by various owners
for the sake of its building materials.

Bishop of Bath and Wells

The former abbey dovecote at Bruton

2 BRUTON DOVECOTE
Off B3081 just S of town centre

[ST 6834]   +

The tall four-gabled stone building on a hill above the town looks at first sight like a northern peel or tower-house that has strayed off course. In fact it is the dovecote of the former Augustinian abbey, of which only a section of wall remains in the town. The size and solid structure of this building indicates the medieval importance of dovecotes – they provided not only meat and eggs for the abbey table but also manure for the fields. This one, now roofless, has mullioned windows. It dates probably from the sixteenth century.

National Trust

3 BURROW MUMP
Beside A361 through Burrow Bridge, 9 miles (14.5 km) NE of Taunton

[ST 3530]   +

The 'Mump' is the conical hill (probably at least partly man-made) in the village of Burrow Bridge, rising above the flat and marshy landscape of the Somerset Levels and visible for miles around, with the remains of St Michael's church on top. The hill's strategic advantages are obvious. There was a small Norman castle on it once, and it may have been one of King Alfred's camps in his ninth-century battles with the Danes. Fondly supposed by ley hunters to be part of a deliberate prehistoric alignment of significant sites across the country, including, naturally, Glastonbury Tor (q.v.).

National Trust

4 CLEEVE ABBEY
Minor road S off A39 at Washford, 2½ miles (4 km) SW of Watchet

[ST 0440]   ★

A small Cistercian monastery was founded here in 1198. Only the foundations of its church are left, but there are remains of some other buildings, and some survive with their roofs intact, so that the place is only marginally ruinous. The site was called *Vallis Florida* – the vale of flowers – and is not at Old Cleeve, as might be assumed, but at Washford, a little to the south-east.

English Heritage

Burrow Mump with its ruined church

5 FARLEIGH HUNGERFORD CASTLE
In village on A366, 3½ miles (5.5 km) W of Trowbridge

[ST 8057]   ★★★

Sir Thomas Hungerford, first Speaker of the House of Commons, built this castle from about 1370, without obtaining a licence – a serious omission for which he was eventually pardoned. His tomb is in the chapel of St Leonard, inside the castle's outer bailey, but here before the castle was built. The castle was of the rectangular courtyard type with angle-towers and a twin-towered gatehouse.

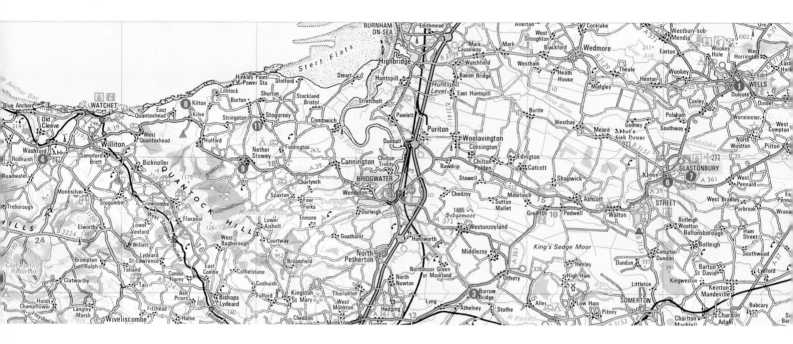

Sir Walter, the first Lord Hungerford, enlarged his father's work, enclosing what was then the parish church as the family's private chapel, and building a new parish church for the townsfolk. Walter also created new water defences. He is said to have spent on the castle the money he obtained by holding to ransom the Duc d'Orleans, whom he captured at Agincourt. The family sold the castle in the seventeenth century. It had been neglected by that time, and was in serious decay by 1730.

English Heritage

6 GLASTONBURY ABBEY
Close to town centre

[ST 5038] ★

Some would say it is the most sacred spot in England – the cradle of Christianity – and the air about it is thick with myths. Joseph of Arimathea is said to have come here with the Holy Grail, and given rise to the famous Glastonbury Thorn; and it is identified with the legendary Isle of Avalon, where King Arthur and Guinevere were reputedly buried. It is also claimed as the burial place of Helen, mother of Constantine the Great, and of St Patrick and St David, among others. But sweep away the legends and the holiness remains intact. The Benedictine foundation can be traced back to the eighth century, and it survived the Saxon

Farleigh Hungerford Castle

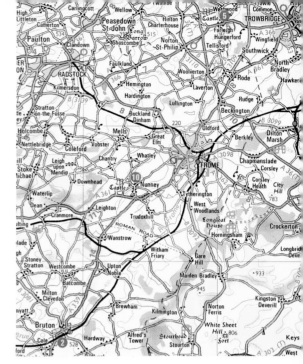

devastation and served English Christianity in its infancy without a break. But the present buildings, of Doulting limestone, date from the twelfth century, when the monastery was rebuilt after a calamitous fire. The monastery was so important that its mitred abbots held the rank of earl, and Henry VIII's commissioners reported that the house was 'great, goodly, and so pryncely as we have not sene the lyke'. But the abbot, Richard Whiting, refused to surrender the monastery, and at length he was tried for treason and, though 80 years old, was hanged, drawn and quartered at the top of Glastonbury Tor. The abbey's remains are fairly sparse, because its stone was plundered in the centuries after the Dissolution, but it is without doubt among the nation's most impressive ruins.

AM

7 GLASTONBURY TOR
SE side of town, off A361

[ST 5138] +

Part of the tower of the thirteenth-century church (inevitably dedicated to St Michael as it is on a hilltop) is all that is left on the summit of this famous eminence, 500 feet (150 m) above sea level. The rest of the chapel built here was destroyed by a landslide. The hill is thick with legend, both pagan and Christian, but what is fact is that the last abbot of the abbey below, Richard Whiting, was dragged up here and

Glastonbury Abbey

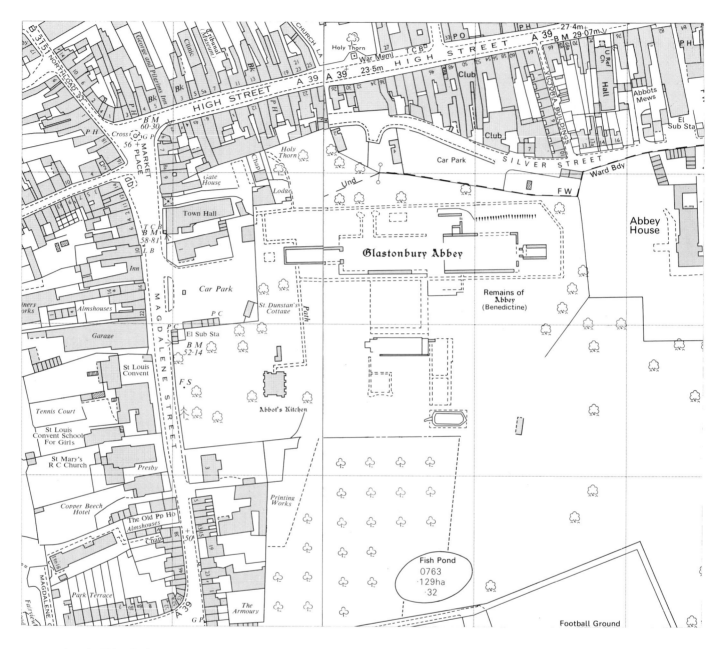

executed at the Dissolution. There is a carving of St Michael on one side of the church's doorway.

National Trust

8 KILVE CHANTRY HOUSE
Minor road N of A39 through village between Williton and Nether Stowey

[ST 1444] +

A creek called Kilve Pill runs down to Bridgwater Bay from near this village, and at its head, near the church, there is a fourteenth-century chantry house built of limestone by Simon de Furneaux, who installed five priests here to pray for him. The building was used later by a local

farmer as a storehouse, but was subsequently burned down, it is said, by smugglers who had used it to hide brandy.

9 NETHER STOWEY CASTLE
In village, minor road S off A39

[ST 1839] +

This Quantocks village, better known for its association with Coleridge, has the fragmentary remains of a twelfth-century castle on a motte. It subsequently passed to the Audley family, and its last owner, James, Lord Audley, was executed for his part in the Perkin Warbeck affair. The castle soon fell into ruin after that.

10 NUNNEY CASTLE
In village, off A361, 3 miles (5 km) SW of Frome

[ST 7345] +

It was built by Sir John de la Mare in 1373 – a moated four-storey tower house raised as a status symbol rather than a fortification, for it stands in the middle of the village, closely accompanied by houses, farms and church. Sir John had served his country well in the Hundred Years War, and was duly made Sheriff of Somerset. Nunney was his stately house built in the French style. It was never threatened – unless by burglars – until the Civil War, when it put up some

Nunney Castle

castle that has been here for over 800 years. It was built around 1180 by Henry II's illegitimate half-brother, Hamelin Plantagenet, on ground undulating with natural mounds and artificial earthworks. The 90-foot (27-m) keep, built of pale ashlar limestone, was of unique design, and its smooth lines and relatively complete appearance give it a fairly modern look compared with the fallen rubble walls of the rest of the castle, but in fact the keep was probably built first. The massive roof-height buttresses had rooms built within them, including part of the chapel, and the castle contains the two earliest hooded fireplaces known in this country.

English Heritage

2 MONK BRETTON PRIORY
Off A633, 2 miles (3 km) E of Barnsley

[SE 3706]   ★

A Cluniac priory which became Benedictine. There was a serious fire here in 1386, but the establishment survived. Relatively little stands to any height, except the fifteenth-century gatehouse, and a house, built after the Dissolution by the 6th Earl of Shrewsbury out of the prior's quarters and the west range of buildings. The ruins are now in the unwelcome embrace of Barnsley's outskirts.

English Heritage

3 ROCHE ABBEY
Just off A634, 1½ miles (2.5 km) SE of Maltby

[SK 5489]   ★★★   Tel: 0709 812739

The ruins are neither as extensive nor as beautiful as some of the other Cistercian foundations in Yorkshire, but what remains is enhanced by the rocky landscape made more picturesque by Capability Brown at the behest of its then owners in the eighteenth century, as part of the grounds of nearby Sandbeck Hall. The abbey was founded in 1147 by neighbouring landowners, one of whom was Richard de Bully of Tickhill Castle (q.v.).

English Heritage

4 THORPE SALVIN MANOR
In village, on minor road from A57, 4 miles (6.5 km) W of Worksop

[SK 5281]   ⊖ No access ⊖

Henry Salford built this manor house of stone during the reign of Elizabeth I. It looks impressive as you approach the southern elevation, three storeys high

resistance before surrendering, and was then slighted. It was left in such weak condition that as recently as 1910 its north wall collapsed, leaving a gaping hole that reveals the interior details of windows and fireplaces, garderobes and an oven, and the altar slab of the chapel on the top floor.

English Heritage

11 STOGURSEY CASTLE
In village on minor road off A39, 2 miles (3 km) N of Nether Stowey

[ST 2042]   +

A few bits of wall and lower courses of two circular gatehouse towers remain of this mainly twelfth-century castle, built

by the local de Courcy family and destroyed during the Wars of the Roses.

---

37 South Yorkshire

See map on page 134

1 CONISBROUGH CASTLE
In the town, off A630 between Rotherham and Doncaster

[SK 5198]   ★

The modern industrial landscapes of Rotherham and Doncaster hardly induce us to seek out medieval remains in this district, but between the two stands a

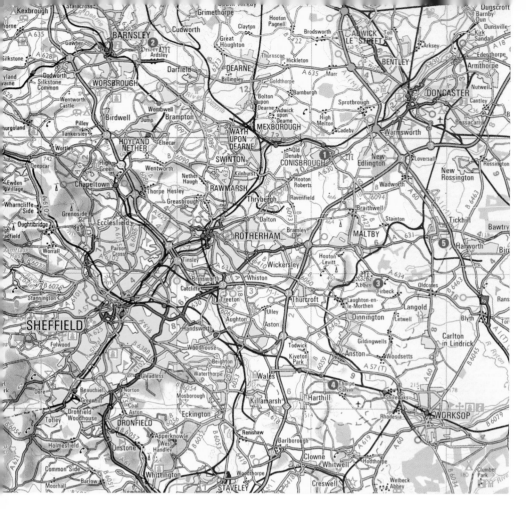

and perfectly symmetrical, with mullioned and transomed windows, giant chimney breasts and round battlemented angle-towers. But this façade is all there is. It stands with nothing at all behind it, like a film set left behind by Metro-Goldwyn-Mayer, with the local residents' allotments round it now. You can see it clearly from the road, where a small gatehouse with a stepped gable punctuates a low wall.

AM

5 TICKHILL CASTLE
S side of village, off A60, 6½ miles (10.5 km) S of Doncaster

[SK 5992] ⊖ *No access* ⊖

Part of the ruin can be seen from the road. An eleven-sided buttressed keep was built on the motte by Henry II, and was owned in turn by his sons Richard I and John, but that has gone except for the foundations. The curtain wall and ruined gatehouse still stand. The castle was demolished in the Civil War.

Private

Conisbrough Castle

38 Staffordshire

See map below

1 CHARTLEY CASTLE

In field beside A518, 7 miles (11 km) NE of Stafford

[SK 0128]   +

The low remaining walls stand on rising ground above the Stafford–Uttoxeter road. The walled bailey enclosed a motte on which a cylindrical keep was built in the thirteenth century by Ranulph Blundeville. Elizabeth I was entertained here by the Earl of Essex, and Mary, Queen of Scots was also entertained later, in rather different fashion. Nothing of the keep is left except the foundations, but the curtain wall and fragments of two towers remain, the towers showing neatly coursed stonework almost like brick. Accessible via a stile in the roadside fence.

Private

2 CRESWELL CHURCH

In field, off A5013 near Seighford, 2½ miles (4 km) NW of Stafford

[SJ 8926]   +

Fragments of a small church remain in a field at the edge of the village now almost absorbed by Stafford. The church has been a ruin for centuries. The location should not be confused with Staffordshire Cresswell, near Stoke-on-Trent.

3 CROXDEN ABBEY

In village, by minor roads off A50, 3 miles (5 km) NW of Uttoxeter

[SK 0639]   +

A Cistercian abbey founded in 1176 by Bertram de Verdun, and now standing among the village cottages and farm buildings. The ruins are of simple architectural quality befitting the early Cistercian philosophy, in the neatly dressed local sandstone. The church has lofty walls with lancets still standing, and the lane cuts through the claustral remains. Trees grow among the broken walls. Staffordshire not being noted as a tourist county, this fine ruin is not as well known as it deserves to be.

English Heritage

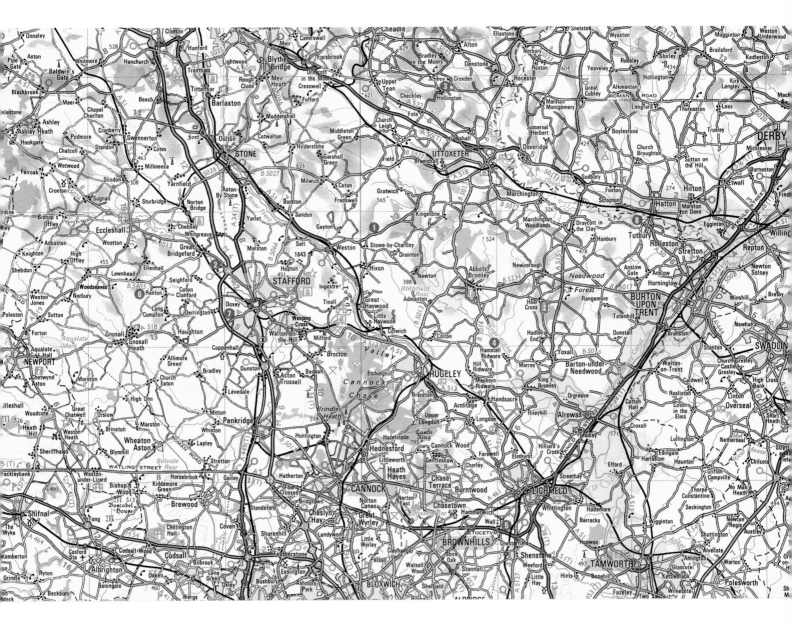

A tower of Tutbury Castle

4 HAMSTALL HALL
At Hamstall Ridware, on minor roads off A515 and B5014, 4 miles (6.5 km) E of Rugeley

[SK 1019] ⊖ *No access* ⊖

The tantalizing ruins of a large Tudor manor house stand just out of reach in a farmyard at Hamstall Ridware, behind the church. The house, built by the Fitzherbert family around 1535, was of red brick with stone dressings. Part of it was incorporated or converted into the farmhouse, but from the churchyard you can glimpse the two turrets of the gatehouse, shaped like pepper-pots, and one tall tower.

Private

5 LETOCETUM
At Wall, just off A5, 1¾ miles (2.8 km) SW of Lichfield

[SK 0906] *** . Tel: 0543 480768

The remains of this Roman garrison and posting station are at the village now known as Wall, just off the A5 (Watling Street) near Lichfield. The excavated remains consist chiefly of a public bath-house and a 'villa', which may have been a hostel for travellers stopping overnight on the principal Roman road. The bath-house is one of the best preserved in Britain, but plundering of stone from the site for other buildings explains why the 12-foot (3.5-m) high walls described by Stukeley in the eighteenth century no longer exist.

English Heritage

6 RANTON ABBEY
Off B5405, 5 miles (8 km) W of Stafford

[SJ 8324] ⊖ *No access* ⊖

This site is complicated by the fact that the name refers to a shooting lodge built in 1820 by the 1st Earl of Lichfield, and subsequently brought to ruin. But the religious house whose site was commandeered was a priory, not an abbey, founded in 1150 or thereabouts for Augustinian canons. The tower of the priory church remains of this, and can be glimpsed from the nearby road, standing in a well-wooded park.

Private

7 STAFFORD CASTLE
Just off A518, W side of town

[SJ 9022] +

The stone castle was built around 1348 on the site of an earlier motte-and-bailey castle to the south-west of the town, and is now a notable landmark for travellers on the nearby M6 motorway. Its builder was Ralph, Lord Stafford, and it consisted of a rectangular keep with four corner towers. The castle was demolished in the Civil War, and then in the early nineteenth century Sir George Jerningham started to convert the remains into a mansion. This work was never finished, however, and at length it was all demolished, leaving only what was left of the original castle after its slighting.

AM

8 TUTBURY CASTLE
NW side of town, off A50, 4¼ miles (7 km) NW of Burton upon Trent

[SK 2029] *

Built soon after the Conquest, Tutbury was held by the Ferrers family and the Duchy of Lancaster for long periods of its history, and John of Gaunt and his son Henry IV were among those who spent some time here. But it is as one of the prisons of Mary, Queen of Scots that the castle is most famous. She was brought here to be kept under lenient house arrest by George Talbot, Earl of Shrewsbury, who leased the castle. It was damp and draughty, and she became chronically ill here, complaining of a refuse heap beneath her windows and the marsh below the castle, from which noxious fumes arose. Talbot's wife, the formidable Bess of Hadwick, was Mary's companion at first, but later grew jealous and spread malevolent rumours of her husband's improper relationship with the State's royal prisoner. The castle was reduced to ruin by order of Parliament after the Civil War. The remains show the progressive enlargement and improvement of the castle, with buildings of both red and white stone.

Duchy of Lancaster

---

39 Suffolk

See maps on page 138

1 BUNGAY CASTLE
Short distance from town centre

[TM 3389] +

Built by the powerful local Bigod family progressively from about 1164, with a great tower or keep of flint and sandstone. In 1173, Hugh Bigod supported Henry II's eldest son Henry's abortive revolt, and the king then confiscated the castle and prepared to demolish it by a well-tried method made familiar to present-day television viewers through its use by steeplejack Fred Dibner in demolishing factory chimneys. The mining gallery begun beneath a corner of the keep at Bungay still remains. The supports would have been set alight, and when the timbers burned through, the tower would have collapsed. But the castle was saved from this operation by Bigod's payment of a large fine. Nevertheless, the castle was in ruins by the fourteenth century. Usually locked, but keys available nearby.

Bungay Town Trust

2 BURY ST EDMUNDS ABBEY
E side of town, off A143

[TL 8564] +

The remains of one of the country's biggest and wealthiest Benedictine abbeys are mightily disappointing for the connoisseur of evocative ruins. Apart from its two gate towers, which remain intact, there are only bits and pieces of rubble walls and the extensive foundations. Difficult to imagine the great church and the monastic buildings alive with the activity of the black monks and the pilgrims to St Edmund's shrine, who included royal visitors such as Edward the Confessor and Richard Coeur de Lion. Here the barons met and resolved to force King John to sign the charter of English liberties. In 1381 the prior, John de Cambridge, was beheaded during the Peasants' Revolt, and his head paraded round the town, for he had been an implacable enemy of the townsfolk. The abbey is 'dead now and dumb', as Thomas Carlyle put it, 'a broken blackened shinbone of the old dead ages'. Accessible during opening hours of the park in which it stands.

English Heritage

3 CLARE CASTLE
E of village, on minor road off A1092 between Sudbury and Haverhill

[TL 7745]   +

A shell-keep on a moated motte was built here, above the Stour, in the thirteenth century, probably by the de Clare family, with two baileys, separated by a ditch, stretching eastward from it. Little remains of the enclosing walls or, indeed, of the keep itself. Elizabeth de Clare lived in the castle in style after being widowed for the third time at the age of 28, and entertained her cousin Edward II here. The town's railway station was built in one of the baileys in the nineteenth century – eventually becoming as redundant as the castle.

Suffolk County Council

4 DUNWICH FRIARY
On coast S of village; minor road off B1125, 4 miles (6.5 km) SW of Southwold

[TM 4770]   ⊖ *No access* ⊖

The ruins are of a house for Franciscan friars, founded about 1277, but rebuilt further inland in 1289 because of the threat from the sea. The ruins, scant and precarious, are on the cliffs beside All Saints' empty churchyard, the church having been consumed by the hungry waves.

Private

5 FRAMLINGHAM CASTLE
Castle Street, B1116 N from town centre

[TM 2863]   *

Roger Bigod, Earl of Norfolk, began this substantial castle around 1190 on the site of an earlier one forfeited by his father

Bungay Castle

because of his involvement in the rebellion against Henry II (see Bungay page 136). The castle had no keep. Its defence depended on the massive curtain walls and the baker's-dozen towers spaced round them. The walls remain to this day over 40 feet (12 m) high and 8 feet (2.5 m) thick, and were surrounded by deep ditches. The castle passed through several royal and noble hands, the Howard family carrying out some modernization; and it was from here in 1553 that Mary Tudor set out with thousands of her supporters to make her triumphal entry into London as Queen of England. The former great hall was absorbed into a seventeenth-century poorhouse built by Pembroke College, Cambridge, which then owned the castle. But this was closed in the 1830s, and then used as a county court for a time. Ornamental brick chimneys of the Tudor period remain on some of the towers.

English Heritage

6 LEISTON ABBEY
Off B1122, 1 mile (1.5 km) N of town

[TM 4464]   +

This abbey for Premonstratensian canons was founded in 1183, but was only transferred here from a previous site in 1363. Nearly 20 years later it suffered a serious fire and had to be largely rebuilt. Not much remains to excite the imagination, though the site is extensive. After the Dissolution it was quarried for building materials, a house being built

partly out of the church, and what was left was used for farming purposes until it all fell into ruin.

English Heritage

7 ORFORD CASTLE
In the village on B1084, 9 miles (14.5 km) E of Woodbridge

[TM 4149]   ***   Tel: 03944 50472

The tall and architecturally unique five-storey keep of this castle is so well

Ruined part of the church at Walberswick

137

England

preserved that one is hesitant to include it in a book of ruins; but the fact remains that it is the last surviving part of a twelfth-century castle whose curtain walls, gatehouse and flanking towers have disappeared. The castle was built for Henry II, using septaria, a local stone dredged up off the Suffolk coast, with dressings of Caen and Oolitic limestone. The revolutionary multi-angular outer walls envelop a cylindrical interior, the buttresses containing kitchens, garderobes, dungeon, chapel and spiral staircase. The designer or 'ingeniator' of the keep was Aluoth, the King's Keeper of Houses. There is an old tale of a twelfth-century lord, Bartholomew de Glanville, who kept a merman, caught by a local fisherman, in the castle for six months as a curiosity.

English Heritage

8 ORFORD CHURCH
In village on B1084, 9 miles (14.5 km) E of Woodbridge

[TM 4249]   +

The nave of St Bartholomew's is intact and in regular use, the chancel in ruins. The chancel dates from the twelfth century. It was the victim of vandalism in the late seventeenth century. The west tower collapsed in 1830, but has been partly repaired.

Church of England

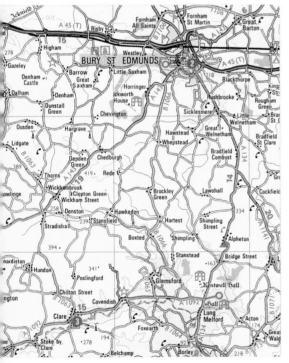

9 WALBERSWICK CHURCH

In village, on B1387, 1 mile (1.5 km)
S of Southwold

[TM 4974]   +

Walberswick was once a thriving fishing port at the mouth of the River Blyth, and its large church was built in the fifteenth century by the local masons Richard Russell and Adam Powle. The town's trade was already in decline when Cromwell's zealous agents began the destruction of the church in 1643, Dr William Dowsing ordering tombs, ornaments and images to be smashed. Later, the townsfolk petitioned for it to be reduced, as they could not afford its upkeep, it being too large for the remaining population. The south aisle of the nave is preserved as the parish church, and the rest is a sparse ruin of flint and stone.

Church of England

10 WALTON CHURCH

In parish churchyard, now N district of
Felixstowe

[TM 3035]   +

The nineteenth-century parish church of St Mary replaced the ancient church here, a fragment of which remains in the churchyard.

Church of England

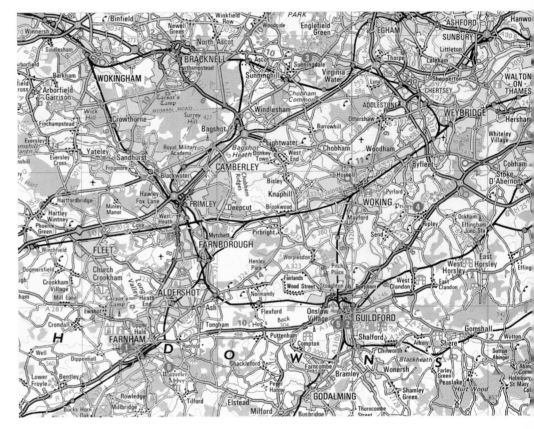

---

40 *Surrey*

See map above

1 FARNHAM CASTLE

On A287 N of town centre

[SU 8347]   ★★

That great ecclesiastical builder Henry de Blois, brother of King Stephen and Bishop of Winchester (see Bishop's Waltham and Winchester in Hampshire), built this castle originally as his palace, but it was slighted by Henry II and then rebuilt in different form, with a shell-keep. It is interesting as one of the most domestic of twelfth-century castles. Much new building went on here within the enclosing walls through the centuries, even after the Civil War when the castle was again slighted, and it continued to be used as the Bishop of Winchester's residence. There is a story that Queen Elizabeth I, dining here once with the Duke of Norfolk, who had designs on marrying Mary, Queen of Scots, suggested sweetly to him on retiring that he should be careful on what pillow he laid his head.

English Heritage

2 GUILDFORD CASTLE

Castle Street, short distance from town
centre

[SU 9949]   ★★

Henry II's great square tower is now hardly more than a broken shell, standing on an earlier motte, but on one side of it, like Clun (q.v.) in Shropshire. In this case, this was evidently done to give the tower firm foundations of rock. An arch of the outer gateway and bits of curtain wall also remain. The castle had strong royal associations, until in about 1368 it was made over as a common gaol for Surrey and Sussex, but eventually it was replaced by the gaol at Lewes in response to protests from the townsfolk, because escapes from it were too frequent. The ruined tower, built mostly of rubble, stands in well-kept public gardens, formerly the bailey.

Guildford Corporation

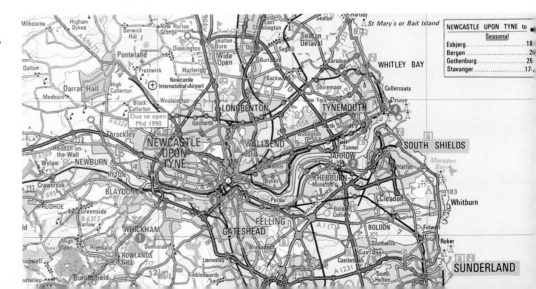

3 LEPCIS MAGNA COLONNADE
S bank of Virginia Water on A329, 5½ miles (9 km) E of Bracknell

[SU 9568]   +

It is arguable that the row of classical columns standing beside Virginia Water should be described as a folly rather than a ruin, since they were brought here from the Roman town in Libya. But they have fallen into a more advanced state of ruin since they arrived, so perhaps deserve a place in this book. They were originally intended for the British Museum's portico, but were put up here instead in 1826, and look quite incongruous.

4 NEWARK PRIORY
B367 just S of Pyrford, 1½ miles (2.5 km) E of Woking

[TQ 0457]   ⊖ *No access* ⊖

In a county with little to offer the ruin-hunter Newark is significant, but too little remains to qualify it as important. The priory was founded for Austin canons in the time of Henry II, beside the River Wey. Flint walls standing in a field present an attractive sight from the road, but, ironically, it was for road repairs that the priory buildings were largely dismantled.

Private

5 ST CATHARINE'S CHAPEL, GUILDFORD
¾ mile (1.2 km) S of town centre beside A3100 Portsmouth road

[SU 9948]   +

Thomas Love Peacock referred to it, in *Gryll Grange*, as a 'picturesque ruin, on the banks of the Wey, near Guildford'. And so it remains. It was a small and simple chapel of sandstone rubble, built early in the fourteenth century, and is now bare and roofless.

6 WAVERLEY ABBEY
Off B3001, 2 miles (3 km) E of Farnham

[SU 8645]   +

Sadly, little remains of this monastery, famous as the first Cistercian foundation in England and only begetter, as it were, of all those monumental Cistercian ruins such as Rievaulx, Fountains, Furness and Tintern. It was founded in 1128 and suppressed after more than 400 years. Its buildings were then plundered for their

The cellarium at Waverley Abbey

materials, and only fragmented remnants are now to be seen, but some of them stand to full height and remain impressive, with lancet windows and some vaulting intact. The ruins occupy a peaceful site in meadows beside the River Wey.

English Heritage

41 Tyne and Wear

See bottom map on page 139

1 HOLLINSIDE MANOR
E bank of River Derwent, 1½ miles (2.5 km) SW of Whickham

[NZ 1860]   +

The ruins of a thirteenth-century fortified manor house stand above the River Derwent. It had a tall entrance tower with a very big archway through it. Approachable by the Derwent country park walk.

Tyne and Wear County Council

2 JARROW PRIORY
In the town, near docks

[NZ 3365]   +

Apart from a part of the ancient church now incorporated in the parish church, only a couple of sections of walling remain of the Anglo-Saxon Benedictine abbey where the scholarly Venerable Bede lived and worked, becoming the 'father of English history'. He died and was at first buried here in 735, having spent nearly all his life in the monastery, before being moved to Durham Cathedral. Modern industry and the adjacent docks of Tyneside mean that there is little left to see, and the walls, of course, do not date from Bede's time, but from after the Conquest, when the place had become a dependent priory of Durham Cathedral.

English Heritage

3 NEWCASTLE UPON TYNE CASTLE
Beside Stephenson's high-level bridge over River Tyne, just S of city centre

[NZ 2463]   ★★★

The name of the city describes precisely

what the building was in the twelfth century, when it was built on the site of an earlier timber castle on a motte on the north bank of the river. Henry II was responsible for the building of this northern fortress, its chief feature being the almost square keep of sandstone, five storeys high with walls up to 18 feet (5.5 m) thick. There is a forebuilding on its east side which, though much altered from the original, has a chapel on the ground floor with richly carved Norman arches. The forebuilding gave access to the second floor of the keep, where the great hall was. This mightily impressive tower originally stood within a triangular bailey, but railway development in Newcastle messed the site about. Stephenson's High Level Bridge begins in the former bailey and a railway line runs at right angles to this, bisecting the bailey between keep and gatehouse. The only other substantial survival is the Black Gate, an outer gatehouse added in 1247 and, with a seventeenth century house attached to it, now part of a museum.

Newcastle Corporation

4 TYNEMOUTH PRIORY
Near town's north pier

[NZ 3769] ★★★ *Tel: 091 257 1090*

At first sight this is something of a novelty – the remains of a priory built inside the remains of a castle. But in fact the ruins represent a novelty of a different kind – a well-fortified monastery. It had good reason to defend itself. The Anglo-Saxon foundation had been attacked by Danish invaders thrice in the ninth century, being burnt and pillaged by the blond pirates. It was re-founded as a Benedictine priory in 1089 or thereabouts, and received licence to crenellate in 1296, although it was then already surrounded by a curtain wall with defensive towers. After the Dissolution, when this long-suffering religious house was plundered yet again, the defensive works were maintained and were taken from Royalist defenders first by the Scots and then by Parliamentary forces, and have been employed even in the present century to guard the mouth of the Tyne. The remains are extensive and also rather impressive, if somewhat confusing, the east wall of the priory church standing almost to its full original height, with Early English lancet windows flanking a pointed oval window.

English Heritage

Kenilworth Castle

42 Warwickshire

See map on page 142

1 KENILWORTH ABBEY
Just off A452 through town

[SP 2872] +

The ruins, between the castle and the parish church, are extensive but not very substantial. It was founded as a priory for Augustinian canons around 1125 by Geoffrey de Clinton, and endowed by Henry I. It was elevated to abbey status some time after 1438. The gatehouse and porter's lodge, and a supposed guest-house, all fourteenth century, are the only remains that stand to any height, the rest being low walls and foundations.

AM

2 KENILWORTH CASTLE
B4103 W of town centre

[SP 2772] ★

This was once the third most stately castle in England, but in the Civil War

Cromwell's men undermined the walls and towers and drained the 'mere', an artificial lake which had been created by Henry III and which extended for a mile to the west of the castle. The red sandstone ruin was clothed with ivy in the nineteenth century, but that romantic veneer has been cleared away, too. There has been talk of restoring the old water defences, which were much more extensive than those at Caerphilly (q.v.). The historic castle at Kenilworth was probably begun about 1174 by Henry II, though there was a motte-and-bailey castle on the site before then. Building continued for a long period in royal ownership, until in 1253 Henry III gave the castle to Simon de Montfort, Earl of Leicester, his brother-in-law and soon his enemy. After a century the castle passed by marriage to John of Gaunt, and was restored to royal ownership when Gaunt's son, Henry IV, acquired it, but then Elizabeth I gave it away again, to Robert Dudley. She came here on at least three occasions, most famous of which was in 1575, when her favourite entertained her in lavish style, with masques and banquets, fireworks and bear-baiting. The queen's retinue

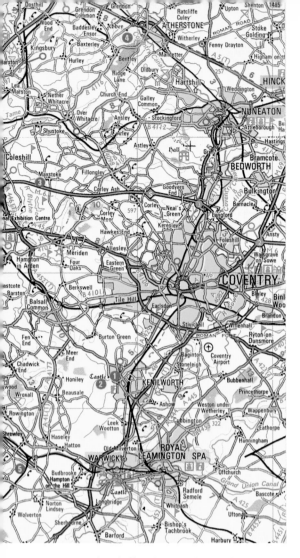

consisted of 33 barons, her ladies-in-waiting and 400 servants, and her three-week stay cost the Earl of Leicester £1000 a day. He had already spent £60,000 before she arrived, improving the castle's comforts and creating new gardens in the fashion of the time (also victims of Cromwell's destruction). The castle's remains are very extensive, and include John of Gaunt's Tower, and his great hall with its huge Gothic windows and five fireplaces. It originally had a fine ceiling of Irish wood. Once described as 'the glory of all these parts', Kenilworth remains one of the best and most fascinating castle ruins in Britain, and thousands of visitors have felt impelled to leave their names or initials on its enduring walls, the soft sandstone lending itself admirably to personal inscription in a page of history.

English Heritage

3 MAXSTOKE PRIORY
W of village on minor road N of A45 between Coventry and Birmingham

[SP 2386]   +

A shattered and insecure-looking section of the priory church's crossing-tower,

which once carried a spire, reaches upward near the village church, the mass of upper masonry seeming too much to be supported by the two Gothic arches below. Little else of significance is left of the priory founded in 1336 for Augustinian canons by Sir William de Clinton and suppressed 200 years later, when the prior and seven canons were in residence.

AM

4 MEREVALE ABBEY
On minor road ½ mile (0.8 km) S of A5 at Atherstone, towards Baxterley

[SP 2997]   ⊝ *No access* ⊝

Inextricably tied up with a farmhouse and its outbuildings, such remains as there are of this Cistercian abbey founded by Earl Ferrers in 1148 do not mean much to the layman, but there is a section of the refectory wall which is interesting, with closely set shafts along one side and buttresses on the other, all of the thirteenth century. The foundations of the church were excavated as long ago as 1849, when a few other details were laid bare.

Private

5 PINLEY ABBEY
Minor road off B4095, 1½ miles (2.5 km) NE of Claverdon

[SU 2165]   *By permission*

Part of Pinley Abbey Farm, an early sixteenth-century half-timbered house which might have been the abbess's lodging, the only other remnant of the Cistercian nunnery is part of the nave's west wall and fragments of adjoining walls. The nunnery was a very early one, founded in the time of Henry I.

Private

---

43 *West Midlands*

See top map on page 143

1 COVENTRY CATHEDRAL
At city centre

[SP 3379]   +

I remember seeing the flames of Coventry from 15 miles (24 km) away on the night in November 1940 when the old cathedral was destroyed by the *Luftwaffe*'s bombing raid. The ancient

church of St Michael had only become a cathedral in 1918, but it had stood here since the fourteenth century, one of the largest parish churches in England, built of sandstone with a 300-ft (90-m) tower and steeple. The church had taken medieval masons 60 years to complete, but it needed only a single night to destroy it. When Sir Basil Spence designed the new Coventry Cathedral, he incorporated the former chancel as a precinct, and it stands as an eloquent witness to more recent devastation than most of our ruins, with bits of jagged glass and twisted lead in windows that still bear their Perpendicular tracery.

Church of England

2 DUDLEY CASTLE
N of town centre, in Dudley Zoo

[SO 9490]   ★

The castle at Dudley is mentioned in the 'Domesday Book', but it was demolished by Henry II after the revolt against him by his eldest son. Roger de Somery and his son John built the new castle of stone from 1265. It commanded a fine position on a hill overlooking the town and surrounding country, and its chief building was a two-storey tower-house on the old motte, surrounded by a high curtain wall with gatehouse. In the fourteenth century, a chapel and new domestic buildings were erected in the bailey by the Duke of Northumberland (who was later executed by Bloody Mary for putting Lady Jane Grey on the throne). The castle was slighted by order of Parliament in 1646. The premises now rather incongruously – as if the Black Country setting were not incongruous enough already – incorporate Dudley Zoo, and cable-cars take you up the hill. The crypt of the medieval chapel houses an aquarium! But the oblong tower, with two of its four original drum-towers remaining in part, is a fine sight, and there are splendid views from it.

Dudley Zoo

3 DUDLEY PRIORY
At foot of Castle Hill

[SO 9490]   +

Founded for Cluniac monks in 1149, it always remained a tiny community, though the ruins show fairly extensive buildings, with remains of the priory church and parts of the ranges on the east and west sides of the cloister.

AM

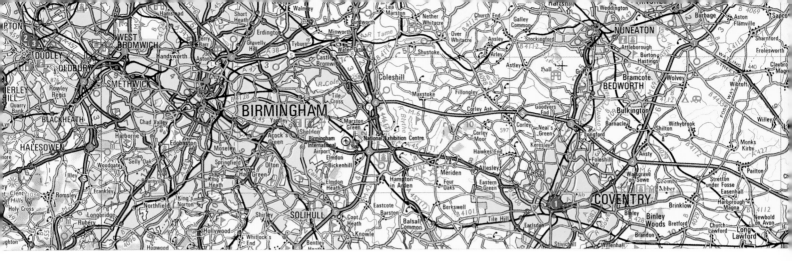

44 West Sussex

See map below

1 AMBERLEY CASTLE
In village, off B2139, 4 miles (6.5 km) N of Arundel

[TQ 0213] ★★★

Not much of this fine battlemented castle is in ruins, having been repeatedly altered and re-occupied since its beginnings as a fortified manor house of the bishops of Chichester in the fourteenth century. The curtain wall and ruined part of a great hall added by Bishop Rede in 1377 are remnants of the early work carried out to make the castle part of the south-coast defences against the French.

Private

2 BRAMBER CASTLE
W of village centre, minor road off A283, 3½ miles (5.5 km) NW of Shoreham-by-Sea

[TQ 1810] +

Built on a chalk knoll overlooking the Adur valley, soon after the Conquest, the wooden palisade was replaced by a stone curtain wall in the twelfth century. Only fragments of this and the eleventh-century gatehouse tower remain.

English Heritage

3 COWDRAY HOUSE
Minor road off A272, ¾ mile (1.2 km) E of Midhurst

[SU 8921] ★

The first builder of Cowdray was, oddly enough, Sir David Owen, son of Owain Glyndwr – an unlikely settler, one might think, in the Establishment corner of England, at the foot of the South Downs. But the estate was purchased in 1529 by Sir William Fitzwilliam, and then passed to the Brown family. Sir Anthony Brown was Henry VIII's Master of the Horse, and he acquired Battle Abbey, Bayham Abbey (q.q.v.) and several other religious houses at the Dissolution. He entertained Edward VI at Cowdray and Queen Elizabeth was a guest of his son, the first Viscount Montague. But in September 1793 a workman left a charcoal fire unattended, and by the end of the day Cowdray House had been gutted by a blaze which swept through every corner. The battlemented ruins present an image of pure Tudor architecture, unspoiled by later interference.

Private

Cowdray House

4 FISHBOURNE PALACE
Minor road off A259, 1½ miles (2.5 km) W of Chichester

[SU 8304] ★★★

Only thorough excavation in the 1960s revealed the true extent and magnificence of what had, up to then, been described simply as a Roman villa. It proved to be, rather, a magnificent palace, of perhaps 100 rooms, all with mosaic floors, and not only the largest Roman domestic building known in Britain, but also a remarkably early one. Speculation inclines to the view that it was built for Cogidubnus, British King of the Reginenses, a Roman citizen and architect of good Romano-British diplomatic relations. The palace and its gardens covered a huge area, but the buildings were demolished late in the third century. Among the surviving mosaic floors, the most famous shows a winged boy riding a dolphin.

AM

5 GREYFRIARS, CHICHESTER
In park, short distance N of city centre

[SU 8605] ★★★

In Priory Park stands the intact Early English choir of a Franciscan friary, founded here in 1269, where Chichester Castle had stood. After the Dissolution,

this remaining part of the church was taken into use as a guildhall and then as an assize court, and in 1804 the extraordinary trial for treason of the mystic poet and engraver William Blake took place here, after he had ejected a drunken soldier from his garden at Felpham. The remnant is now used as an archaeological museum. Nothing more of the friary is to be found.

City of Chichester

6 HALNAKER HOUSE
In the grounds of Little Halnaker, in village on A285 near Chichester

[SU 9008] ⊖ No access ⊖

Originally a medieval house, it was rebuilt in the sixteenth century by Earl de la Warr. Passing to the Duke of Richmond, it became redundant with the building of Goodwood, and fell into ruin fairly rapidly.

Private

7 HARDHAM PRIORY
½ mile (0.8 km) S of hamlet, off A29, 1¼ miles (2 km) SW of Pulborough

[TQ 0317] +

Little known, because indeed rather sparse, this small priory for Augustinian canons, founded in 1248, has one superb remnant – the chapter house with its fine

triple-arched entrance, beautifully carved and proportioned, the arches supported on marble shafts. The priory's demise came through the deaths of the last remaining canons before the Dissolution. The refectory was later converted into a farmhouse which was gutted by fire in 1912, and by burning plaster off the walls, the heat revealed ancient wall paintings, which were then neglected and lost.

AM

8 KNEPP CASTLE
Off W side of A24, 5½ miles (9 km) S of Horsham

[TQ 1620] ⊖ No access ⊖

The castle was built by the powerful de Braose family. A chunk of the keep, of Henry II's time, stands on a motte. It can be seen from the A24 near West Grinstead.

AM

9 NYMANS
Just off B2114 at Handcross, 4½ miles (7 km) S of Crawley

[TQ 2629] ★★★ Tel: 0444 400321

Only part of this house is a ruin, the rest being still occupied by the descendants of Leonard Messel, who built it in medieval style in the late 1920s, to

The ruined wing of Nymans

replace the earlier house round which Ludwig Messel had begun the fine and now famous gardens in 1890. But in 1947 the south side of the house was gutted by fire and has never been rebuilt, though its outer walls and windows look in perfect shape among the trees and shrubs of one of the great gardens of England. Visible from outside only.

National Trust (Garden)

10 TREYFORD CHURCH
In village on minor road betwen A286 and B2141, 4¼ miles (7 km) SW of Midhurst

[SU8218]   +

The ruins of the thirteenth-century church of St Mary remain in the heavily overgrown old churchyard, both being deserted when a new church was built, in a new churchyard, in 1849. The latter was demolished in 1951, leaving the village with two churchyards but no church.

Church of England

---

45 *West Yorkshire*

See map on page 146

1 ALL SAINTS CHURCH, PONTEFRACT
Off A645 to NE of town centre

[SE4622]   +

The old parish church stands close to the castle (q.v.), and its destruction happened during the castle's defence against siege in the Civil War, when the Royalists, who were holding the church as well, turned their own guns on it when they were forced to withdraw. The church was left derelict for 200 years until part of it was restored for worship in 1838, and then in 1964 a new nave of brick was built inside the dark stone walls of the old one – a strange sight. But the old tower is intact, and the former nave and chancel remain in ruins.

Church of England

2 EAST RIDDLESDEN HALL
In village on minor road 1 mile (1.5 km) NE of Keighley

[SE0742]   ★★★   *Tel: 0535 607075*

Part of this seventeenth-century gabled stone mansion is intact, but one range is ruined, and that, ironically, the latest part of the house, which was built originally in 1648 for the Murgatroyd family, wealthy clothiers of Halifax. The range, now in ruins, was added towards the end of the century.

National Trust

3 HAREWOOD CASTLE
Harewood House grounds, off A61, 7 miles (11 km) N of Leeds

[SE3245]   ★★★   *Tel: 0532 886225*

You can catch a glimpse of it high above the road and river as you approach the village from the west on the A61. It was a courtyard castle, licensed in 1367, and had a great hall, solar and chapel, as well

Kirkstall Abbey, Leeds

Pontefract's ruined medieval church

as the service rooms and private quarters. It now stands in the landscaped park of Harewood House.

The Earl of Harewood

4 HEPTONSTALL CHURCH
In village, on minor road off A646, ½ mile (0.8 km) NW of Hebden Bridge

[SD 9828]   +

The old church of St Thomas à Becket, in this stone industrial village on a steep hill above Hebden Bridge, was so severely damaged by a storm in 1847 that a new one was built, in the same churchyard, and the ruins of the old remain among the closely-built weavers' cottages. It was a fifteenth-century building, and its nave and tower were left instead of being completely demolished. The floor of the ruin is paved with old headstones laid face-down. It has a rather eerie atmosphere.

Church of England

5 KIRKSTALL ABBEY
On A65 (Abbey Road), 3½ miles (5.5 km) NW of city centre

[SE 2636]   +

Today Kirkstall stands in the city of Leeds, protected within a formal park, making it difficult to believe that, when it was founded in the twelfth century as a daughter house of Fountains, it was in a 'solitary vale' such as the Cistercians loved. But the growth of Leeds is a relatively recent phenomenon, and a well-known watercolour by Thomas Girtin shows Kirkstall Abbey still in rural surroundings as late as 1800. Little of substance remains of the monastic buildings, but the abbey church is the most complete and unaltered Cistercian ruin in the country, and it stands to a greater height than either Fountains or Rievaulx, with one side of its crossing tower intact. Though built of dour grey Pennine stone, further discoloured by the belching smoke of the Industrial Revolution, the remains are noble and fascinating, and architecturally closer to the early Cistercian ideal than the more famous abbeys.

Leeds Corporation

6 PONTEFRACT CASTLE
NE of town centre, off A645

[SE 4622]　★

This castle, the most important in medieval northern England, and the scene of the displaced Richard II's death by starvation, either voluntary or enforced, is now only a shadow of its former self. Demolished in response to a petition from the townsfolk after the Civil War, and no doubt subsequently quarried for its building stone, the castle of 'Bloody Pomfret' eventually became a liquorice field for Pontefract cakes, and only parts of its curtain wall and keep of uncertain shape remain above ground. Begun by the de Lacys not many years after the Conquest, Pontefract was built on rock foundations, and for most of its history was a royal residence and a northern royal arsenal. It had many towers and elaborate defences, and withstood two sieges in the Civil War before finally surrendering.

AM

7 SANDAL CASTLE
1½ miles (2.5 km) S of Wakefield town centre, on minor road off A61

[SE 3318]　★

'Little remains except for the earthworks', Sir Nikolaus Pevsner was able to say in his 1959 volume on Yorkshire's West Riding in *The Buildings of England* series. But in the early 1960s, systematic excavation began on this overgrown site marked only by a few fragments of walls and the surrounding earthworks. After ten years' work, archaeologists had revealed extensive remains of an important castle built

originally in the twelfth century by the Warenne earls of Surrey and maintained up to the Battle of Bosworth, Richard III having extended its buildings considerably. After his death it was neglected to the point of ruin, though defended for a time by the Royalists in the Civil War, after which it was slighted and left to become derelict and mostly hidden by vegetation. The complete layout of the castle and the foundations and some more substantial fragments of the castle can now be seen.

Wakefield Corporation

46 Wiltshire

See map on page 150

1 IVYCHURCH PRIORY
Just N of Alderbury, on minor road off A36, 3 miles (5 km) SE of Salisbury

[SU 1827]　⊜ *No access* ⊜

Only fragments remain *in situ* of the Augustinian priory founded by King Stephen, some other parts having been built into an adjoining farmhouse, and its materials used in the drinking-trough and fountain on Alderbury's village green. The priory was already foundering when it was formally dissolved in 1536, having suffered grievously from the Black Death.

Private

2 LUDGERSHALL CASTLE
In village, off A342, 7 miles (11 km) NW of Andover

[SU 2651]　+

There is nothing here to excite the passions of the romantic – just a few remains of a castle built in the eleventh century. In the thirteenth it was converted into a kind of palatial hunting lodge by Henry III, and used as such by the king and his sons Edward (later Edward I) and Edmund Crouchback. After Henry's death, it passed to his widow, and was then a royal manor house, but by the late Tudor period it had fallen into ruin, John Leland reporting that it was 'clene down'.

English Heritage

3 MALMESBURY ABBEY
Town centre

[ST 9387]　+

Founded as a Celtic monastery, or perhaps a nunnery in the seventh century, Malmesbury became a great Benedictine abbey in the ninth, the Saxon King Athelstan, one of its benefactors, being buried here in 940. The medieval historian William of Malmesbury was a monk here. After the Dissolution, part of the great church having collapsed, most of the abbey gradually disappeared, largely through plundering of its materials, but a wealthy clothier, William Stumpe, bought the church and, after setting his looms up in it for a while, and building streets of houses for his workers within the former abbey precincts, gave it to the town as its parish church. Only the nave was employed for this purpose, however, and the substantial walls of the rest, built of Cotswold stone, remain as ruinous attachments, partly filled with masonry to enclose the rescued nave.

Church of England

4 OLD SARUM
Off A345, 1½ miles (2.5 km) N of Salisbury

[SU 1332]　★

This amazing site, occupied continuously from the Iron Age to AD 1226, is – from the point of view of the ruin-hunter – a Norman scene, with the foundations of the cathedral built between 1075 and 1092, and fragments of the castle's fortifications. A palace was built here for the bishop, too; but in 1226 the see was moved to Salisbury, and gradually the whole site fell into ruin, helped by the taking of materials from the old cathedral to build the new one. It is impossible to ignore the massive earthworks of this terraced site, first an Iron Age hill fort, then a Roman settlement and then an Anglo-Saxon burgh, Searobyrg, before it became a Norman town. The Saxon name means 'dry town', and it was partly due to the difficulty of obtaining water here that the place was abandoned, Leland noting in the sixteenth century that: 'There is not one house … inhabited.' Samuel Pepys found the place somewhat unnerving in the following century. 'I saw a great fortification,' he wrote, ' … and find it prodigious, so as to frighten one to be in it all alone at that time of night.'

English Heritage

Old Wardour Castle

Part of the castle at Old Sarum

5 OLD WARDOUR CASTLE

Minor road from Donhead St Andrew, off A30, 5 miles (8 km) NE of Shaftesbury

[ST 9326]   ***   Tel: 0747 870487

Yet another victim of the Civil War, Wardour was defended for a while against the seige of 1000 Parliamentary soldiers by the 60-year-old Lady Blanche Arundell and a handful of servants and retainers, but the walls were undermined and the house plundered, and then the Royalists did more damage in trying to recover it. The Arundells finally abandoned it for a new mansion nearby. The original castle, or fortified house, had stood since the fourteenth century, when it was built by a branch of the Lovell family round a central hexagonal courtyard. It was given some classical remodelling late in the sixteenth century, which shows particularly in the courtyard portal to the steps of the great hall, with its Tuscan columns and lions' heads.

English Heritage

6 STONEHENGE

At present from A344 near junction with A303, 2 miles (3 km) W of Amesbury (changes to the present road and access layout are imminent at the time of writing)

[SU 1242]   *

Most famous of all the ruins of Britain, and indeed one of the outstanding prehistoric remains of the world, it is also one of the most tantalizing – a dramatic witness to the fact that monumental building was taking place here soon after the Egyptian pharaohs had erected the first pyramids, and its pagan site on Salisbury Plain is a place of pilgrimage quite as potent as any in Christendom. Yet we do not know what it is, and no doubt its mystery is a large part of its attraction. Even before 2000 BC the first builders evidently created the circle of pits known to us as the Aubrey Holes inside a bank and ditch, and some of these were found to contain burnt human bones. Then the so-called 'Beaker people' probably erected a double circle of bluestones, perhaps transported here from Wales, around 1800 BC (although some doubt has been cast in recent years on this long-held theory of Stone Age man transporting gigantic boulders across the Bristol Channel on rafts). The axis of the circle pointed to the rising sun at the summer

Stonehenge: the Hele Stone seen through monument's axis

Stonehenge

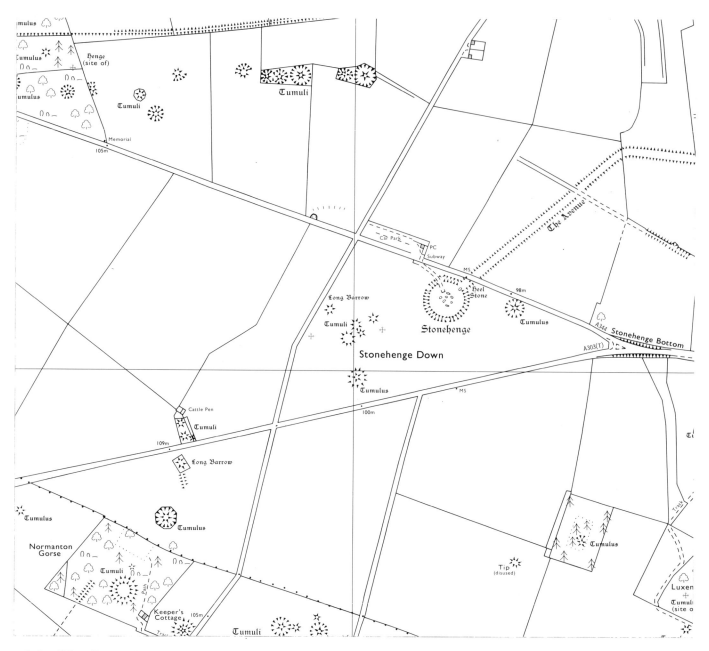

solstice. Then Bronze Age men brought huge grey sarsen stones from the Marlborough Downs and erected them in an outer circle and an inner horseshoe-shape, with curved lintels, secured by mortice and tenon joints carved in the stones, forming a continuous architrave. It is this later work which qualifies Stonehenge as architecture and its remains as a ruin, unlike the many circles of standing stones scattered about the country. Legend abounds here – it is the tomb of Boudicca, or of King Arthur's father, Uther Pendragon, or it was spirited whole to this spot from Ireland by the magician Merlin, or it is a Druid temple. Actually, it was here long before

Boudicca, or Arthur, or the Druids, but its stones resolutely refuse to give up the real secrets of antiquity. It was undoubtedly a building of religious significance, probably in connection with tribal ceremonies and fertility ritual.

English Heritage

7 WEST KENNET LONG BARROW
Footpath S from A4, 5¼ miles (8.5 km) W of Marlborough

[SU 1067]   +

The dramatic remains (reconstructed) of this neolithic tomb help to form one of

the most concentrated prehistoric complexes in Europe, along with the Avebury stone circle and Silbury Hill. Dating from around 3400 BC, the barrow consists of a central corridor with chambers off both sides, formed with massive boulders and all covered over with chalk and turf, its entrance blocked by a 12-foot (4-m) high stone. Excavation revealed the burial of at least 20 adults and 12 children here, probably over a period of several centuries. One man was killed by an arrow in his neck. The skulls of others were missing.

English Heritage

Wales

Caerphilly Castle, Mid Glamorgan

47 Clwyd

See map on page 158

1 BASINGWERK ABBEY
Beside A548, 1¼ miles (2 km) NE of Holywell

[SJ 1977] +

Founded by the Earl of Chester as a Savignac house in 1131, Basingwerk became Cistercian 16 years later. The layout of the buildings was the standard Cistercian arrangement, but the site was unusual, on high ground near the sea at Holywell, and because of this situation the abbey was given some fortification. Edward I made his headquarters here while Flint Castle was in the course of completion. The remains of the church are not very great, but there are extensive ruins of the domestic buildings, the refectory being the best preserved.

Cadw

2 CAERGWRLE CASTLE
In village on A541, 4½ miles (7 km) NW of Wrexham

[SJ 3057] +

Fragments of the enclosing wall and towers of a small thirteenth-century castle built within Iron Age earthworks, and given by Edward I to Eleanor of Castile.

3 CASTELL DINAS BRAN
Minor road off A542 just N of Llangollen

[SJ 2243] ★★★

Prominently sited on a lofty hilltop overlooking Llangollen, it was also known as Crow Castle, and was once the fortress of the warlord Madoc ap Gruffyd Maelor, who founded Valle Crucis Abbey (q.v.), doubtless from anxiety at the prospect of meeting his maker. It was captured by the English, and was in ruins before the end of the sixteenth century. Little remains but the enclosing wall and fragments of towers, but the views from the ruins are worth the climb.

AM

4 DENBIGH CASTLE
Short distance from town centre

[SJ 0565] ★

Henry de Lacy, Earl of Lincoln, built this castle as a supplement to the king's own castles in subduing the Welsh, although the Welsh captured it not long after its completion. They did not, however, hold on to it for long. Sir Henry Percy (Hotspur) made it his HQ in 1399, and in Elizabeth I's time Robert Dudley, Earl of Leicester, included it among his possessions, entertaining the queen here on one occasion. It was slighted after surrendering in the Civil War, following an 11-month siege. The remains are fairly substantial and extensive, but what catches and holds the attention is the north-east gatehouse, triangular in plan and formed of three polygonal towers, replete with portcullises, spy-holes and a drawbridge. Although badly ruined, this building is highly interesting and attractive, with a weathered statue above a great entrance arch, representing perhaps de Lacy himself, or possibly Edward I.

Cadw

5 EWLOE CASTLE
Off B5125, 1 mile (1.5 km) NW of village, 7½ miles (12 km) W of Chester

[SJ 2867] +

Llewellyn the Great built this stone castle early in the thirteenth century, but it was made strategically redundant by the building of Flint Castle (q.v.) late in the same century, and it has no significant history after that. The ruin, however, is quite attractive, with the lower part of its D-shaped keep, known as the Welsh Tower, on a mound with a stone retaining wall above the bailey or outer ward, where other walls remain.

Cadw

6 FLINT CASTLE
Off A548 just N of town centre

[SJ 2473] ★★

It was the first of Edward I's castles in north Wales, begun during the campagin of 1277 and designed by the king's military architect James of St George. It was built beside the River Dee and defended by a moat on the sides not protected by the river. The rectangular inner enclosure had three circular angle-towers and at the fourth corner a huge circular keep which doubled as a gatehouse to the inner ward. Fateful meetings took place here between Edward II and Piers Gaveston in 1312 and between Richard II and Henry Bolingbroke in 1399. The castle passed back and forth in the Civil War until, finally surrendered to Parliament in 1646, Cromwell's demolition gang did so thorough a job that it was said later to be 'almost buried in its own ruins'. Nevertheless, there is enough left of its walls and towers to make its exploration interesting.

Cadw

7 HAWARDEN CASTLE
Short distance S of village-centre, off B5125, 6 miles (9.5 km) W of Chester

[SJ 3165] ★★★

Ruins of the medieval castle stand in the park of the eighteenth-century mansion of the same name which was Gladstone's home. The remains are of a circular keep and a hall of the thirteenth century. The castle changed hands three times in the Civil War – once after a letter to the occupants from the Royalist commander warning them to 'expect no quarter for man, woman, or child', and declaring that 'our intents are not to starve you, but to batter and storm you, and then to hang you all'. But the Roundheads took the castle back again later, and it was then efficiently slighted by Parliamentary troops.

Private

8 LEICESTER'S FOLLY
In Denbigh near castle

[SJ 0565] ⊖ *No access* ⊖

The outer walls of a church begun by Robert Dudley, Earl of Leicester, in 1579, but never finished, stand in the grounds of Castle House, Denbigh, and can be seen from the road. It is said that Leicester intended it to replace St Asaph's Cathedral, which had at that time undergone repair after being burnt down by Owain Glyndwr. Leicester, however, died before the new church was finished, and the work was then abandoned.

Private

9 MOEL FAMAU TOWER
Minor road off A494, 5 miles (8 km) SW of Mold

[SJ 1662] +

On the peak of the hill is the stump of a stone pyramidal monument which was built – none too well, it would seem – to commemorate the jubilee of George III in 1810. In 1862 it was blown down in a storm. The climb is rewarded more by the views than by the ruin, perhaps.

Clwyd County Council

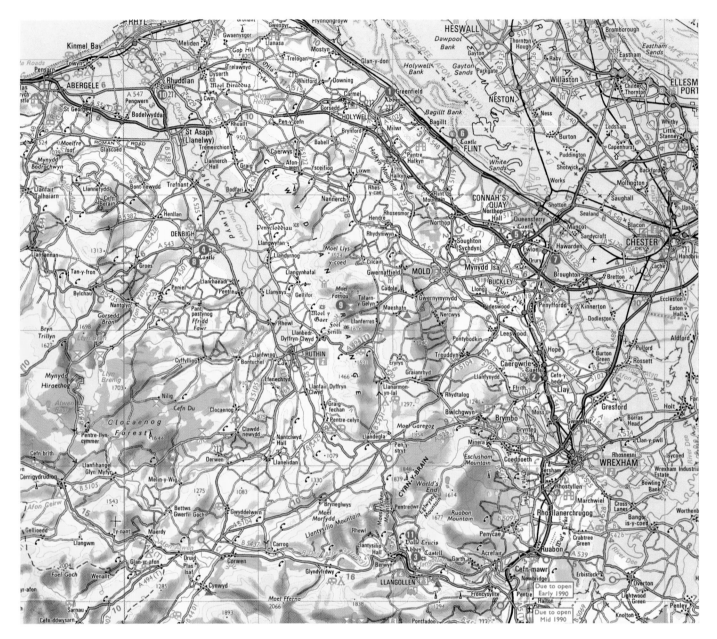

10 RHUDDLAN CASTLE

On minor road, short distance S of village centre

[SJ 0277] ★

Rhuddlan's story is the familiar one in north Wales – built by James of St George for Edward I, and knocked down by order of Parliament after the Civil War, the life-span of 400 years in between being partly occupied in resisting Welsh attacks. The ruins here are more substantial than those of many castles in Wales, and show a concentric plan with twin circular-towered gatehouses at opposite corners of the inner enclosure and single towers at the other two. The most impressive work of Master James at Rhuddlan, however, was the diverting of the River Clwyd's course so that building materials and supplies, not to mention reinforcements, could be brought to the castle by ship. You can still see the dock gate.

Cadw

11 VALLE CRUCIS ABBEY

A542 just NW of Llangollen

[SJ 2044] ★

Valle Crucis – the Valley of the Cross – gets its name from an isolated column now known as Eliseg's Pillar, an ancient monument to a prince of Powys which was once thought to have been a cross, and thus a religious relic. The abbey was founded in 1201 by a Welsh warlord, Madoc ap Gruffyd Maelor, no doubt to ease his conscience after a lifetime of warfare and plunder. The Cistercian abbey's water supply came from a small tributary of the River Dee. Henry VIII did not need much excuse to suppress this establishment. It had expensive sculptures in the church, and a reputation for lavish hospitality far removed from the asceticism which was supposedly the Cistercian norm. One visitor reported dining on four courses of meat off silver dishes, washed down with claret, in the company of an abbot who wore rings on his fingers. The most impressive parts of the ruins are the chapter house, remaining largely intact

Valle Crucis Abbey

with vaulted aisles and Decorated windows (there was still glass in them at the beginning of the twentieth century), and the nave of the church with its lofty west wall and fine rose window. One can see clearly that the gabled upper part of this wall is a later addition, being built in ashlar stonework unlike the thinly coursed rubble below.

Cadw

48 Dyfed

See maps on pages 163 and 166

1 ABERYSTWYTH CASTLE
Promontory near sea-front in town

[*SN 5781*]   +

One of the earliest of Edward I's Welsh castles, it was contemporary with Flint and Rhuddlan (q.q.v.) in Clwyd. Built on a promontory, and triangular in plan, one of the original baileys has disappeared through coastal erosion, but there are extensive remains, some parts fragmentary and some substantial. The latter include the gatehouse and one or two towers, and some of the curtain wall. Owain Glyndwr captured the castle in 1403 but it was retaken by the English in 1409. After the Civil War, when it was

Bishop's Palace, St David's

used as a royal mint (coins being made from locally-mined silver), the castle was undermined, having been besieged and taken by Cromwell's army.

AM

2 BISHOP'S PALACE, ST DAVID'S
Close to cathedral

[*SM 7525*]   ★

Henry de Gower was elected Bishop of St David's in 1328, and during the next 19 years, until his death, he supervised the building of the magnificent palace whose ruins stand close to the cathedral, still showing the style and splendour in which he and his successors lived. The palace looked towards the cathedral on one side and on another towards Ramsey Island, where the wealthy bishops kept herds of cattle and flocks of sheep, as well as horses. In the sixteenth century, however, Bishop Barlow proposed the removal of the see to Carmarthen, and

the palace began to decay from that time, when he stripped the lead from the roof of the great hall. Some of the buildings were demolished by a later bishop, and the place was derelict before the end of the seventeenth century. But even in its ruined state its stylishness can be appreciated, its buildings of buff and purplish sandstone, with fine arcaded parapets, arranged round three sides of a square courtyard in which an elaborate porch with an ogee arch has a flight of steps leading up to the great hall. The palace is undoubtedly one of the finest medieval ruins in Wales.

Cadw

3 CAREW CASTLE
A4075, 4½ miles (7 km) E of Pembroke

[*SN 0403*]   ★★★

This is one of the most substantial, striking and fascinating of the countless ruins of Welsh castles, though it does

not look as much like a mighty fortress as most of them. Standing on a rocky site above a tidal inlet, it is one of the castles of the so-called Landsker, that southern part of what was formerly Pembrokeshire, settled largely by the English and French rather than the Welsh. The castle was begun by the Carew family as an authentic fortified stronghold in the twelfth and thirteenth centuries, with a dungeon and a curtain wall with four towers surrounding a keep. But in the fifteenth century it was partly converted into a splended fortified mansion by Sir Rhys ap Thomas, who entertained Henry Tudor here during his progress to Bosworth Field. Then it was altered again in the sixteenth century by Sir John Perrott. He was the spitting image of Henry VIII, so everyone – including himself – drew the obvious conclusion, but that did not save him from being thrown into the Tower of London for treason by Elizabeth I. The castle was besieged and brought to ruin in the Civil War, and the ruins present a curious hotch-potch of more than three centuries of baronial architecture, with medieval walls and battlements adjoining Tudor state apartments and wide mullioned and transomed windows.

Private

4 CARMARTHEN CASTLE
Near town centre

[SN 4119]   +

The gateway is practically all that is worth notice among the ruins of this thirteenth-century castle, though it had a keep and a curtain wall with five towers and was Edward I's administrative headquarters for the region. The castle was thoroughly slighted in the Civil War, and local authority offices now occupy much of the site.

AM

5 CARREG-CENNEN CASTLE
¾ mile (1.2 km) E of Trapp, on minor road off A483 3 miles (5 km) SE of Llandeilo

[SN 6619]   *

The builder of the original castle here is unknown, but it was granted by Edward I to John Gillard, who rebuilt it on this rocky hilltop, commanding fine views in what is now peaceful Welsh countryside, though its paramount consideration then, of course, was defence. It was seriously damaged by Owain Glyndwr's forces, and afterwards repaired, being taken by the Lancastrians during the Wars of the Roses. Then it became a haunt of bandits, and was largely destroyed by its owner in 1462, William Herbert, to preserve the local country from medieval hooligans. One of the ruin's most famous features is a long tunnel through the solid rock beneath the castle to a cave where a spring supplied water in times of siege.

Cadw

6 CILGERRAN CASTLE
In village, on minor road off A478, 2½ miles (4 km) SE of Cardigan

[SN 1943]   *

The second Earl of Pembroke, William Marshall, who captured the town from the Welsh in 1223, rebuilt an existing castle here, standing in a spectacular position high above the River Teifi, which later drew artists of the Romantic period to the spot to paint the scene. It was only the view of the castle at a distance, as a feature in a landscape, that could have turned it into a work of art. At close quarters its ruins are dour and aggressive. It was built of thin, slatey Welsh stone, with voussoirs in the arches of gateways jutting ferociously inwards. The castle was abandoned in the fourteenth century by its then owners, the Vaughan family, and was further damaged by slate quarrying before being repaired and taken into care as an ancient monument.

Cadw

7 DOLAUCOTHI MINE
Near Pumsaint, on minor road off A482, 7 miles (11 km) SE of Lampeter

[SN 6640]   ***   Tel: 055 85 359

This unique industrial ruin is the excavated site of a Roman gold mine. There were both opencast and underground workings, and an elaborate system of reservoirs and aqueducts to provide the water needed at the site for washing ore and driving a water-wheel that drained the galleries. The mine was the second-largest gold mine in the

Cilgerran Castle

Carreg-Cennen Castle

Roman Empire, and the British were probably working it before the Romans came.

National Trust

8 DYNEFWR OLD CASTLE
Lane off A40 just W of Llandeilo

[SN 6121] ⊖ *No access* ⊖

From the road south of Dynefwr Park, going west from Llandeilo, the ivy-covered ruins of a castle can be seen on a hilltop, consisting of a circular keep and flanking tower with part of a curtain wall. It was of Welsh origin and before the Conquest south Wales was ruled from it by the Welsh princes.

Private

9 KIDWELLY CASTLE
Short distance from town centre on A484, 6½ miles (10.5 km) S of Carmarthen

[SN 4007] ★

The castle at Kidwelly is as fine a concentric castle ruin as one could wish for, being well preserved and showing with extreme clarity the layout and buildings of a late thirteenth- and early fourteenth-century fortification. It was begun by Payn de Chaworth around 1275 and completed by Edward I's nephew, Henry of Lancaster. The first building operations created an enclosure within a square curtain wall with round towers at the corners and a chapel extending outwards towards the river. This was then enclosed on the landward

sides by a semi-circular outer curtain with flanking towers and a gatehouse at each end of the semi-circle. The north-east gatehouse was burnt down by Owain Glyndwr early in the fifteenth century, but the by then neglected castle escaped the wrath of Cromwell, and a great deal of Kidwelly survives, including part of a later hall added to the outer ward, and one can profitably study the layout of halls, kitchen, solar and chapel, dungeons and the brute of the remaining gatehouse, which had sufficient accommodation to serve as an independent fortress in an emergency.

Cadw

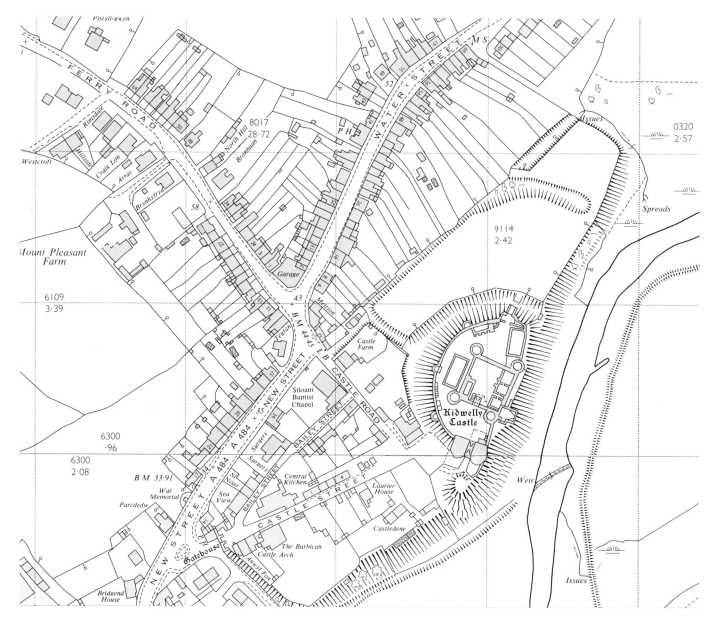

10 LAMPHEY PALACE
Off A4139, 2 miles (3 km) E of Pembroke

[SN 0100] ★

The bishops of St David's built this fine country seat from the thirteenth century. Bishop Gower, who built the palace at St David's (q.v.) was responsible for much of this one, too. Note the similar arcaded parapets. Lamphey was, however, smaller than and architecturally inferior to the St David's palace. Lamphey was sold to the Devereux family by Henry VIII, and Robert Devereux, Elizabeth's well-beloved Earl of Essex, lived here when he was a boy. The ruins are substantial and interesting, rather than beautiful.

Cadw

11 LLANDOVERY CASTLE
Short distance S of town centre

[SN 7634] +

Only fragments remain on a knoll in the town. It was built in the twelfth century, and passed back and forth like a shuttlecock between the Welsh and English until Edward I's conquest of Wales. Standing behind the Castle Hotel, the ruin has recently had the cattle market and a car park as its neighbours.

AM

12 LLANSTEPHAN CASTLE
Minor road S from B4312 in village, 7 miles (11 km) SW of Carmarthen

[SN 3510] +

Substantial remains of the walls, towers and gatehouse stand on a steep hill overlooking the mouth of the Afon Tywi. The castle was the scene of several encounters between the English and Welsh, and it often changed hands, being captured by Glyndwr in the fifteenth century. The thirteenth-century gatehouse is the most interesting survival. It is a ruin more striking when seen from a distance, perhaps, than at close quarters.

Cadw

13 LLAWHADEN CASTLE
In village, minor road off A40, 7 miles (11 km) E of Haverfordwest

[SN 0717] ★

The castle built in the early thirteenth century was later converted into a palace for the bishops of St David's, but the rather notorious Bishop Barlow (see Bishop's Palace, St David's) is generally

accused of bringing it to ruin by stripping the lead from the roof and abandoning it to nature. The ruins are fairly extensive and are reached by a steep lane opposite the churchyard.

Cadw

14 MANORBIER CASTLE
Near village centre, on B4585, 5½ miles (9 km) SE of Pembroke

[SS 0697] ★★★

Attractively situated and very well preserved (part is still inhabited), the ruins of Manorbier are among the most fascinating and instructive of castles in Wales. It was the birthplace of the Welsh scholar and churchman Giraldus de Barri, known as Giraldus Cambrensis, who wrote topographical works on Wales and Ireland in the twelfth century, and he described this castle as 'excellently well defended' and its site 'the pleasantest spot in Wales'. The castle's curtain walls and flanking towers are largely intact, and the remains of its domestic and service quarters are very clear, with the great hall and chapel built over vaulted undercrofts, and stable blocks and a gatehouse. Elizabeth I sold the castle to one Thomas Owain, and his descendants have owned it ever since. When occupied, it must have been one of the most practical and peaceful of Welsh castles.

Private

15 NEWCASTLE EMLYN CASTLE
On A475 just NE of town centre

[SN 3140] +

Partly built by the Welsh and partly by the English, the castle was raised in a loop of the Teifi and changed hands several times in the course of its history, finally being slighted in the Civil War, so that little of it now remains but part of a twin-towered gatehouse and other fragments of a later conversion into a fortified house. You could easily mistake the gatehouse for a folly, its remaining overgrown shape looking almost calculated to catch the eye.

16 PEMBROKE CASTLE
W end of town

[SM 9801] ★★★

Henry Tudor, later Henry VII, was born here in 1457 on 28 January – 'this day of St Agnes,' as his mother wrote later, 'that I did bring into this world my good and gracious prince'. It is among the finest of Welsh castles, dating from the

late twelfth century, when a bailey with a stone hall was enclosed by the earls of Pembroke on a site above the river estuary, where a timber castle had formerly stood within the earthworks. Half a century later, an outer bailey was added. A massive circular keep of four storeys, with a splayed plinth, still stands more or less to its original height of nearly 80 feet (24 m), its walls being 16 feet (5 m) thick in places, and the roof unusually domed. It could be entered only at first-floor level via a detached stone staircase and a drawbridge. A narrow stairway gave access from the castle's hall to a natural cave, ominously called a Wogan, in the cliff below, possibly used as a cold store and also available as an emergency exit. This extremely well-defended castle never fell into enemy hands until the Civil War, when it was brought to ruin after a long siege conducted by Cromwell himself. It was afterwards much quarried for building materials.

Private

17 ST DOGMAEL'S ABBEY
In village, on B4546 just W of Cardigan

[SN 1645] +

This was a Celtic site sacked by the Vikings, and succeeded in 1115 by a Benedictine priory of the reformed Order of Tiron, made an abbey within five years. The remains are such as we dismiss as 'sparse', and we have to remind ourselves that black-habited monks lived out their lives here over a period of more than 400 years, the time that separates us from the young Elizabeth I. St Dogmael's, founded by Robert FitzMartin, Lord of Cemaes, is associated with the Segranus Stone, now in the parish church, from which the ancient Irish Ogham alphabet was deciphered. Parts of the priory church's nave remain, with a moulded entrance arch and carved corbels.

Cadw

18 SLEBECH CHURCH
Footpath S of A40, 5½ miles (9 km) E of Haverfordwest

[SN 0314] +

What a change from all the feudal intimidation of the countless castles in this part of Wales is presented by this attractive ruin in wooded parkland by the Cleddau estuary. It was the church of a hospice of the Knights Hospitallers, founded in the twelfth century, which

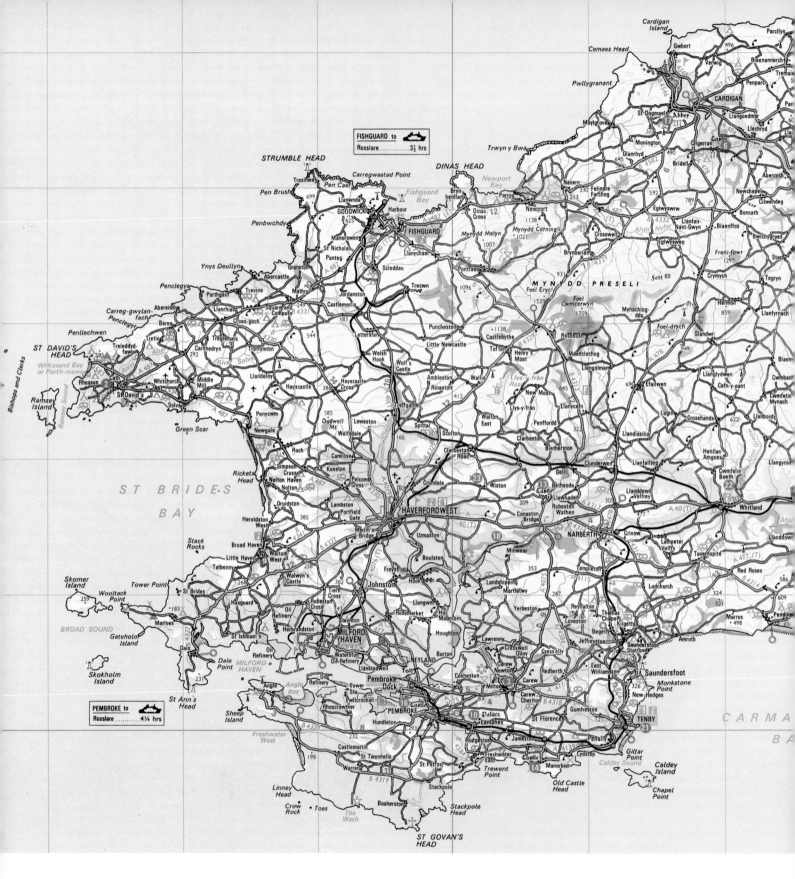

FISHGUARD to
Rosslare............3½ hrs

PEMBROKE to
Rosslare............4¼ hrs

was the largest such establishment in the west of Britain, and famous for its hospitality to pilgrims on their way to St David's. You need to be a pilgrim to see it, walking 2 miles (3 km) along a forest path.

Private

19 STRATA FLORIDA ABBEY
Minor road E of B4343, 20 miles (32 km) W of Llandrindod Wells

[SN 7465]   ★

Its name ('vale of flowers') and its history are rather more romantic than its grey

stone ruins, which are fairly sparse. But it was 'a wonderful place once', as George Borrow said. Founded on its present site in 1200, it was, of course, a Cistercian monastery which, despite rough handling in the wars between English and Welsh, as well as natural disaster (fire) and piracy by a rival abbey, became a major centre of Welsh learning, although it was commercially very active as well, dealing in lead and wool. Some of the stone may have been brought all the way from Somerset, and the abbey, burial place of Welsh princes and poets, was reputedly a splendid building. Relatively little remains, the church being the most interesting, with fine tiled pavements and a unique west doorway with five orders of moulding interrupted by regularly spaced narrow bands ending in whorls like bishops' croziers.

Cadw

20 TALLEY ABBEY

Off B4302, 6½ miles (10.5 km) N of Llandeilo

[SN 6332]   ★

Part of the church's simply-built crossing remains to some height among other fragments, but this Premonstratensian abbey – the only one of this order in Wales – was despoiled and burnt in the fifteenth century, but survived in diminished form, and after the Dissolution it was quarried for building the parish church, among other things. The abbey was founded about 1197 by the Welsh prince, Rhys ap Gruffydd.

Cadw

21 TENBY CASTLE

Overlooking town's harbour

[SN 1300]   +

There are minimal remains on Castle Hill, overlooking the harbour, of this twelfth-century castle, which became largely redundant when the town itself was fortified with walls and towers, some of which survive.

AM

22 WHITLAND ABBEY

1¾ miles (2.8 km) NE of village on minor road off A40, 12½ miles (20 km) W of Carmarthen

[SN 2018]   +

A fragment of the church stands forlorn and insignificant, but this is the remnant of the first Cistercian foundation in Wales, called Alba Landa, from which sprang more famous daughters – Strata Florida and Cwmhir (q.q.v.). About 1151 the abbey was moved here from Tregarn, whence the monks had come direct from Clairvaux in 1143, and Leland described the abbey later as standing in a vast wood, as in a wilderness.

AM

23 WISTON CASTLE

In village, on minor road off A40, 4¼ miles (6.8 km) E of Haverfordwest

[SN 0218]   ⊜   No access   ⊜

The stump of a cylindrical keep of the thirteenth century remains on a motte. It was built probably after Llewellyn the Great had destroyed the earlier castle on the site, one of the Landsker castles of 'Little England beyond Wales'.

AM

---

49 Gwent

See map below

1 ABERGAVENNY CASTLE

Short distance SW of town centre

[SO 2913]   ★★★

The castle was the scene of an act of infamous treachery in the late twelfth century, when William de Braose, who had recaptured the castle from the Welsh, invited a number of prominent Welsh lords to dine with him at Christmas and had them all slaughtered while they were sitting at his table. The

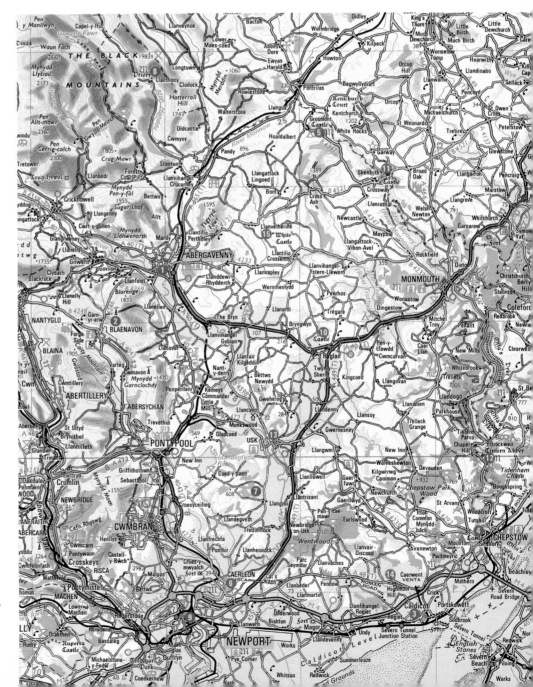

present ruins post-date this event, and there is not much of them – bits of the curtain wall, gatehouse and two towers. The local museum is in the castle.

AM

2 BLAENAVON IRONWORKS
In the town, on B4246, 4½ miles (7 km) SW of Abergavenny

[SO 2509]   ★★

A fine bank of five blast furnaces survives at this important industrial site, where iron working was first established in the mid-eighteenth century, and expanded rapidly when it was discovered that the local coal could be used for smelting instead of the increasingly scarce timber used up to that time.

Cadw

3 CALDICOT CASTLE
In village, on minor road off B4245, 10 miles (16 km) E of Newport

[ST 4888]   +

Partly in ruins and partly a museum, Caldicot was built in the twelfth and thirteenth centuries by the de Bohun earls of Hereford. It was a fine and extensive castle, as its remains still show, and was owned by Dukes of Gloucester and Buckingham before becoming neglected. The last private owners were the Cobb family, who presented the castle to the public, and it is now part of a country park.

Gwent County Council

4 CHEPSTOW CASTLE
Short distance from town centre

[ST 5394]   ★

One of the first castles to be built in stone after the Conquest, Chepstow was the work of William FitzOsbern, Earl of Hereford, and was built on a limestone platform above the River Wye, consisting then of a two-storey great tower to which was later added a wall and towers enclosing baileys on both sides along the ridge and, later still, a barbican at the western end and a further bailey at the eastern end. The castle was in the ownership of the Herbert family, earls of Pembroke, from the fifteenth century to the twentieth. Jeremy Taylor, the Royalist divine and author of *Holy Living* and *Holy Dying*, was imprisoned here for a while. After the Restoration, Henry Marten, one of the signatories to Charles I's death warrant, was imprisoned here for 20 years until his death at 78 in a D-shaped tower at the

extreme eastern end of the castle, which was then called Bigod's Tower, but now is known as Marten's Tower. The ruins are full of interest, having gone through more than 900 years relatively unscathed, though latterly neglected. Chepstow is now one of Europe's oldest ruined stone castles. The remains look friendly enough from the town side, but more intimidating from the river.

Cadw

5 GROSMONT CASTLE
In village, B4347, 7½ miles (12 km) NE of Abergavenny

[SO 4024]   +

Grosmont, Skenfrith and White Castles (q.q.v.) are known as the Trilateral Castles, built to guard the routes in and out of Wales between the River Wye and the Black Mountains. All three were begun by Hubert de Burgh, to whom the existing timber castles in 1201 were granted by King John, but in the 1260s they passed to the Earl of Lancaster. None of them were by any means lavish in the provision of living accommodation, and were clearly intended for military purposes only, so that in spite of withstanding attacks by Owain Glyndwr, all three were in decay by the sixteenth century. At Grosmont, Prince Henry (later Henry V) inflicted a crushing defeat on Glyndwr's army when he marched from Hereford to relieve the besieged castle in 1405. One of the most interesting features of the ruin is a fine octagonal chimney, dating from about 1330, which served fireplaces in a new three-storey range built about that time.

Cadw

6 ISCA
At Caerleon, on B4236 just NE of Newport

[ST 3390]   ★

From this fortress at Caerleon the Roman Empire brought south Wales into the *Pax Romana*. It was a characteristic imperial military headquarters, rectangular, orderly, and covering 50 acres (20 ha) of ground. Its remains were described by Giraldus Cambrensis as: 'handsomely built of masonry, with courses of bricks . . . a town of prodigious size, remarkable hot baths, relics of temples and theatres all enclosed within fine walls'. The fortress was established in the first century AD and was occupied by the 2nd Augustan Legion until the end of the third century, the garrison town gradually growing around it from

Roman origins as a civil settlement alongside the barracks, which accommodated more than 5000 men. The best of the remains is undoubtedly the amphitheatre, which has been thoroughly excavated, and consists of an oval-shaped area surrounded by raised earth banks and stone walls, some stones bearing inscriptions recording the progress of the building from about AD 80. The earth banks would have supported wooden seating for several thousand spectators at, perhaps, military parades and blood sports.

Cadw

7 LLANGIBBY CASTLE
In village, on minor road off A472, 2¾ miles (4.5 km) S of Usk

[ST 3697]   +

A fairly small and simple fourteenth-century castle also known as Tregrug Castle, it was never completed and played no role in history. It stands on an overgrown hilltop defended on one side by a deep ditch, but has no sign of buildings within its stone outer defences.

8 LLANTHONY PRIORY
In village, on minor road N from A465, 8½ miles (13.5 km) N of Abergavenny

[SO 2927]   +

I loved thee by thy streams of yore,
By distant streams I love thee more.

These ironical words on Llanthony are those of the poet and essayist Walter Savage Landor, who purchased the priory remains early in the nineteenth century and intended to incorporate them in a model estate, over which he would preside as a latterday country squire, but his plans came to grief over local disputes and refusal of permission to restore the priory, and he eventually gave up and went abroad. The priory had begun as a religious community, growing up from a hermit's cell about 1103, and it became a regular Augustinian priory 15 years later, but had a turbulent history, suffering from both Welsh and English depredation. Re-establishing itself at Gloucester, Llanthony became for a time a mere cell again, though it did recover somewhat. There are considerable remains, although a farm absorbed the gatehouse and a hotel the prior's quarters. The church, sacristy and chapter house, mostly Transitional, are especially remarkable, but perhaps the setting, in a deep valley in the Black Mountains, does as much for the atmosphere of this ruin as its fine architecture.

Cadw

9 NEWPORT CASTLE
W bank of River Usk between Newport Bridge and railway

[ST3188]   +

Despite having only one side left to any extent of its former quadrangular curtain wall and surrounding towers, this castle has the virtue of a highly interesting detail which many such smaller Welsh castle ruins could badly do with. The castle was built originally in the twelfth century, rebuilt in the fourteenth and re-modelled in the fifteenth, after being destroyed by Owain Glyndwr. It had a long frontage on the west bank of the River Usk, and the waterfront side is the one with the substantial remains – three towers linked by the curtain wall. The central tower is a water-gate, with an arched entrance defended by two portcullises, which allowed water into the ground floor of the tower at high tide so that boats could sail right into it. At the top of this gate-tower was a chapel. The castle was brought to ruin for the second time by Cromwell.

Cadw

10 RAGLAN CASTLE
Off A40 just N of village, 7 miles (11 km) SW of Monmouth

[SO 4108]   ★

The poet Thomas Churchyard referred to it as a 'rare and noble sight', and indeed it was one of the most sumptuous of Welsh palaces, which one would call a fortified mansion rather than a military fortress, were it not for the fact that, in the Civil War, it held out for a long time against a siege by 3500 Parliamentary soldiers led at the end by Fairfax himself, commander of Cromwell's New Model Army. The castle was begun in 1435 by Sir William ap Thomas, and after his death his son William Herbert, subsequently Earl of Pembroke, continued the work. The oldest building is the separate moated keep known as the Yellow Tower of Gwent, possibly erected so that the lord of the castle could isolate himself in the event of a change in the loyalty of his household during the Wars of the Roses. Beyond the main castle's gatehouse, with its machicolated towers, are fine courtyards known as the Pitched Stone Court and

Skenfrith Castle

the Fountain Court, on either side of the great hall, with its great oriel window which once contained heraldic glass. Before the Civil War, Charles I was entertained here by the Marquis of Worcester, reputed to be the richest man in England, who had a large and unique library containing the finest collection of Welsh bardic manuscripts. But when the castle was surrendered to Fairfax in

August 1646, the library was burnt and the octogenarian millionaire imprisoned, though with a promise that he would be buried in St George's Chapel at Windsor, as befitted his rank. 'God bless my soul,' he exclaimed, 'they will give me a grander castle when dead than they took from me when living.' Be that as it may, Raglan remains one of the most picturesque and evocative castles in the country, though we no longer see it as the Romantics did, with ivied towers lending the moated ruins an aspect of medieval chivalry rather than twentieth-century conservation.

Cadw

11 SKENFRITH CASTLE
In village, on B4521, 6 miles (9.5 km) NW of Monmouth

[SO 4520] +

After Raglan it is rather pathetic – a sandstone round tower on an artificial mound with a quadrilateral curtain wall round it, originally moated. It was built in Henry III's time, replacing an earlier castle probably of timber, and was the middle one of the so-called Trilateral Castles guarding the routes in and out of Wales between the River Wye and the Black Mountains. Its neighbours were Grosmont and White Castle (q.q.v.). It was owned by the Duchy of Lancaster until the fourteenth century, and evidently became derelict soon afterwards, for it must have been a miserable place, with its western range of living quarters below ground level and always damp, if not actually flooded, in the winter months.

Cadw

12 TINTERN ABBEY
Beside A466, 4 miles (6.5 km) N of Chepstow

[SO 5300] ★

Tintern was one of the earliest of the great Cistercian foundations in Britain. It was founded, a year before Rievaulx, by Walter de Clare, in heavily wooded country of the Wye valley, 'remote from

The presbytery of the abbey church at Tintern Abbey

the traffic of men'. But its architecture is not, as we might expect, the restrained work of Cistercian austerity, because it was largely rebuilt in the thirteenth century, by which time the white-cowled monks' pure principles had rather fallen by the wayside. Because of the limitations of the site, the monastic buildings were erected on the north side of the church rather than the south, departing from the customary Cistercian layout. Tintern became a rich establishment deriving most of its wealth from sheep-farming. Abbot Richard Wyche surrendered the property to the king's commissioners in 1536, and the abbey's isolation protected it from the excesses of plunder, although the royal agents themselves stripped the lead from the roof and removed the bells from the crossing tower, and some of the stone was used in local houses. Then vegetation gradually engulfed what remained and it was in this state that Tintern was 'discovered' by the Romantic movement, with Wordsworth and Turner in the vanguard. Both poet and painter convince us that the great ruin looked far more romatic then than it does today, but we can still appreciate the stately beauty of the abbey church and trace the buildings where so many men spent the largest parts of their lives in what they conceived as their duty to God.

Cadw

13 USK CASTLE
In town, 5 miles (8 km) E of Pontypool

[SO 3701] +

Built by the de Clares in the twelfth century, taken by Simon de Montfort in the thirteenth, besieged by Glyndwr in the fifteenth, and slighted by Cromwell in the seventeenth, Usk's ruins show a curtain wall with a round tower and gatehouse and a keep, all in poor state except the gatehouse, which is part of a modern residence.

AM

14 VENTA SILURUM
Caerwent, off A48, 4¼ miles (6.8 km) SW of Chepstow

[ST 4690] +

The remains of the Romano-Welsh town, close to the former tribal capital of the Silures, are now part of Caerwent. The Roman walls and gates enclosed about 45 acres (18 ha) divided up into blocks of buildings by a regular street grid. It was the only Roman walled town

in Wales. The southern wall with its bastions is the most impressive part of the visible imperial work, built in the third and fourth centuries. In addition to the usual Roman buildings – forum, basilica, baths, temples, etc. – a shop has been identified as a fish-stall or oyster-bar, and among other archaeological finds was a Celtic mother-goddess figure, possibly an object of worship at a shrine here. (It is now in the Newport Museum.) This civil settlement is only 7 miles (11 km) from the military one of Isca (q.v.) with which it makes an interesting contrast.

Cadw

15 WHITE CASTLE
Minor road N off B4233 at Llantilio Crossenny, 6 miles (9.5 km) E of Abergavenny

[SO 3816] ★

White Castle is the largest of the Trilateral Castles, though not the most sophisticated in terms of living accommodation. Its name is a consequence of its stone walls having once been coated with white plaster. Unlike its neighbours, it stands in isolation from a town or village, although it was once called Llantilio Castle.

Cadw

Gatehouse of Beaumaris Castle, Anglesey

50 Gwynedd

See maps on pages 174 and 175

1 BEAUMARIS CASTLE
In village, on A545 on E coast of Anglesey

[SH 6076] ★

Begun on the Anglesey shore in 1295, overlooking the Menai Strait, Beaumaris was one of the last castles built by Edward I during his subjugation of the Welsh, but it did not near completion until after the king's death. Its name means 'beautiful marsh' – a contradiction in terms, one might think. The castle was built with concentric defensive walls, an outer curtain wall with frequent towers enclosing the thick high walls of the inner castle, which had angle-towers, semi-circular towers in the east and west walls, and mighty twin-towered gatehouses in the north and south walls. In its early stages, 3000 men were at work on it. The moat was fed from the sea, and boats could dock in the moat to land supplies in the event of approaches by land being cut off by the enemy. But this great piece of military engineering was never put to the test, and in fact it was abandoned before it was finished. It remained in royal ownership, however, until the Civil War, when it was surrendered to Parliamentary forces. The ruin is one of the more attractive of castles in Wales, built of light-coloured stone reflected in the moat, and with views of the hills of Snowdonia.

Cadw

2 BRYN-CELLI-DDU

Footpath from minor road off A4080, 3½ miles (5.5 km) SW of Menai Bridge

[SH 5070] +

The best example in England and Wales of a megalithic passage grave. The chamber is built of upright stone slabs with rubble infill. It was formerly covered with earth, and is still surrounded by a ditch and a stone circle. There is a monolith inside the chamber, which may be a phallic symbol, and standing stones at the entrance were found to bear inscribed and no doubt symbolic spirals and wavy lines. The remains are in an Anglesey field close to a farmhouse (signposted), to which you must walk from the minor road 1 mile (1.5 km) east of Llanddaniel Fab.

Cadw

3 CAPEL LLIGWY

Minor road off A5108, 1 mile (1.5 km) W of Moelfre

[SH 4986] +

A little west of Moelfre, on the island of Anglesey, is the ruin of an ancient chapel, probably of the twelfth century, standing on a hill. Stone steps lead down to a crypt.

Cadw

4 CASTELL Y BERE

Minor road N off B4405, 7 miles (11 km) SW of Dolgellau

[SH 6608] +

The ruins, on a formidably uneven and rocky spur below Cader Idris, vaguely reminiscent of Tintagel, are hardly anywhere more than mere foundations. The castle was built by Llewellyn the Great, and captured and utilized by Edward I, but seems to have been neglected by the end of the thirteenth century, possibly as a result of attack by Welsh rebels, for excavation revealed evidence of burning.

Cadw

5 CONWY CASTLE

E of town centre by river

[SH 7877] ★

Edward I's military architect and engineer, Master James of St George, built this castle at the entrance to the River Conwy in four years from 1283, at a cost equivalent in modern money to well over £3 million. It was one of the most expensive of the king's castles in Wales, and one of the most formidable – a compact enclosure with eight mighty cylindrical towers round its 15-foot (4.5-m) thick curtain walls, linked to the town walls, and with a barbican at each end of its east-west axis. Although Owain Glyndwr captured it in 1401 (while the garrison was in church on Good Friday!) its strength was never really challenged until the Civil War, by which time its defences were out of date and the castle was, in any case, 'utterly decayed'. It was dismantled in 1665. The remains have been described as among the finest castle ruins in Europe, and have attracted many artists to paint them, most notably, perhaps, Thomas Girtin and John Sell Cotman.

Cadw

Bryn-celli-ddu, Anglesey

6 CRICCIETH CASTLE

In town, off A497, 8 miles (13 km)
E of Pwllheli

[SH 5037] *

Like Castell y Bere, Criccieth was a Welsh castle captured and utilized by Edward I. This one, however, is chiefly an English building as far as its remains are concerned, the only Welsh parts being the vaguely triangular outer curtain wall and two rectangular towers, one of which, called the Engine Tower, was used for launching missiles, such as boulders, at attackers. The Welsh and English structures are distinguished by their different materials, the Welsh ruin being of grey stone and the English of reddish sandstone. The castle seems to have been burnt down after its capture in 1404 by Owain Glyndwr.

Cadw

7 CYMER ABBEY

Minor road off A470, 1 mile (1.5 km)
N of Dolgellau

[SH 7219] *

Some ruins of a Cistercian monastery founded at the end of the twelfth century

Harlech Castle

remain near Llanelltydd, though much of it was long ago commandeered by a farmhouse. The name (pronounced 'cummer') means 'waters meet', and the abbey was established in a characteristic Cistercian situation near the confluence of the rivers Mawddach and Wnion. It was never a large or wealthy house, and its church was never, in fact, finished.

Cadw

8 DINAS EMRYS CASTLE

Off A498, 1¼ miles (2 km) NE of
Beddgelert

[SH 6049] +

Built by Llewellyn the Great in the thirteenth century, its purpose was to protect the rich deposits of copper in the area. Nothing remains but the base of a rectangular tower, but the wooded hilltop site was occupied by an Iron Age fort, and is associated in legend with Merlin and Vortigern.

9 DIN LLIGWY

Minor road off A5108, 1 mile (1.5 km)
W of Moelfre

[SH 4986] +

This is an Iron Age settlement, close to

Capel Lligwy, consisting of both circular and rectangular stone huts or houses within an enclosing wall. The village was occupied throughout the Roman occupation of Britain, and one of the huts was an iron-smelter's workshop.

Cadw

10 DOLBADARN CASTLE

A4086, 1 mile (1.5 km) E of Llanberis

[SH 5859] **

This small and simple thirteenth-century Welsh castle stands on a cliff overlooking the entrance to the Llanberis Pass, and was abandoned after Edward I's conquest of Wales, its materials being used for other building works. Its chief remain is a circular great tower in the boomerang-shaped curtain wall. It is of three storeys, and still stands 40 feet (12 m) high, with modern steps replacing the original ones which gave access to first-floor level. Turner painted a highly romanticized view of the castle, accompanied by a poem commemorating the 23-year imprisonment here of Owain Goch, brother of Llewellyn the Last.

Cadw

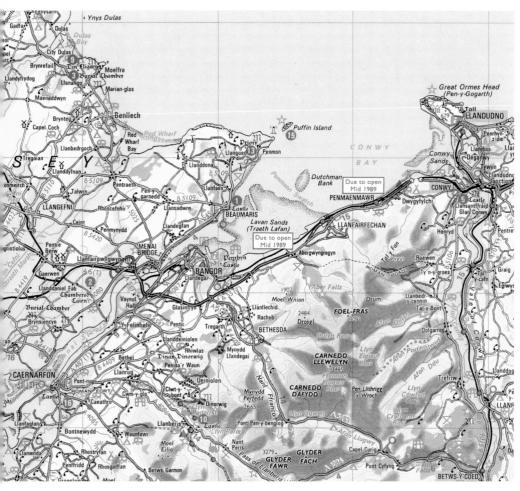

The remains of Segontium, Caernarfon

11 DOLWYDDELAN CASTLE

A470 W of village, 4½ miles (7 km) N of Blaenau Ffestiniog

[SH 7252]　★

The rectangular keep, which still stands to its full height (though restored), was built in the twelfth century, the rest in the thirteenth. Standing on a rocky ridge high above the Afon Lledr, the castle was captured by the English in 1283. It is significant chiefly as the probable birthplace in 1173 of Llewelyn ap Iorwerth, later known as Llewellyn the Great, Prince of All Wales.

Cadw

12 HARLECH CASTLE

Town centre

[SH 5831]　★

As you look at it from north, south or west, it appears impregnable, perched on its cliff overlooking the sea, but from the town side – the east – have come all its long troubles, for it has had to withstand siege on several occasions, the most famous of which inspired the song 'Men of Harlech', when the Lancastrian occupants held out for seven years against Yorkist forces in the Wars of the Roses, and Edward IV was said to be 'possessed of all Englonde, excepte a castelle in North Wales called Harlake'. At length the Welsh constable, Dafydd ap Jevon ap Einion, was forced to yield by famine, and Sir Richard Herbert, who had led the siege, had such respect for his adversary that he negotiated with the king to have Dafydd's life spared. The castle was built by Edward I, needless to say, perhaps, his architect or 'ingeniator' being Master James of St George, who became the castle's constable when it was completed around 1288. Originally, it stood above a river estuary. It was Owain Glyndwr's stronghold for a few years early in the fifteenth century, after he had taken it by treachery. The castle was reduced to its present condition by Cromwell, but the strength of its walls and towers can still be appreciated, even as you enter via the massive gatehouse, reached by a huge bridged ditch from the town's market place.

Cadw

13 PENMON PRIORY

Minor road off B5109 at E tip of Anglesey

[SH 6380]　+

The Celtic monastery founded by St Seiriol at the eastern tip of Anglesey in the sixth century was refounded as an

Augustinian priory, perhaps in the thirteenth century. The church survives as the local parish church, and there are remains of some of the domestic buildings, most notably a three-storey block with refectory and dormitory above a cellar. There are also remains of a hut nearby where St Seiriol is supposed to have lived, and of a well where he is supposed to have baptized converts.

Cadw

14 PORTH-Y-NANT
Minor road and footpath from Llithfaen, village on B4417, 5 miles (8 km) N of Pwllheli

[*SH 3444*] +

Above the bay, south-west of Trevor, is a deserted settlement which grew up in the nineteenth century as a granite-quarrying village, where only farms had existed before. It had its own Methodist chapel, a population of about 100 at its height, and a jetty from which ships carried the granite to Liverpool. But by the middle of the twentieth century demand for the granite had declined to such an extent that the quarry owners packed up, and by the 1960s the village was deserted and in ruins. Though partly restored, the site is a melancholy scene of industrial decay.

15 PRIESTHOLM PRIORY
On Puffin Island, off E tip of Anglesey

[*SH 6582*] +

On the island now uninhabited and known as Puffin Island, there are the remains of a church tower which was part of a priory cell for Austin canons. It was developed from an earlier Celtic religious settlement founded by St Seiriol and destroyed by the Danes. The island was granted to Penmon Priory (q.v.) in 1237, and women were not permitted to set foot on it.

Private

16 SEGONTIUM
On A4085 at SE edge of Caernarfon

[*SH 4862*] +

Sir Mortimer Wheeler was responsible for the excavation in the 1920s of this Roman auxiliary fort at what is now

175

Caernarfon. Much plundering of its stone had occurred over the centuries since its abandonment, and all that remain are low walls defining the layout, but they give a very clear picture of the considerable size and complexity of the site. The red sandstone was brought from Cheshire to rebuild the original timber fort aimed at defending the empire from potential Irish attack, and protecting local copper mining interests. The Welsh believed the Emperor Constantine had lived here once, and called the place *Caer Custenit*, the City of Constantine.

Cadw

51 Mid Glamorgan

See top map on page 178

1 CAERPHILLY CASTLE
Town centre

[ST 1587]   ★

It is one of the two or three largest castles in Britain, covering 30 acres (12 ha) of land, and one of the country's best examples of medieval military architecture and engineering. Begun in 1268 by a powerful Marcher lord, Gilbert de Clare, it was built on a concentric plan, with elaborate water

defences. The outer curtain wall, flanking the town's Castle Street, also serves as a dam, holding back the water of two streams to form a lake, the level of which is maintained by sluices. The mighty castle sits in the middle of this lake, and was built to be capable of withstanding a long siege. Only the south-east angle tower, leaning startlingly out of vertical, shows signs of frailty in the castle's defences, even today. But even that withstood attempts to demolish it altogether. No wonder when Edward I saw this mighty fortress, he took it as a pattern for rebuilding the Tower of London.

Cadw

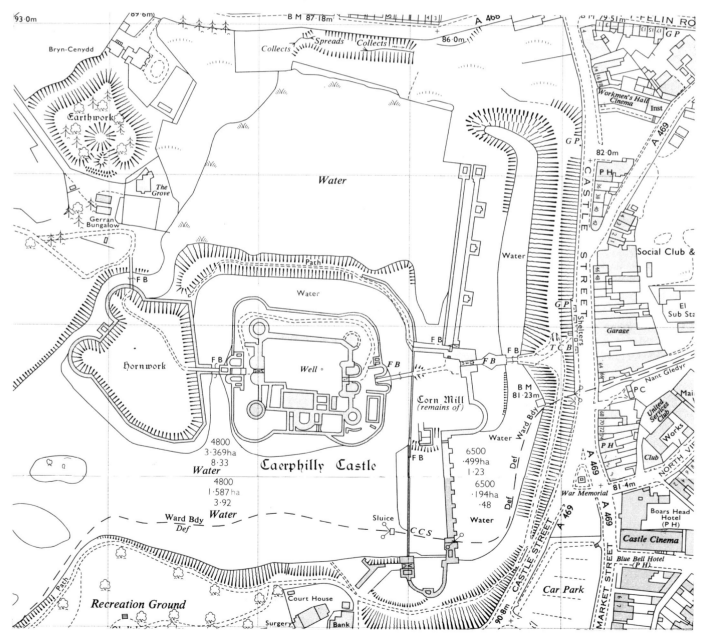

2 CANDLESTON CASTLE

End of minor road beyond Merthyr Mawr, off A48, 2 miles (3 km) SW of Bridgend

[SS 8777]   +

The ruin of a fifteenth-century fortified manor house, this 'castle' was the sometime seat of the Cantalupe family. Surrounded by trees, the neglected ruin is the sad relic of a courtyard house with a square tower, which was still occupied as recently as the nineteenth century.

3 COITY CASTLE

In village, 1½ miles (2.5 km) NE of Bridgend on minor road off A4061

[SS 9281]   *

Legend says that Coity was given to Payn de Turbeville, a Norman knight, on condition that he married the daughter of Lord Morgan, who owned it at the time. Be that as it may, a stone castle grew up

Caerphilly Castle

on the site from the twelfth century, intermittent alteration and extension continuing until the Tudor period. The castle consisted of a circular moated inner bailey with an outer bailey of roughly rectangular shape extending to the west. A thirteenth-century oval tower projecting from the inner bailey wall over the ditch to the south, though having defensive advantages when required, was primarily, to put it bluntly, a four-storey jakes (latrine), with three latrines on the ground floor, two on the first, and one on the second, all draining into the moat via the basement. (Perhaps this tower was one of the original 'outside loos'.) The castle, for some time the seat of the Gamage family, whose heiress Barbara married the brother of Philip Sidney, against the wishes of Elizabeth I, was deserted by the early seventeenth century.

Cadw

4 LLANTRISANT CASTLE

In village off A4119, 10 miles (16 km) NW of Cardiff

[ST 0483]   ⊖ *No access* ⊖

Little more than a fragment of a cylindrical keep remains of this thirteenth-century castle of the de Clare family, though it evidently had a high curtain wall. It was already in ruins by the Tudor period.

AM

5 NEWCASTLE, BRIDGEND

On hill NW of town centre

[SS 9080]   ***   *Tel: 0656 2964*

It is a fairly simple twelfth-century castle consisting of two rectangular towers in a curtain wall enclosing a ward or bailey, and having a decorated arched entrance alongside the southern tower. Some new building was carried out in the sixteenth

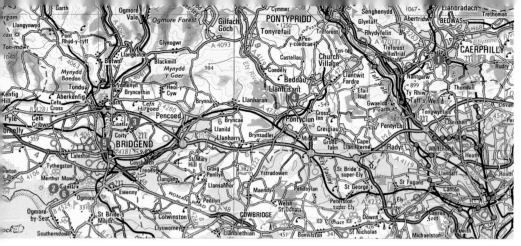

5 KNUCKLAS CASTLE

On B4355, 2¾ miles (4.5 km) NW of Knighton

[SO 2574]   +

It is fondly supposed by some that this is where King Arthur married Guinevere, but the hilltop ruin we see now, possibly on the site of a prehistoric hill-fort, is of

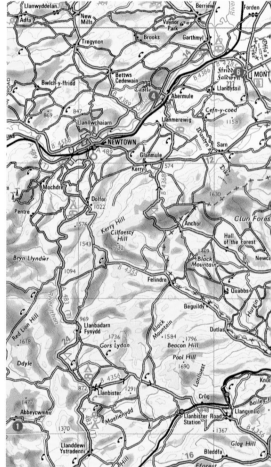

century, but – despite its name – this is locally known as the 'old' castle, the 'new' one being that at Coity (q.v.) which post-dates it.

Cadw

6 OGMORE CASTLE

N of village, off B4524, 2½ miles (4 km) SW of Bridgend

[SS 8877]   +

This partly-moated site on the south bank of the River Ewenny consists of an enclosing wall with four rectangular buildings of various dates within it, the earliest being a twelfth-century keep. The stonework is primitive, this being one of the earliest stone castles in south Wales. In the late fourteenth century a courthouse was built in the outer bailey. The castle was apparently built originally to guard a ford, where there is now a stepping-stone crossing of the river.

Cadw

---

52 *Powys*

See maps right and above right

1 ABBEY-CWM-HIR

In village of that name on minor road off A483, 5½ miles (9 km) NE of Rhayader

[SO 0571]   +

Little more than fragments of rubblestone walls and a few scattered stones remain in a meadow in the village of the same name near Rhayader, but this was once the greatest church in Wales. Said to have been founded in 1147, it stood in 10 acres (4 ha) of ground and had a nave 240 feet (73 m) long. Llywellyn ap Gruffydd, the last native Prince of Wales, is believed to have been buried here in 1282, and it almost goes without saying that legend has a hawthorn tree growing above the decapitated Llywellyn's grave. But in

1401 Owain Glyndwr completed the demolition job begun by Henry VIII as revenge for alleged treachery by the Cistercian monks.

2 BRECON CASTLE

Part in Castle Hotel grounds, part opposite

[SO 0428]
By application to Castle Hotel

'Brecknock' Castle is where Henry Stafford, Duke of Buckingham, plotted with his prisoner John Morton, Bishop of Ely, to overthrow his former ally, King Richard III, and set out with that end in mind only to lose his head at Salisbury. The twelfth-century castle's scattered remains are partly in the grounds of a hotel and partly in the Bishop of Brecon's private grounds. It was destroyed chiefly by the townspeople so that neither side should use it in the Civil War.

Private

3 BRONLLYS CASTLE

Just SE of village, on A479, 7½ miles (12 km) NE of Brecon

[SO 1434]   +

A three-storey round tower or keep is the only remnant of a late twelfth-century castle that Henry III visited in 1223, and which was captured by the Welsh ten years later. It stood on the high motte of an earlier castle, probably of timber, which Giraldus Cambrensis says was burnt down.

Cadw

4 DOLFORWYN CASTLE

Minor road W of A483, 3½ miles (5.5 km) NE of Newtown

[SO 1595]   ***   Tel: 0222 465511

Built in 1273 by Llewellyn ap Gruffydd, called Llewellyn the Last, it fell to Edward I and passed to the Mortimer lords of the Marches. It consisted of a circular tower surrounded by a curtain wall. Little survives, but there are fine views from its hilltop site.

Cadw

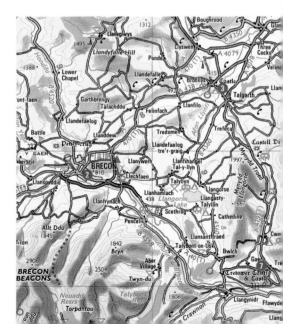

the thirteenth century, and was held by the Mortimer Marcher lords for a long period. There are remnants of a square enclosure wall with angle-towers.

6 MONTGOMERY CASTLE
Short distance from town centre

[*SO 2296*]   +

No great shakes as a fortress, it was nevertheless built by Henry III on a site recommended to him as a 'suitable spot for the erection of an impregnable castle', and it was held by the Mortimers for a time – one of that great string of castles along the Welsh border. But it was then already in a poor state of repair as a military stronghold, one report saying that only one 'lytle peece of waynscotte remayninge in the grett hall or dyning Chamber'. The chief interest of its fragmentary remains is as the subsequent home, for four centuries, of the Herbert family. Lord Herbert of Cherbury built a new house in the castle's grounds, but this was demolished some years afterwards. His brother, the poet George Herbet, was born in the castle, and John Donne was a guest here. He was a close friend of the Herbert brothers' mother, Magdalene, and at her funeral service, chose to comfort her grieving family and friends with the reflection that her corpse was 'mouldring, and crumbling into lesse, and lesse dust, and so has some motion, though no life'. Access to the remains is via a farmyard, where the official guide is obtainable.

Cadw

7 TRETOWER CASTLE
In village, on A479, 10 miles (16 km) SE of Brecon

[*SO 1821*]   ★

One of the many small ruined border castles, this one was built to guard the Usk valley against Welsh rebels. Originally a timber castle of the motte-and-bailey type, it was owned by the Picard lords of the manor for two centuries, and in the mid-twelfth century they built a stone shell-keep to replace the former wooden palisades, and later added inside this a circular three-storey keep. The castle was defended for the king against Glyndwr's revolt in 1403, but was badly damaged, and was duly abandoned for the fortified manor house of Tretower Court, beyond which the ruin still stands.

Cadw

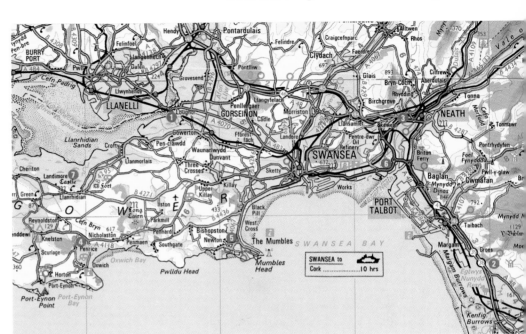

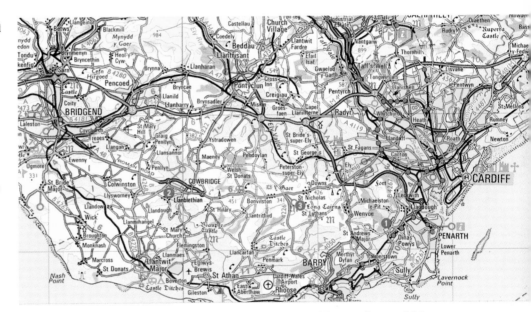

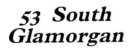

53 South Glamorgan

See map directly above

1 DINAS POWIS CASTLE
In village, off A4055 3½ miles (5.5 km) S of Cardiff

[*ST 1571*]   +

The twelfth-century castle here replaced an earlier timber one which was not, however, on the same site. The stone castle was a simple affair comprising a high curtain wall with gate, enclosing a square keep. The remains are fairly scanty. Welsh castles were, as Gwyn Thomas wrote, 'small affairs, easily kicked over and flattened'.

AM

2 LLANBLETHIAN CASTLE
In village off A48 just S of Cowbridge

[*SS 9874*]   +

The twin-towered three-storey gatehouse is the best feature of this eighteenth-century fortification also known as St Quintin's Castle, on account of a local family of that name being wrongly believed to have built it. It was

Montgomery Castle

actually built by Gilbert de Clare, and was never completed. It seems to have been basically a curtain wall with flanking towers, two of which were round and one square, showing the transition to round towers which were less vulnerable to undermining than cornered ones.

3 TINKINSWOOD
Minor road off A48, 6½ miles W of Cardiff, ½ mile (0.8 km) S of St Nicholas village

[ST 0973]   +

This is a fine chambered neolithic long barrow, dating from around 2500 BC, and one of the best preserved of its type in Britain. It is of the kind known to archaeologists as 'Severn-Cotswold' tombs, differing from others in several important respects – dry-stone walls, wedge-shaped mound, burial practised instead of cremation (about 50 skeletons were found in this one). The entrance was in the side rather than at the end, and a chamber inside has three vertical slabs supporting a gigantic capstone weighing around 40 tons. Flint implements and pottery were also found when the tomb was excavated in 1914.

Local folklore held that some of the upright stones were local maidens turned to stone for dancing on the Sabbath – a common-enough myth in various parts of Britain.

Cadw

54 West Glamorgan

See top map on page 179

1 LOUGHOR CASTLE
W side of village near river bridge on A484 between Swansea and Llanelli

[SS 5698]   +

Built on a Roman site, Lencarium, the thirteenth-century castle stands on a Norman motte and shows the remains of one square tower projecting from an enclosing wall.

Cadw

2 MARGAM CASTLE
In Margam Park, on foot from A48, 5 miles (9 km) SE of Port Talbot

[SS 8186]   ★★★

This is the shell of a mock-Gothic mansion built by Thomas Hopper in 1840 and badly damaged by fire in 1977. The house replaced the Mansel family's sixteenth-century mansion, a fragment of which also remains here, to say nothing of the chapter house of Margam Abbey, one of the largest Cistercian houses in Wales, and the excavated site of the original village of Margam, well away from the modern steel town. All these remains are within what is now Margam Park, providing a veritable field-day for ruin-hunters. What is more, there is a small ruined fifteenth-century chapel on the hill above the former abbey church, the nave of which now serves as the parish church.

West Glamorgan County Council

3 NEATH ABBEY
W bank of River Dulais, near bridge

[SS 7597]   ★

Leland called it 'the fairest abbey in all Wales' before the Dissolution, and though much abused by wars, industry and later owners, it still makes a fine sight, if you can ignore the industrial surroundings which shocked George Borrow when he came upon the remains in the nineteenth century: 'a ruin of vast size with window holes, towers, spires and arches' rising from the pandemonium of stacks of smoking chimneys, heaps of cinders and black rubbish. The abbey had been founded as a Savignac house about 1129, but became Cistercian, and very wealthy. King John and Edward I visited it and, ironically enough, the abbot at the time of Henry Tudor's progress to Bosworth went out to bless the cause of the future king whose son was to bring destruction on all the religious houses in half a century. Sir John Herbert built a mansion out of the abbot's lodging in the sixteenth century, and this was duly used as a lodging for iron foundry workmen, while beggars also made a den of the ruins at one time.

Cadw

4 OLD PENRICE CASTLE
Just off A4118, 10½ miles (17 km) SW of Swansea

[SS 4988]   On application

A roughly triangular bailey contains remains of a circular great tower which was part of a multi-towered gatehouse complex, and a later great hall at the northern end. The castle was the property of the Norman Mansel family, who evidently had to move between floors of their three-storey tower by means of ladders and trap-doors, since it never had a staircase. Not surprisingly, when they no longer felt threatened, the Mansels built themselves more comfortable accommodation not far away, at Oxwich.

Private

5 OYSTERMOUTH CASTLE
On hill at N end of town, on A4067, 4 miles (6.4 km) SW of Swansea

[SS 6188]   ★★★

Standing on a hill above the rather incongruous setting of boarding houses and seaside holiday attractions, and facing the Port Talbot steelworks across Swansea Bay, this ruin is nevertheless worthy of examination, having remains – not unduly tidied up – of gatehouse, barracks, kitchen, banqueting hall, chapel and so on, the latter having a piscina. The castle was built by the de Braose family, and was twice extensively

The shell-keep of Tretower Castle

damaged in Welsh attacks. Edward I was here in 1284, and later owners were the Mowbrays and the Beauforts, who made alterations to increase the domestic comforts of the original fortification. The hall, on the second floor of the keep or great tower, has fine Early English windows.

Swansea Corporation

6 SWANSEA CASTLE
Castle Street, town centre near Tawe Bridge

[SS 6593]   +

What we can see now is the remnant of a fortified manor house built in the fourteenth century, with a circular turret and arcaded parapets characteristic of the builder, Bishop Henry Gower (see Bishop's Palace, St David's and Lamphey Palace, both in Dyfed). This building replaced the earlier castle built

by the Beaumont lord of Gower. At the time of writing, this ruin is visible from the outside only.

Cadw

7 WEOBLEY CASTLE
Minor road off B4295, 11 miles (17.5 km) W of Swansea

[SS 4792]   ★

A fortified manor house, rather than a military fortification, Weobley Castle stands on high ground on the Gower Peninsula. It was the property of the De la Bere family until damaged by Owain Glyndwr's forces in the fifteenth century. Afterwards it passed to the Herberts, and was partly rebuilt. Chapel, kitchen, solar and great hall remain, along with the original tower and gatehouse, and this is an interesting relic of a well-to-do medieval lord's dwelling.

Cadw

Scotland

Glenluce Abbey, Dumfries and Galloway

55 Borders

See maps on page 186

1 CROSS KIRK, PEEBLES
Close to town centre

[NT 2540] ★

Fairly scant remains of a friary founded by Alexander III about 1296 for Trinitarian or 'Red' friars. Only the nave and west tower of the church stand to any height, the nave having been used as the parish church after the Reformation until the late eighteenth century. Exposed foundations of conventual buildings show the layout.

SDD

2 DRYBURGH ABBEY
B6356 off B6404 near St Boswells, 7½ miles (12 km) E of Selkirk

[NT 5931] ★

Beautifully set in a loop of the River Tweed, Dryburgh is one of the Scottish border monasteries which suffered repeatedly from English attack in the fourteenth–sixteenth centuries, and was finally burnt down in 1544. Dating from about 1152, when it was founded by Hugh de Morville, Constable of Scotland, the church is fairly fragmentary, but there are excellent remains of the claustral buildings. The monastery was a house of Premonstratensian canons. The abbey lands were in possession of Sir Walter Scott's ancestors after the Dissolution, and he was buried in the church.

SDD

3 EDROM CHURCH
In village off A6105, 10½ miles (17 km) W of Berwick-upon-Tweed

[NT 8255] +

Behind the modern parish church stands the Norman chancel arch of a church founded early in the twelfth century by Thor Longus.

SDD

4 HERMITAGE CASTLE
Minor road off B6399, 12 miles (19.5 km) S of Hawick

[NY 4995] ★

Built in the thirteenth century, it was held in turn by the de Soulis, Douglas and Hepburn families. It is a grim and eerie ruin, standing in a lonely spot beside Hermitage Water in Liddesdale. The Earl of Bothwell belonged to the Hepburn family, and he came here severely wounded in a border skirmish in 1566, Mary, Queen of Scots riding from Jedburgh to see him.

AM

5 JEDBURGH ABBEY
High Street, town centre

[NT 6520] ★★★ *Tel: 031 244 3101*

This Augustinian abbey was founded as a priory by King David I around 1118. Like the other border monasteries, it suffered continually from the English invasion, but while the monastic buildings are fairly fragmentary, the

Jedburgh Abbey

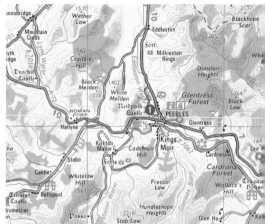

abbey church is a magnificent ruin. The fine rose window in the west wall of the church is popularly known as St Catherine's Wheel. Beneath it there is a Norman doorway with rich decorative carving, and the nave walls have layers of impressive arcading.

SDD

6 KELSO ABBEY
Bridge Street, short distance from town centre

[*NT* 7333]   +

Although it was the largest of the border monasteries, founded by David I in 1128 and occupied by monks of the Order of Tiron, it is now the most completely ruined of them, having been destroyed by the Earl of Hertford in 1545. Its Transitional architecture is unique in Scotland.

SDD

7 MELROSE ABBEY
Main Square, town centre

[*NT* 5433]   ★

Generally regarded as the most spectacular of Scotland's ecclesiastical ruins, Melrose dates from 1136, when it was founded by David I and colonized by Cistercian monks from Rievaulx. But, as with the other border monasteries, it was a long-suffering target of English aggression, and the church had to be rebuilt after destruction by Richard II's troops in 1385. The ruins of both the church and the monastic buildings are substantial and highly impressive, the working of red sandstone by the medieval masons being breathtaking. The heart of Robert the Bruce is said to have been buried here, having failed to reach the Holy Land as intended. The abbey church remained in use by the

parish until early in the nineteenth
century. Official opening hours preclude
taking the advice of Sir Walter Scott
which is also applicable to many more of
our finest ruins:

> If thou would'st see fair Melrose
> aright,
> Go visit it by the pale moonlight.

SDD

Dryburgh Abbey

56 Central

See map below

1 CASTLE CAMPBELL
*Minor road off A91 at Dollar, 11 miles
(17.5 km) E of Stirling*

[NS 9699]   ***   Tel: 031 244 3101

It was known as Castle Gloom once – a
fifteenth-century tower-house built by
the first Earl of Argyll. The original
castle was extended in the sixteenth
century, but burnt by Montrose in 1645.

SDD

2 DOUNE CASTLE
*Off A84 in village, 6¾ miles (11 km)
NW of Stirling*

[NN 7201]   ***   Tel: 031 244 3101

Partly a ruin, partly unfinished and
partly restored, the castle was built, or at
least commenced, at the end of the
fourteenth century by the Regent of
Scotland, Robert Stewart, Duke of
Albany. Later it was held by the earls of
Moray, and Bonnie Prince Charlie used
the castle as a prison during the rising of
1745. The well-preserved remains are of
an irregular enclosure wall with a huge
gatehouse-tower at one corner with other
buildings extending from its western
flank.

SDD

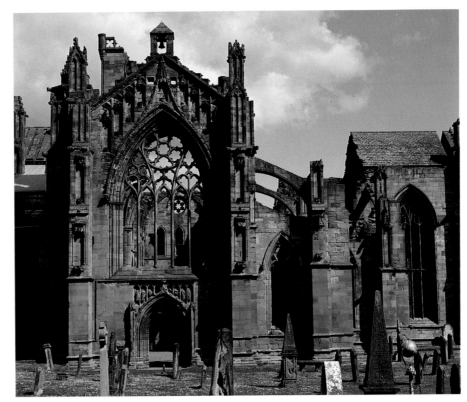
Melrose Abbey

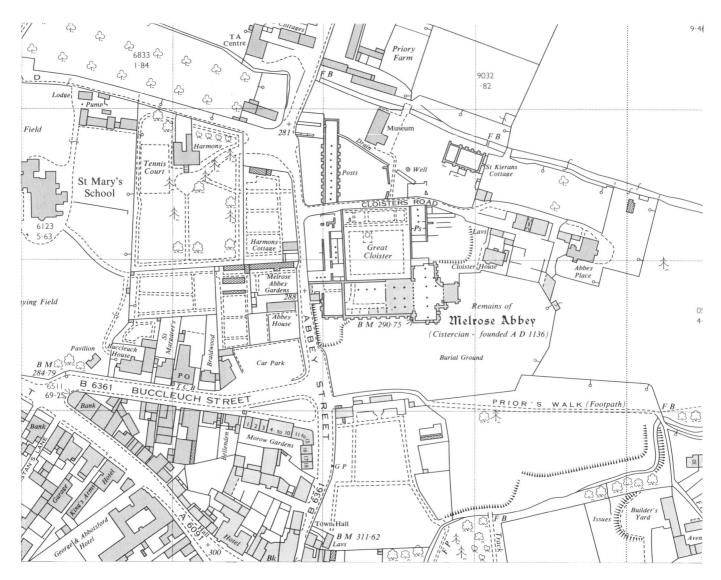

3 INCHMAHOME PRIORY

On isle in Lake of Menteith, off A81, 3 miles (5 km) E of Aberfoyle (access from Port of Menteith on main road)

[NN 5700] ★★

This priory for Augustinian canons was founded on the island in the Lake of Menteith in 1238. It was the scene of David II's second marriage and in 1547 the infant Mary, future Queen of Scots, was brought here for safety after the English defeat of the Scots at the Battle of Pinkie. The priory was suppressed in 1604, and its island site saved it from the worst excesses of both Protestant destruction and plundering of its materials, so that the remains are substantial. Access is by boat from Port of Mentieth.

SDD

57 Dumfries and Galloway

See maps on page 190

1 CAERLAVEROCK CASTLE

Off B725, 7½ miles (12 km) S of Dumfries

[NY 0265] ★

This castle, triangular in plan and unique in Scotland, was built towards the end of the thirteenth century on the north shore of the Solway Firth, and some say it was designed by Edward I's 'ingeniator', Master James of St George, though others believe it to have been built by the Scots. It changed hands a few times in the border wars, and was finally abandoned after destruction by

the Covenanters in 1640, the castle having held out for the king for three months. The substantial ruins show high walls enclosing the triangle with round towers at two corners and a twin-towered gatehouse at the third.

SDD

2 CARDONESS CASTLE

On A75 near Gatehouse of Fleet, 7 miles (11 km) NW of Kirkcudbright

[NX 5855] ★

Nothing of significance is left standing except a fifteenth-century four-storey keep with a corridor by which two rooms are reached. The great hall and solar have elaborate wall fireplaces, and there is a vaulted basement. The castle was the home of the McCulloch family.

SDD

Caerlaverock Castle

3 DUNDRENNAN ABBEY
In village, on A711, 5 miles (8 km)
SE of Kirkcudbright

[NX 7447] ★

Established in 1142 and colonized by
monks from Rievaulx, this Cistercian
abbey has Norman and Transitional
architecture and a fine thirteenth-century
chapter house, but relatively little of the
abbey church remains standing, the
buildings having been much quarried
after the abbey's suppression in 1606.

SDD

4 GLENLUCE ABBEY
Minor road N off A75 from village, 8½
miles (13.5 km) E of Stranraer

[NX 1858] ★

Fairly scant ruins remain of the
Cistercian monastery colonized from
Melrose in 1128 and suppressed in 1602.
The vaulted chapter house is the most
interesting survival, dating from about
1470, but generally speaking, the wooded
riverside site is more appealing than the
ruin. There is a story that a wizard,
Michael Scott, lured the plague to this

abbey in the thirteenth century and
locked it up in a vault so that it could do
no more harm.

SDD

5 LOCHMABEN CASTLE
S shore of Castle Loch, B7020 S of village,
8 miles (13 km) NE of Dumfries

[NY 0881] ★

Several Scottish castles lay claim to
being the birthplace of Robert the Bruce
– this one among them – and you can

Scotland

take your pick. Lochmaben's claim is based on the fact that his de Brus ancestors built a wooden castle here before the present one, a fourteenth-century stone enclosure castle that saw a great deal of military action during its lifetime, as well as receiving royal visitors – James IV and, of course, Mary, Queen of Scots.

AM

6 MACLELLAN'S CASTLE
In Kirkcudbright, off High Street

[NX 6851]   ***   Tel: 031 244 3101

This was more a fortified mansion than a true castle, built late in the sixteenth century overlooking the harbour at Kirkcudbright. It still stands high, though it has been in ruins since 1752, and its walls contain stones from a convent which stood derelict when the 'castle' was being built.

SDD

7 ST NINIAN'S CHAPEL
End of A747 at Isle of Whithorn, 12 miles (19.5 km) S of Wigtown

[NX 4736]   +

The ruined twelfth- or thirteenth-century chapel at the so-called Isle of Whithorn (it *was* a tiny island once), is dedicated to St Ninian, who is supposed to have made an oratory in a cave on the other side of the peninsula in the fifth century.

SDD

8 SWEETHEART ABBEY
Beside A710 at New Abbey, 6 miles (9.5 km) S of Dumfries

[NX 9666]   *

The name of this Cistercian monastery came from the fact that the embalmed

Glenluce Abbey

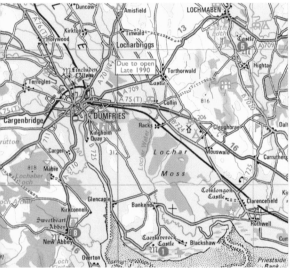

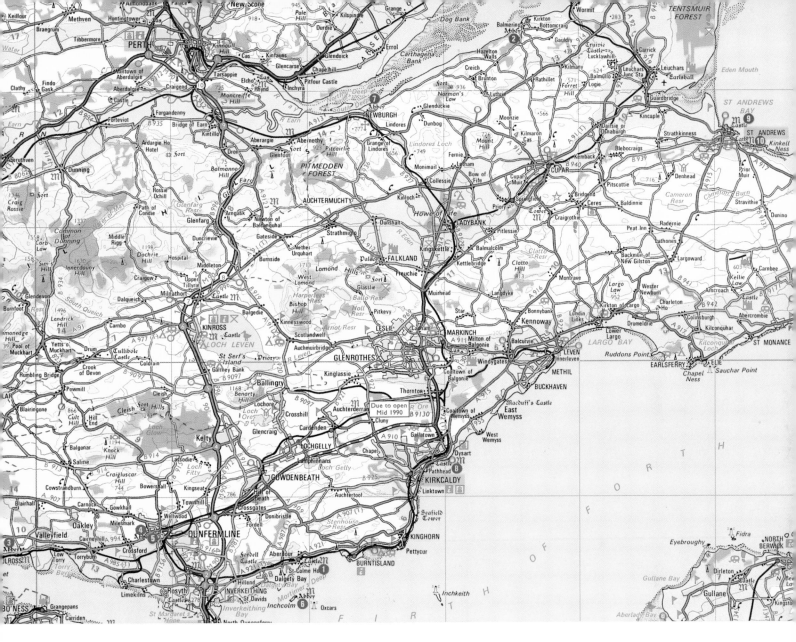

heart of John Balliol was buried here with his widow, Devorgilla, Lady of Galloway – who founded the abbey in 1273, and also Balliol College, Oxford – and was interred, with the morbid relic, her 'sweet, silent companion' in its casket, laid on her bosom. There is relatively little of the monastic buildings, but within the precinct wall built of huge boulders the ruined abbey church stands glorious in red sandstone, with scarcely a rival for beauty among the ruined churches of Britain.

SDD

9 THREAVE CASTLE
On island in River Dee, N of A75 at Bridge of Dee, near Castle Douglas

[NX 7462]   +

This ruin on an island in the River Dee west of Castle Douglas is the remains of a mighty private fortress of the Black Douglases. The 70-foot (21-m) keep,

with walls 10 feet (3 m) thick, was built in the fourteenth century by Archibald the Grim, 3rd Earl of Douglas, and in the following century the defences were reinforced by what was probably the first artillery wall in Britain. Nevertheless, the castle eventually fell to James II, the king's siege being aided by the Flanders gun known as Mons Meg, now to be seen at Edinburgh Castle.

SDD

10 WHITHORN PRIORY
On A746 through village, 9½ miles (15 km) S of Wigtown

[NX 4440]   ★★★   Tel: 031 244 3101

St Ninian, who is credited by the Venerable Bede with leading the southern Picts to forsake the errors of idolatry and embrace the truth, founded the first church in Scotland here in AD 397, and on the site a priory for Premonstratensian canons was

established in the late twelfth century. It was wealthy because of its attraction for pilgrims, who included Robert the Bruce, James IV, and Mary, Queen of Scots. It survived until 1612, but there is little left except the ruins of the priory church, which was used by the parish until the nineteenth century. Many valuable finds here can be seen in the attached museum, however.

SDD

---

58 Fife

See map above

1 ABERDOUR CASTLE
Near village harbour, off A92, 6¼ miles (10 km) E of Dunfermline

[NT 1985]   ★★★   Tel: 031 244 3101

The remains cover a building period of

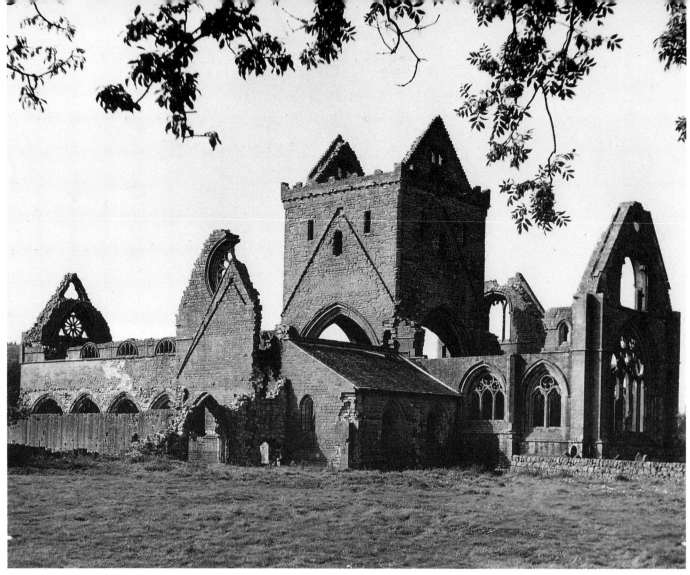

Sweetheart Abbey

more than two centuries, the oldest part being a ruined great tower built in the fourteenth century by the Earl of Moray.

SDD

2 BALMERINO ABBEY
In village, minor road N off A914, 11 miles (17.5 km) NW of St Andrews

[NO 3524]   +

The monastery beside the Firth of Tay was a Cistercian foundation of around 1227. It was ruined in 1603. The fairly sparse remains are now connected with a farm, but can be seen from the outside.

National Trust for Scotland

3 CULROSS ABBEY
Minor road off A985, 6½ miles (10 km) W of Dunfermline

[NS 9885]   +

It was a Cistercian abbey, founded by Malcolm, Earl of Fife, on the site of an earlier monastery, but apart from the choir of the church, which is now used by the parish, the remains are few and insignificant.

AM

4 DUNFERMLINE ABBEY
Monastery Street in town

[NT 0987]   ★★★   Tel: 031 244 3101

The Benedictine abbey was founded shortly after the Norman Conquest, on the site of a Celtic monastery, by Queen Margaret, wife of Malcolm III who overthrew the usurper Macbeth. The remains are substantial, part of the abbey church now being the parish church. Robert the Bruce was buried here (minus his heart – see Melrose Abbey, page 186). After the Dissolution the abbey guest house was rebuilt as a royal palace (see below).

SDD

5 DUNFERMLINE PALACE
Monastery Street in town

[NT 0987]   ★★★   031 244 3101

Adjacent to the abbey, it was converted from the monastery's guest house in the sixteenth century, and became the home of James VI and Anne of Denmark, who gave birth here to the future Charles I in 1600.

SDD

6 INCHCOLM ABBEY
On island in Firth of Forth (access from Queensferry)

[NT 1982]   ★★★   Tel: 031 244 3101

This Augustinian abbey on the island of Inchcolm in the Firth of Forth dates from about 1153, and has well-preserved monastic buildings of what has been called the 'Iona of the East', on account of its reputation for holiness going back to an ancient Christian hermitage. The foundation was a priory at first, and became an abbey in 1235. Although it suffered depredation in the wars with the English, its island site finally protected the buildings from worse attack by plundering after the Reformation.

SDD

7 LINDORES ABBEY
Minor road off A913 at Newburgh, on S bank of Firth of Tay

[NO 2418]   +

An abbey of the Order of Tiron, founded at the end of the twelfth century by David, Earl of Huntingdon, the brother of William the Lion. It was an establishment of note, and kings paid homage here, but its remains are not among the best of ecclesiastical ruins.

SDD

8 RAVENSCRAIG CASTLE
On N bank of Firth of Forth at Kirkcaldy

[NT 2992]   ★

This ruin at Kirkcaldy is interesting, as it is possibly the first castle in Britain to be built specifically for defence by guns. Built by James II of Scotland in 1460 to guard the coast against attack from the Firth of Forth, and provided with cellar armouries, the four-storey keep stood on a high cliff and was armed with many gun-ports. This prototype artillery castle later passed to the earls of Orkney.

SDD

9 ST ANDREWS CASTLE
Town sea-front

[NO 5116]   ★

What stories could be told, if only they could be induced to speak to us, by the stones of this thirteenth-century castle on the sea shore at St Andrews. Protected on the landward side by a deep moat, it is often referred to as an 'ecclesiastical castle', because it may have been built originally as a bishop's residence and was certainly rebuilt by Bishop Trail at the end of the fourteenth century. In 1546 the Cardinal-Archbishop of St Andrews, Cardinal Beaton, was assassinated here, and later the castle was attacked by French ships, and prisoners were taken, including the Protestant prophet John Knox, who spent two years chained to an oar as a galley slave. There is a fearful dungeon beneath one of the towers, deep and wide at the bottom with only a narrow opening at the top through which prisoners were lowered into the damp rat-hole, few of them, I should think, ever seeing the light of day again.

SDD

10 ST ANDREW'S CATHEDRAL
Near sea-front between castle and harbour

[NO 5116]   ★

It was once the largest church in Scotland, and was built over a period of more than 150 years from 1161, then stood through many trials and tribulations until 1559, when its destruction began with the Protestant suppression and continued with plundering of its stone until the nineteenth century. There are some interesting remnants, despite the savagery of the destruction of what was once a noble building and the heart of the old faith in Scotland.

SDD

59 Grampian

See map on page 195 and left-hand map on page 198

1 AUCHINDOUN CASTLE
Off A941, 1½ miles (2.5 km) SE of Dufftown

[NJ 3437]   +

It is an impressively large ruin on a hilltop that was a prehistoric hill-fort. Built in the fifteenth century, it was the scene of a Jacobite council of war after the Battle of Killiecrankie. Undergoing preparation for public access, it is visible from the outside only, at the time of writing.

SDD

2 BALVENIE CASTLE
Just N of Dufftown on B9014

[NJ 3240]   ★★

This substantial and extensive castle was begun in the thirteenth century and considerably added to in the sixteenth. It was protected on three sides by a moat which was 40 feet (12 m) wide and stone-faced, and by a high curtain wall. It was among Scotland's earliest stone castles, and was clearly built to last. Originally the stronghold of the Comyn family, it was later held by Douglases and Stewarts, the latter family undertaking the extensive sixteenth-century rebuilding which included a three-storey tower house, known as the Atholl building after John Stewart, 4th Earl of Atholl. The castle fell into ruin after about 1724, when it was already roofless.

SDD

3 CORGARFF CASTLE
Off A939, 11 miles (17.5 km) NW of Ballater

[NJ 2508]   ★

It was a tower-house when built originally in the sixteenth century, but extensions were made in the eighteenth century. Famous, or notorious, as the castle where Margaret Forbes and her children and servants were burned to death in 1571, when one of the Gordons of Auchindoun (q.v.) set fire to the castle, via a garderobe drainage channel, during a quarrel between the two families.

SDD

4 DEER ABBEY
In village of Old Deer, A9950, 10 miles (16 km) W of Peterhead

NJ 9647   ★★★   Tel: 031 244 3101

Remains of a thirteenth-century Cistercian monastery, which stands near the site of a Celtic settlement where the earliest known Gaelic manuscript, the *Book of Deer*, was produced in the ninth century, and rediscovered at Cambridge University Library 1000 years later. The Cistercian abbey was founded by William Comyn in 1218, and there are extensive ruins of the monastic buildings as well as the church.

SDD

5 DUFFUS CASTLE
Minor road off B9012, 3 miles (5 km) NW of Elgin

[NJ 1867]   ★

Originally a motte castle, it was built in stone in the first years of the fourteenth century, with a three-storey keep and a curtain wall surrounded by a moat. The foundations, however, were inadequate, and eventually one corner of the keep broke loose and shifted its position, as can still be seen. A range extending eastwards was added to the castle in the fifteenth century, and the moated ruins of this Moray stronghold are impressive.

SDD

6 DUNNOTTAR CASTLE
On coast 1¼ miles (2 km) S of Stonehaven, off A92

[NO 8883]   ★★★   Tel: 0569 62173

Its site is spectacular – a promontory 160 feet (49 m) above the North Sea connected to the mainland only by a low isthmus. But the castle is really a conglomeration of ruined and restored

Dunnottar Castle

buildings starting from a twelfth-century castle, then a fourteenth-century tower-house which became the home of the Earls Marischal of Scotland, and finally a courtyard residence of the sixteenth and seventeenth centuries. During the Civil War, Dunnottar was the last castle in Scotland to be held for the king, and in the year after Cromwell crossed into Scotland the Scottish regalia were hidden there, being smuggled out by the governor's wife and a local minister's wife when the castle came under siege by Cromwell's troops. The castle was dismantled in 1718 after being forfeited following the Jacobite rebellion of 1715.

Private

7 ELGIN CATHEDRAL
North College Street in town

[NJ 2262] ★

It was known as the 'Lantern of the North', founded originally in 1224, though much rebuilt in the fifteenth century after it was burnt in 1390 by Alexander, Earl of Buchan, the Wolf of Badenoch, in revenge for his excommunication. Much beautiful Transitional and early Gothic building remains, however. The road to final ruin was commenced by the Scottish Privy Council in 1567, when it stripped the lead from the cathedral's roof to raise money to pay its army. The towers of the west front still rise to make an impressive sight from a considerable distance away. *See photograph and map on pages 196 and 197.*

SDD

8 HUNTLY CASTLE
Castle Street, NE of town centre

[NJ 5340] ★

The complicated building history of this castle does nothing to interfere with the immediate impact it makes as a highly impressive ruin with great architectural distinction. It has been called, with justice, one of the finest baronial remains in Scotland. It was the seat of the powerful Gordon earls and marquesses of Huntly, and one of the last strongholds of Scottish Catholicism. It began with a late fourteenth-century tower built close to a Norman motte on which a timber castle had stood. The tower, referred to afterwards as the 'auld werk' was burnt out in 1453 and the 'new werk' was then commenced – a V-shaped block with a five-storey round tower at the elbow. It was later extended to the east, and rebuilding went on until the seventeenth century, especially after the 'new werk' had been blown up by James VI late in the sixteenth century. The south range with the cylindrical tower has fine oriel windows and heraldic inscriptions dating from the first years of the seventeenth century, and there are superb armorial bearings and carved fireplaces.

SDD

9 KILDRUMMY CASTLE
Off A97, 7¾ miles (12.5 km) W of Alford

[NJ 4516] ★

A thirteenth-century enclosure castle with flanking cylindrical and D-shaped towers, to which a twin-towered gatehouse was added later. The seat of the earls of Mar, the castle was captured by treachery in 1306 when the resident blacksmith was bribed by the English into setting it on fire. The castle's military commander, Sir Nigel Bruce, brother of Robert the Bruce, was taken to Berwick for execution, and when someone protested that he was of the blood royal, King Edward I said, 'Hang him on a gallows thirty feet higher than the rest!'. The castle was finally dismantled in 1715, being the source of the Jacobite rising of that year, and afterwards the castle became a quarry. Little remains to any height except the round tower at the northern corner, and the red sandstone ruins are extensive and the layout clear and interesting.

SDD

The west doorway of Elgin Cathedral

10 KINKELL CHURCH
Minor road off B993, 1½ miles (2.5 km) S of Inverurie

[*NJ 7819*]   +

The church whose ruins stand by the River Don near Inverurie was built early in the sixteenth century, and has interesting details of the period.

SDD

11 LOIRSTON CHURCH
Near Girdle Ness, Aberdeen, on minor road off A956 on S bank of River Dee

[*NJ 9604*]   +

The ruined medieval church dedicated to St Fittick stands where the disciple of St Ninian was shipwrecked and, according to legend, built a cell or hermitage in the seventh century. There is a leper squint in one of the remaining walls.

City of Aberdeen

12 OLD RATTRAY CHAPEL
S end of Loch of Strathbeg, near Rattray Head, on minor road off A952, 7½ miles (12 km) NW of Peterhead

[*NK 0857*]   +

The fragmentary ruins of St Mary's Chapel are all that remain visible of what was once the port of Rattray. The town, on a windswept sea inlet, was created a royal burgh by Mary, Queen of Scots, to prevent a territorial dispute between two clans, but a great storm in the early eighteenth century created a sand barrier at the mouth of the navigation channel, and the former port was fairly rapidly depopulated, the houses gradually disappearing and only the melancholy gravestones, and parts of the chapel's walls, remaining upright.

13 SLAINS CASTLE
Coast at Port Erroll, by minor road off A975, 7 miles (11 km) S of Peterhead

[*NK 1036*]   +

The 'vast ruined castle' of Transylvania

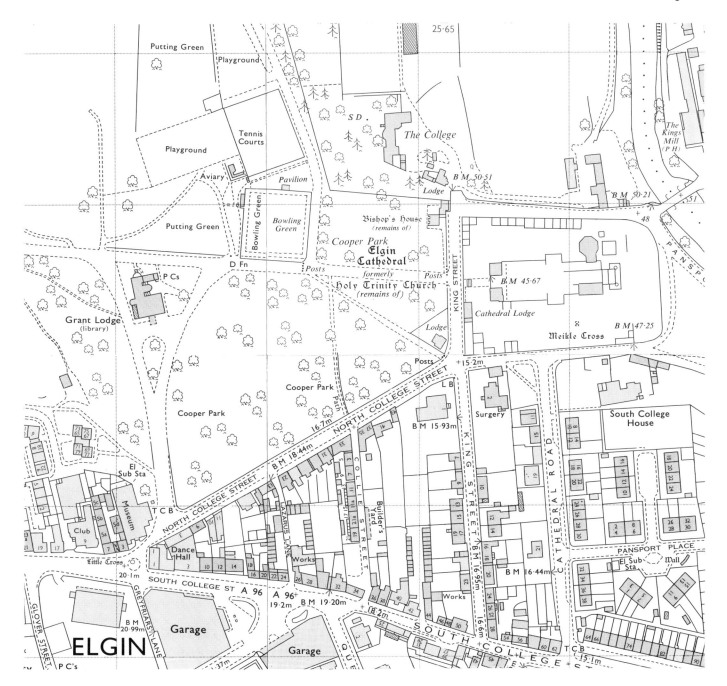

in Bram Stoker's *Dracula*, a building 'from whose tall black windows came no ray of light', was actually modelled on Slains, Stoker having written the novel at Cruden Bay. This seventeenth-century ruin hardly induces scenes of Gothic horror in the minds of visitors today. It was built to replace a shattered castle on the rocky coast 4 miles (6 km) to the south, brought to ruin by James VI of Scotland in 1594. Samuel Johnson visited the 'new' castle – really a mansion – with Boswell in 1773. They were guests of the Earl and Countess of Errol, and sat in a bow window here looking out to sea.

AM

14 TOLQUHON CASTLE
Off B999 just N of A920 between Ellon and Oldmeldrum

[NJ 8728] ★

A rectangular tower of the late fifteenth century was incorporated a century later by the Forbes family into a much larger baronial fortified courtyard mansion, an inscription on which states that all the castle 'excep the auld tour' was begun by William Forbes, '15 Aprile 1534. and endit be him. 20 October 1589'. If only *all* ruins had such precise building records carved in their masonry! We know the name of the master mason too – one William Leiper – who built the castle of roughly coursed granite. The gatehouse has coats of arms above a round-arched entrance, flanked by semi-circular turrets with gun-ports. The ruins stand in a wooded dell.

SDD

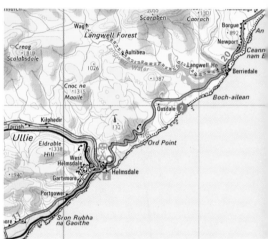
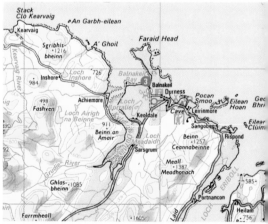
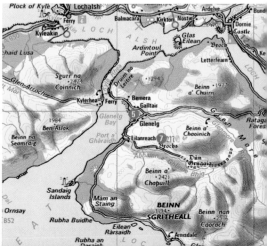

60 Highland

*See four small maps left and maps above
and right*

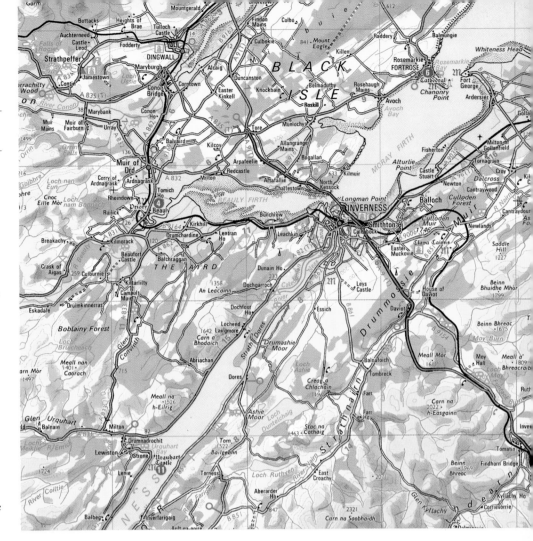

1 ARDVRECK CASTLE

*E shore of Loch Assynt, off A837, 9½ miles
(15 km) E of Lochinver*

[NC 2423]   +

It was built on the shore of Loch Assynt
at the end of the fifteenth century by the
MacLeods, with a three-storey keep, and
it was here that the captured James
Graham, Marquess of Montrose, was
handed over to Parliament in 1650, duly
to be executed in Edinburgh. Some say
he was delivered into the hands of the
authorities by treachery, having thrown
himself on the mercy of the Macleod of
the time.

AM

2 BADBEA TOWER

*On coast near Ousdale, off A9 between
Helmsdale and Berriedale*

[ND 0819]   +

This small stone tower on the cliffs of the
Caithness coast – sole remnant of a lost

Ardvreck Castle, Loch Assynt

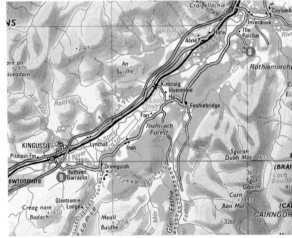

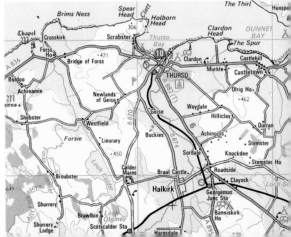

village – sheltered crofters driven off their land in the brutal Highland clearances of the Sutherland estates in the nineteenth century. It is said that children, as well as cattle, were tethered to prevent them falling over the cliff-edge.

3 BALNAKEIL KIRK

At Balnakeil Bay, by minor road off A838 at Durness

[NC 3968] +

The ruin of an early seventeenth-century church close to Scotland's northern Atlantic coastline. The churchyard contains a monument to the Celtic bard Rob Donn.

4 BEAULY PRIORY

In village on A862, 9 miles (14.5 km) W of Inverness

[NH 5246] ★★

Founded around 1230 as a priory for Valliscaulian monks by Sir John Bissett, it became Cistercian after Pope Julius II dissolved the order in 1510.

SDD

5 BERNERA BARRACKS

8 miles (13 km) W along minor road off A87 at Shiel Bridge

[NG 8119] +

These very curious remains are of barracks erected around 1720 for English

troops and German mercenaries protecting General George Wade's military road-building and civilizing works in the glens. The barracks were thus occupied until almost the end of the century. Afterwards the barracks provided shelter for victims of the Highland Clearances.

AM

6 FORTROSE CATHEDRAL

Town centre, on A832, 8 miles (13 km) SW of Cromarty

[NH 7256] +

Only a fragment of the church founded by David I remains (parts of the nave and sacristy), but there are some

Loch-an-Eilean Castle

interesting details in the pink sandstone ruin, including monuments and the burial chapel of the MacKenzies of Seaforth. The building fell into dereliction at the Reformation, and Cromwell completed the ruination by quarrying the remaining parts for building material.

SDD

7 GLENELG BROCHS
Minor road SE of village, 6½ miles (10.5 km) W of Shiel Bridge

[NG 8317] +

Two fine examples of the Iron Age broch, a circular defensive tower of dry-stone walling most common in the north and west of Scotland, stand to a height of more than 30 feet (9 m), beside a valley road east of Eilanreach. They are known as Dun Telve and Dun Troddan. The brochs have concrete walls with slabs of stone between them forming galleries reached by staircases.

SDD

8 LOCH-AN-EILEAN CASTLE
On isle in loch, by minor road off B970, 2 miles (3 km) S of Aviemore

[NH 8907] +

The medieval castle's remains occupy an islet in the loch, and the castle was once one of the strongholds of Alexander Stewart, known as the Wolf of Badenoch. Ospreys nested in one of the ruined towers in the last century. The castle is clearly visible from the shore of the loch.

AM

9 RUTHVEN BARRACKS
B970 just S of Kingussie

[NN 7699] +

These extensive barracks on the south bank of the River Spey near Kingussie were built in 1716–18 to house troops employed in controlling the Highlands after the Jacobite rising. They were extended by General Wade in the 1730s, but blown up by Bonnie Prince Charlie's men soon after the Battle of Culloden.

SDD

10 ST PETER'S CHURCH, THURSO
[ND 1168] +

A medieval church much rebuilt in the seventeenth century, the ruin stands in the old part of the town near the harbour, and was once the chapel of the bishops of Caithness. One window has its tracery intact.

AM

11 URQUHART CASTLE
W shore of Loch Ness, off A82, 13½ miles (22 km) SW of Inverness

[NH 5328] ★

Built on the west bank of Loch Ness, mostly in the sixteenth century, it was one of the largest castles in Scotland. It is unusually irregular in plan. Its turbulent history came to an end when it was destroyed in 1692 to prevent its use by Jacobite rebels, and though much plundered for building stone, the ruins are extensive, with a bridge across a huge ditch leading into the castle via a twin-towered gatehouse.

SDD

61 Lothian

See maps on page 202

1 CRAIGMILLAR CASTLE
Minor road between A68 and A695, 3 miles (5 km) SE of Edinburgh city centre

[NT 2870] ★★★ *Tel: 031 244 3101*

This famous baronial castle of the Preston family at the south-eastern fringes of Edinburgh was built in the

Dirleton Castle

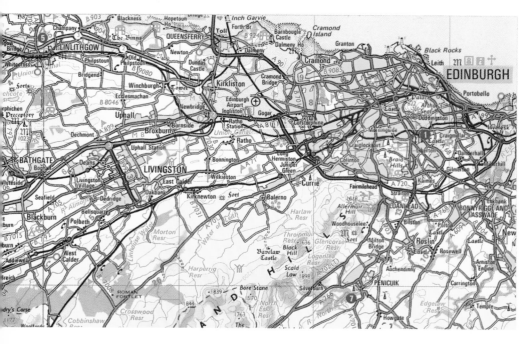

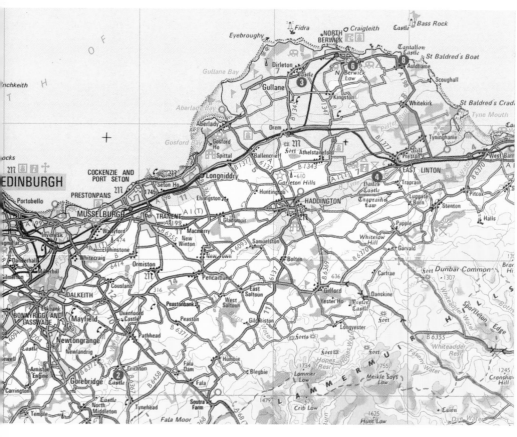

of her husband, Lord Darnley. The original keep is well-preserved, and the ruins substantial and impressive.

SDD

2 CRICHTON CASTLE
S of village, by minor road off B6367, 5 miles (8 km) SE of Dalkeith

[NT 3861]   ***   Tel: 031 244 3101

Partly built by Francis Stewart, Earl of Bothwell, the older parts date from the fourteenth and fifteenth centuries. One of Scotland's largest castles, its buildings were erected round a more or less square courtyard on a site overlooking Tyne Water. Bothwell's additions were elaborate extensions to the north range in Italianate fashion, and are said to be copied from the palace at Ferrara.

SDD

3 DIRLETON CASTLE
In village, on B1345, 2 miles (3 km) W of North Berwick

[NT 5183]   *

The ruins are of a thirteenth-century castle with alterations and extensions that went on until Cromwell brought it to ruin in the seventeenth century. It seems innocuous enough today, standing close to the village green with a bowling green and gardens in its grounds. But it was built to guard the chief military route into Scotland from England, and the massive red and grey walls of its towers rise straight out of its rock foundations. The castle was taken by Edward I and by Robert the Bruce in its early years.

SDD

4 HAILES CASTLE
Minor road S off A1 at East Linton

[NT 5775]   ***   Tel: 031 244 3101

A thirteenth-century castle which later came into the possession of the Hepburn earls of Bothwell, who reinforced its defences, it was attacked by the Percys in the border wars. It has two pit dungeons, and a chapel added in the sixteenth century. Cromwell dismantled the castle in 1650.

SDD

5 LINLITHGOW PALACE
Short distance from town centre, on S shore of loch

[NT 0077]   *

This splendid royal palace overlooking the loch was begun by James I of

fourteenth century as an L-shaped tower-house, then later enclosed within a high wall with angle-towers, inside which were new ranges of domestic buildings and a courtyard. In the seventeenth century, a further courtyard within a curtain wall was added to the north side. After the castle had been badly damaged by the Earl of Hertford in 1544, restoration was carried out, and Mary, Queen of Scots stayed here on several occasions. It was while she was in residence in 1566 that Bothwell and his fellow-conspirators plotted the murder

Tantallon Castle

Scotland after an earlier fortified palace had been burnt down in the fifteenth century. The chapel and great hall date from the earliest rebuilding, and the palace was gradually extended until its completion by James V, whose daughter Mary – Queen of Scots within a week – was born here in 1542 to Mary of Guise, in a room in the north-west corner. The palace played a significant role in the Stuart history of Scotland and England, but was already falling into dereliction by the beginning of the seventeenth century, and was finally destroyed by fire

in 1746, probably by accident rather than design, when occupied by troops.

SDD

6 NORTH BERWICK TOWER
On North Berwick Law (hill just S of town) off B1347

[NT 5584] +

This is the ruin of a watch tower built during the Napoleonic wars. It stands on what is called North Berwick Law, a volcanic rock from which there are fine views.

7 PENICUIK HOUSE
Off A766 just SW of town

[NT 2259]   By appointment

The house was built in the early eighteenth century for the local laird, Sir John Clerk, a patron of the arts who has been called 'the Maecenas of his age'. But the mansion was gutted by fire in 1899. The shell has a splendid Augustan façade. The family still lives on the estate, having converted the former stables into a residence after the fire.

Private

8 TANTALLON CASTLE
On coast off A198, 3 miles (5 km)
E of North Berwick

[NT 5985]   ★★★   Tel: 031 244 3101

This was the fortress of the Black Douglas family – a rose-coloured stone castle standing on a sheer clifftop above the Firth of Forth. Built in the fourteenth century, its landward side was protected by a wall 50 feet (15 m) high and 12 feet (3.5 m) thick, having a central entrance tower with drawbridge and portcullis, and flanking towers. The castle, which features in Scott's *Marmion*, withstood several sieges, but was bombarded by General Monck in 1651 and surrendered after 12 days, being then brought to ruin.

SDD

---

62 Orkney and Shetland

See map on page 206 and left-hand map on page 207

1 BIRSAY PALACE
On A966 at Birsay, NW coast of Orkney's Mainland

[HY 2427]   +

The ruins of a stone palace built by Earl Robert Stewart around 1580.

SDD

2 BROUGH OF BIRSAY CHURCH
On island off A966 at NW corner of Mainland

[HY 2328]   ★★★   Tel: 031 244 3101

Accessible at low tide, the uninhabited island has the ruins of a small Romanesque church where Vikings settled.

SDD

3 EYNHALLOW PRIORY
On island in Eynhallow Sound, between Mainland and Rousay

[HY 3528]   +

The ruins of the church and monastic buildings, such as they are, tell us little about the origins of this Benedictine priory on the tiny island between Mainland and Rousay, though the church is of the twelfth century.

SDD

4 JARLSHOF
S end of Shetland's Mainland, off A970 at Sumburgh

[HU 3909]   ★★★   Tel: 031 244 3101

This is unquestionably one of Britain's most remarkable prehistoric and medieval remains. Close to Shetland's airport are the ruins of a series of settlements dating back to origins around 2000 BC, the location being occupied more or less continuously, it seems, from the Stone Age to the Viking period. There are stone walls of oval Bronze Age huts, Iron Age houses with underground passages, a Pictish 'broch' or defensive tower, a sub-divided wheel-house, and Viking long-houses. Also on the site is the ruin of a mansion built in the sixteenth century by Earl Patrick Stewart, and it was this that Scott called 'Jarlshof' in *The Pirate* (1821), the name since becoming generally adopted for the prehistoric remains. The remarkable condition of the remains is due to their having been buried for centuries beneath sand, from which archaeologists have recovered them.

SDD

5 KIRKWALL PALACES
Close to cathedral

[HY 4410]   ★★

In 1607, Earl Patrick Stewart, whose name is synonymous with feudal tyranny in Scotland, and who was hanged in Edinburgh seven years later, built here a palace whose ruins have been called the 'finest relic of domestic Renaissance architecture in Scotland'. Nearby are the ruins of a thirteenth-century bishop's palace.

SDD

6 MIDHOWE BROCH
W coast of Rousay, off minor road 1¼ miles (2.8 km) NW of Westness

[HY 3730]   +

This Iron Age broch is on the island of Rousay, within a walled enclosure on a coastal promontory defended by a ditch cut into the rock.

SDD

7 MOUSA BROCH
On island of Mousa off E coast of Shetland's Mainland near Sandwick

[HU 4523]   +

A 43-foot (13-m) high round tower of dry-stone walling, regarded as the best preserved of the Iron Age brochs, consisting of a double shell with slabs forming a gallery within the walls, and with a stone staircase which can be climbed to the parapet. The island of Mousa can be reached by hired boat from Sandwick on Mainland.

SDD

8 ORPHIR CHURCH
S of village, on minor road off A964, Mainland, Orkney

[HY 3304]   +

This twelfth-century church of St Nicholas on Orkney's Mainland is

Jarlshof, Shetland

Earl's Palace, Kirkwall, Orkney

circular – the only medieval example in Scotland.

SDD

9 SCALLOWAY CASTLE
On coast at Scalloway, A970, 5 miles (8 km) W of Lerwick

[HU 4039] ★

It sticks up like a rotten tooth from the shore across Mainland island from Lerwick – a sixteenth-century tower-house built by the notorious Earl Patrick Stewart, whom legend accuses of mixing the mortar with human blood. He was executed in Edinburgh in 1615, and the castle fell into dereliction.

SDD

10 SKARA BRAE
W coast of Mainland, Orkney, off B9056, 6½ miles (10.5 km) N of Stromness

[HY 2318] ★

The ruins of this neolithic village lay hidden beneath a natural sand cover for 4,500 years, and were laid bare for archaeologists by a storm which shifted much of the sand in the nineteenth century. Investigation revealed about eight stone houses of around 3000 BC, with stone beds and hearths, privies and drainage channels, and all linked by paved passages. Clay-lined tanks in the floors are thought to have been used for soaking limpets for use as fishing bait. It may have been the drifting sand which drove the inhabitants away from the settlement by about 2700 BC.

SDD

Skara Brae, on Mainland, Orkney

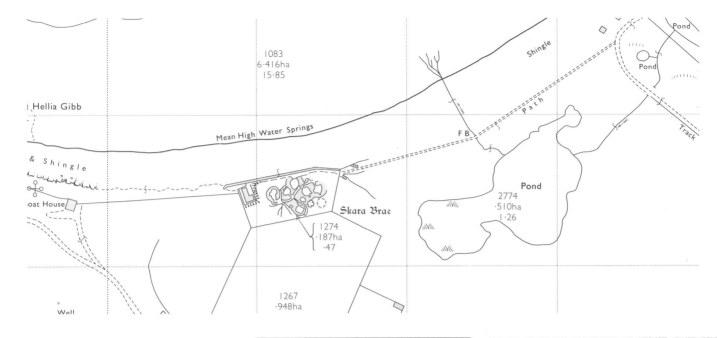

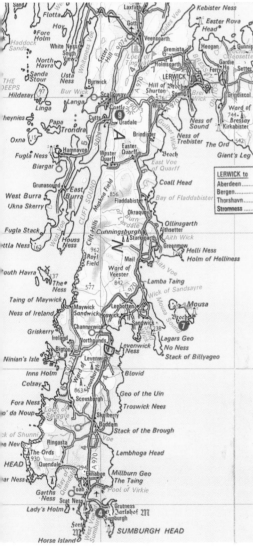

63 Strathclyde

See maps right and on pages 210 and 211

1 ALLOWAY KIRK

Next to Burns Centre in village, 2 miles (3 km) S of Ayr

[NS3318]

By arrangement: Tel: 0292 41252

This kirk in Robert Burns' birthplace was already falling into ruin in his time. It features in the poem *Tam o' Shanter*, Tam seeing witches and warlocks through its windows. The poet's father was buried in the graveyard.

Private

2 ARDCHATTAN PRIORY

N bank of Loch Ettive, by minor road off A828, 7½ miles (12 km) NE of Oban

[NM 9734]   +

Scant remains of a thirteenth-century priory of the Valliscaulian order, the scene of a Scottish Parliament in 1308. Suppressed in 1602, the church was burned down by Cromwell's troops in 1654, the house converted from the prior's lodging, still intact beside it.

SDD

3 ARDROSSAN CASTLE

In village, overlooking bay, on A738, 6 miles (9.5 km) NW of Irvine

[NS 2342]   +

Little remains but part of a gatehouse

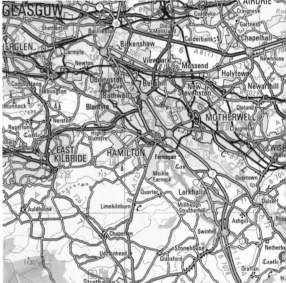

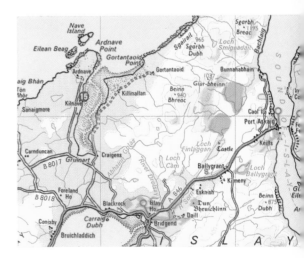

tower and other fragments, but there are good views from its hilltop site. It was a twelfth-century courtyard castle, brought to ruin by Cromwell.

AM

4 BOTHWELL CASTLE
On E bank of River Clyde just NW of town, 7½ miles (12 km) SE of Glasgow (M74 junction 5)

[NS 6859]   ★★★   *Tel: 031 244 3101*

A thirteenth-century castle built on the south bank of the Clyde by the Moray family, it was at one time the largest and best stone castle in Scotland. It passed back and forth between Scots and Sassenachs, being taken in turn by Edward I, Wallace, Edward again, Robert the Bruce, Edward III, and Moray. Then it came into possession of the Black Douglas family, who rebuilt it after its slighting by Bruce and Moray to render it useless to the English, and further building was done up to the sixteenth century. The remains show fine ashlar stonework, which some believe to have been done by French masons.

SDD

5 CARNASSERIE CASTLE
S of village, off A816, 1 mile (1.5 km) N of Kilmartin

[NM 8300]   +

A sixteenth-century tower house, once the home of John Carswell, whose translation of John Knox's *Liturgy* in 1567 became the first book printed in Gaelic. The castle was blown up in 1685.

SDD

6 CASTLE LACHLAN
Near E shore of Loch Fyne, off B8000, 6¼ miles (10 km) SW of Strachur

[NS 0195]   +

A fourteenth-century courtyard castle, though it looks from outside like a tower-house, it was the seat of the MacLachlans until the rising of 1745, when it was bombarded by naval gunfire and abandoned.

Private

7 CASTLE SWEEN
On E shore of Loch Sween off coastal road 11 miles (17.5 km) SW of Lochgilphead

[NR 7178]   +

One of the oldest of all Scotland's stone-built castles, it dates from the early twelfth century, and is in the form of a roughly rectangular enclosure with corner buttress towers or turrets. The castle was destroyed in 1647.

SDD

8 CRAIGNETHAN CASTLE
Minor road off A72 near Crossford, 4 miles (6.5 km) W of Lanark

[NS 8146]   ★

A formidable castle of the sixteenth century on a promontory above the Clyde, it was built by the Hamiltons, and had artillery defences in its massive

The former nunnery on Iona

Lochranza Castle, Isle of Arran

western rampart protecting a three-storey tower-house. Because the Hamiltons supported Mary, Queen of Scots, the castle was slighted in 1579 after repeated harassment by the Protestant party. The castle was the model for Tillietudlem in Sir Walter Scott's *Old Mortality* (1816).

SDD

9 CROSSRAGUEL ABBEY
Beside A77, 2 miles (3 km) SW of Maybole

[NS 2708] ★★★ *Tel: 031 244 3101*

Founded as a Cluniac priory in 1244 by the Earl of Carrick, it became an abbey in 1270. Its remains are substantial and its architecture impressive, thanks

largely to the fact that it was out of reach of English cross-border raids. The choir of the church has a three-sided apse, and there is a fine battlemented gatehouse as well as other highly interesting remains.

SDD

10 DUNSTAFFNAGE CASTLE
On coast off A85, 3½ miles (5.5 km) N of Oban

[NM 8834] ★★★ *Tel: 031 244 3101*

The remains, on a promontory north of Oban, are of a thirteenth-century fortress in the form of an enclosure wall with angle-towers rising from solid rock foundations. It was built by Alexander II as a base for his attack on the Vikings in the Hebrides, and was later held by

Robert the Bruce, before passing to the Campbell Earls of Argyll, whose home it was until the gatehouse tower was destroyed by fire in 1810. The finely decorated castle chapel, outside the walls, is also in ruins.

SDD

11 DUNURE CASTLE
On coast in village, on minor road off A719, 6 miles (9.5 km) SW of Ayr

[NS 2515] +

Relatively little remains of this thirteenth-century coastal castle where, in 1570, Gilbert Kennedy, Earl of Cassillis, roasted the Commendator of Crossraguel Abbey to induce him to sign over the abbey lands to him.

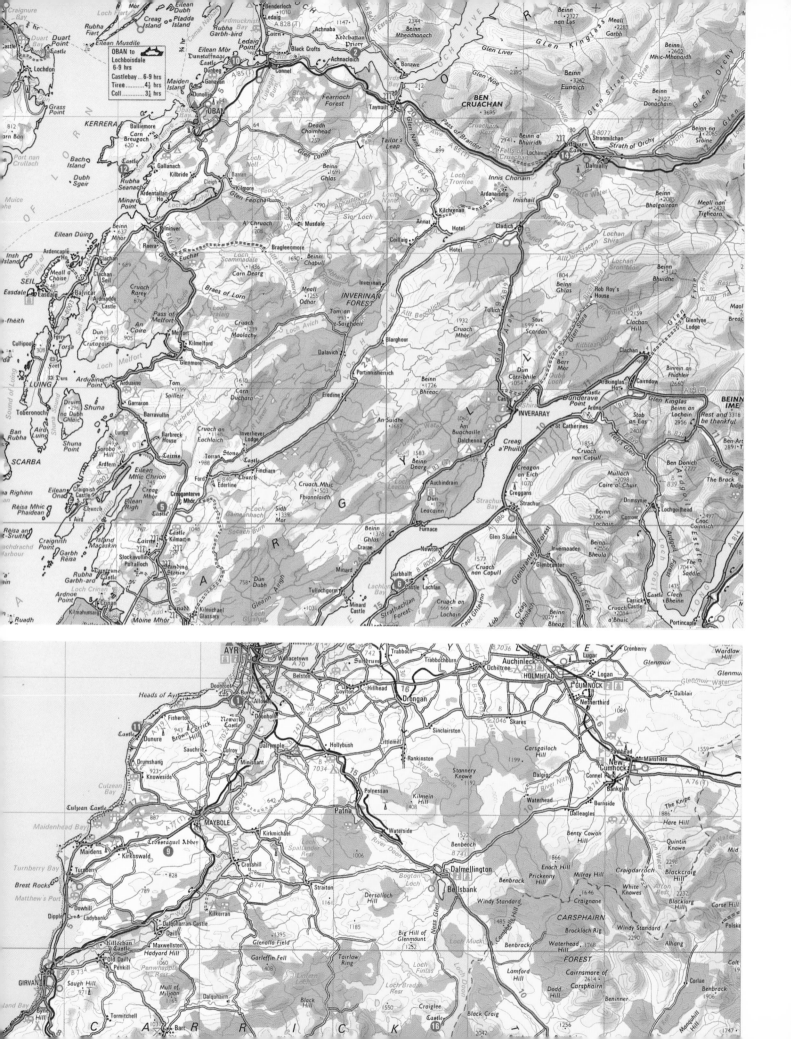

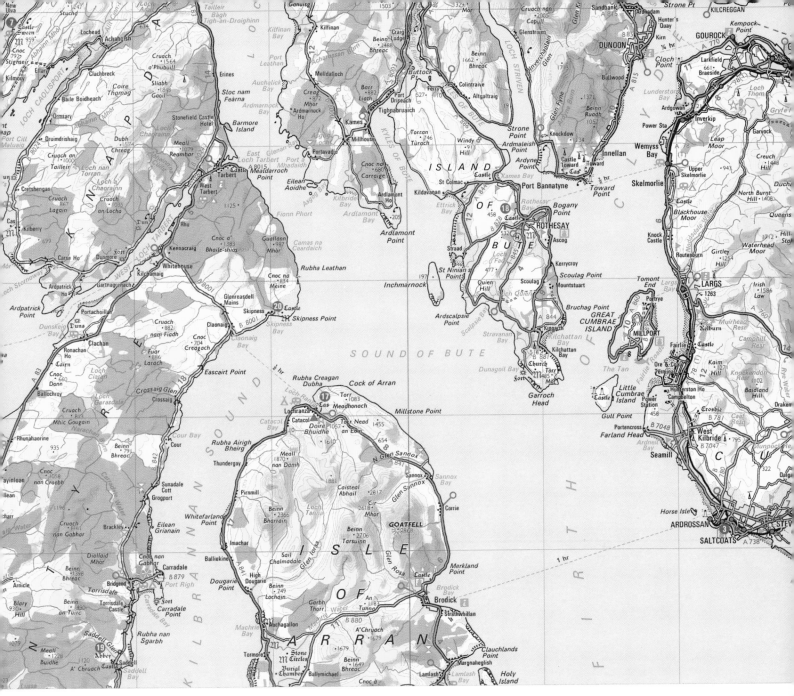

12 GYLEN CASTLE
S coast of Isle of Kerrera, off Oban

[NM 8026]   +

The island of Kerrera, across the Sound from Oban, has at its southern end the ruins of a late sixteenth-century castle, built by the MacDougalls, which survived for less than a century, as it was destroyed by Cromwell's troops in 1645.

SDD

13 IONA NUNNERY
E coast of island, off Ross of Mull

[NM 2824]   +

The ancient and world-famous abbey church and other monastic buildings have been gradually restored during the present century, but the associated nunnery remains in ruins, and is an attractive and atmospheric relic of the cradle of Christianity in Britain, with round Norman arches in walls of coursed rubble.

Iona Community

14 KILCHURN CASTLE
N end of Loch Awe, off A85, 1¾ miles (2.8 km) W of Dalmally

[NN 1327]   +

It might reasonably be called the 'Calendar Castle', so often has it formed a picturesque scene on calendars of Bonnie Scotland or Beautiful Britain. Built in the fifteenth century on a peninsula in Loch Awe, it was the work of Sir Colin Campbell of Glenorchy and

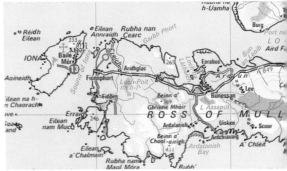

his descendants of the Breadalbane family. The top of one of its towers was blown down in 1879 by the same gales that destroyed the Tay Bridge (q.v.), 80 miles (130 km) east.

SDD

15 KILNAVE CHAPEL
*Island of Islay, on minor road off B8017,
6 miles (9.5 km) NW of Bridgend*

[NR 2871]   +

There is little enough of it left to see, but that is because the Macdonalds burnt the place down in 1598 with thirty of the rival Macleans inside. Gravestones and a forlorn Celtic cross dating from the eighth century stand round the rough gable and low walls of dark thinly-coursed stone that were the scene of the horrific clan vengeance, on the shore of Loch Grinart on Islay.

AM

16 LOCH DOON CASTLE
*On W shore of loch, on minor road off
A713, 6½ miles (10.5 km) S of
Dalmellington*

[NX 4895]   +

Long before the great Abu Simbel temple in Egypt was carved up and re-erected above the rising waters of the Nile created by the Aswan Dam, this Scottish castle was dismantled stone by stone and rebuilt elsewhere for the same reason. It was originally built early in the fourteenth century on an island in the loch, which was to be submerged by a new hydro-electric plant. The castle, except for a sixteenth-century addition, was taken down in 1934-5, every stone being numbered, and re-erected on the loch's western shore. Does that make it a folly, one wonders?

SDD

17 LOCHRANZA CASTLE
*N coast of Isle of Arran, off A841 through
village*

[NR 9350]   ★

The ruins of the castle stand on a spur in a sea-inlet at the northern end of the island of Arran. Though the existing work is mainly of the sixteenth century, the castle was originally erected in the thirteenth or early fourteenth century, and Robert the Bruce stayed in it when he returned from Ireland in 1306.

AM

18 ROTHESAY CASTLE
Close to town centre, on Isle of Bute

[NS 0864]   ★★★   Tel: 031 244 3101

The thirteenth-century castle at Rothesay is something rare in Scotland – a shell-keep. In 1240, the castle was besieged by Vikings, who breached the walls by penetrating the masonry with their axes, as can still be seen in the ruins. Later in the century, after Haakon of Norway had captured the castle and held it briefly, four round towers were built round the shell wall, and James IV subsequently built a gatehouse tower projecting from the north side over the moat. The shell of the castle's chapel remains in the courtyard.

SDD

19 SADDELL ABBEY
*In village near E coast of Kintyre, by
B842, 8 miles (13 km) NE of
Campbelltown*

[NR 7832]   +

Scant ruin of a Cistercian monastery founded on Kintyre about 1150 by a Lord of the Isles, but so poor that in 1508 its revenues were transferred to the bishopric of Argyll by permission of Pope Julius II. Its remains were afterwards ruthlessly quarried for building materials, and only parts of the church walls are left.

AM

20 SKIPNESS CASTLE
*Near Skipness Point, on E coast of Kintyre
7½ miles (12 km) SE of Tarbert*

[NR 9157]   ⊜ No access ⊜

Originally built in the thirteenth century, it was a Campbell stronghold, and overlooks the Kilbrennan Sound which separates Arran from the mainland. The dark stone ruins, with their characteristic baronial tower, can be viewed clearly from outside the grounds.

AM

---

64 *Tayside*

See maps on page 214

1 ARBROATH ABBEY
Short distance from town centre

[NO 6441]   ★

Founded as a Cluniac priory in 1178 by William the Lion (who was buried here), and dedicated to his friend Thomas Becket, it had become an abbey of the Order of Tiron by 1233, and it was here in 1320 where the famous Declaration of Arbroath took shape pronouncing Scotland an independent kingdom under Robert the Bruce. The ruins are mainly of the thirteenth century and are splendid, the gable of the abbey church's south transept standing to its full height with the rose window known as the O of Arbroath, once used to aid navigation.

SDD

2 BURLEIGH CASTLE
*Near N end of Loch Leven, off A911 just
E of Milnathort*

[NO 1204]   ★

A small sixteenth-century tower-house, it was the home of the Balfours of Burleigh, who entertained King James VI here. A gatehouse was added later in the century with gun-ports.

SDD

3 DUNKELD CATHEDRAL
*High Street in village, on A923, 9½ miles
(15 km) W of Blairgowrie*

[NO 0242]   +

Not completed until the first years of the sixteenth century, it was in ruins within 60 years, a victim of the Reformation. The cathedral had been started 200 years earlier, and some of its bishops held powerful positions. The choir remains in use as the parish kirk, having been restored. The rest is an impressive ruin, though curiously primitive in style for its time, and it stands in a somewhat isolated, though beautiful, position, because of a shift in population after the Jacobite wars.

SDD

4 EDZELL CASTLE
*W of village, on minor road off B966,
5½ miles (9 km) N of Brechin*

[NO 5869]   ★

It began as a fine tower-house of the Stirling family in the sixteenth century, and was then extended with ranges round a courtyard to the north. In the early seventeenth century, Sir David Lindsay added a 'pleasance' to the south – a walled Renaissance garden with a summer-house and a bath-house tower. The garden walls have unique heraldic decoration and carvings representing the cardinal virtues, and fortunately remain intact, the castle itself having been the victim of Campbell vandalism after the Jacobite rising of 1745.

SDD

Arbroath Abbey

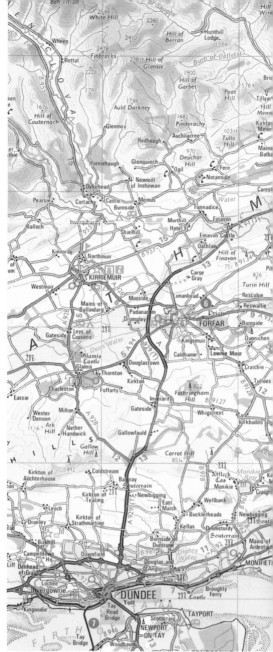

5 MUTHILL CHURCH

In village, on A822, 3 miles (5 km)
S of Crieff

[NN 8616]   +

The main body of this ruined church is late fourteenth century, but the tower is much older – possibly eleventh century. It is 70 feet (21 m) high, with crow-stepped gables.

SDD

6 RESTENNETH PRIORY

Beside B9113 just E of Forfar

[NO 4851]   +

David I is said to have founded this Augustinian priory on the site of an earlier Celtic monastery, around 1153. It was destroyed by Edward I, but then rebuilt, to remain active until 1606.

Little other than the church remains, this having a square tower with broach spire intact.

SDD

7 TAY BRIDGE PIERS

Firth of Tay between Dundee and Wormit

[NO 3926–9]   +

Alongside the present Tay railway bridge, built in 1883–7, are the concrete stumps which supported the original bridge completed in 1878, then the longest in the world. Just after Christmas in 1879, the bridge collapsed in a fearful gale while a train was crossing, and 75 people lost their lives. Twelve iron columns and thirteen spans gave way and over 1000 yards (900 m) of the bridge disappeared into the raging firth in a matter of seconds.

65 Western Isles

See maps right and below

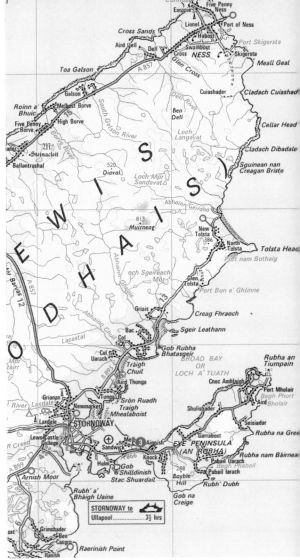

1 CILLE BARRA
N end of Barra on minor road at Eoligarry

[NF 7007] +

The most westerly inhabited island of Scotland has the remains of a church dedicated to St Barr, from whom the island takes its name. It is the fragmentary ruin of a medieval monastery.

AM

2 TRINITY TEMPLE
S end of North Uist, on minor road off A865 near Carinish

NF 8159 +

This ruin on North Uist is what is left of a monastic settlement, founded in the thirteenth century, which had a college attached to it, and where Duns Scotus, the medieval philosopher and divine, is said to have studied as a Franciscan friar.

3 UI CHURCH
On Eye Peninsula, Isle of Lewis, on minor road off A866 at Aignish, 3½ miles (5.5 km) E of Stornoway

[NB 4832] +

Near Stornoway on the island of Lewis, the ruin of this church contains tombs of the local Macleods. The name is pronounced 'Eye', like the peninsula on which it stands. It is a church of uncertain origin, now under threat from Hebridean storms.

AM

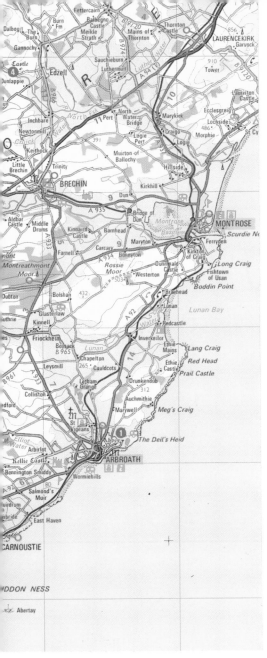

Historical and Architectural Glossary

Almonry Room or office for distribution of alms

Amphitheatre Space for ceremony or performance with rows of seating rising around it

Arcade A row of arches supported by columns

Architrave Moulded frame round window or doorway

Ashlar Finely dressed and jointed stonework

Bailey A court or ward in a castle

Balustrade Length of rail or coping carried on short pillars

Barbican Structure defending gate of castle

Baroque Exuberant or extravagant style of decoration, mainly seventeenth and eighteenth centuries

Barrow A prehistoric grave-mound

Basilica Roman approximation to town hall

Bastion Projecting defensive tower of castle, not designed for habitation

Bastle-house Fortified house (Scotland)

Broch Circular stone dwelling-tower with chambers and stairways in walls (Scotland)

Bronze age Prehistoric period between Stone and Iron Ages, approx. 1800–500 BC

Buttery Storeroom for provisions, especially wine

Cellarium Monastic equivalent of buttery – store for provisions and office of cellarer

Chancel East end of church beyond nave, with altar, choir, etc.

Chapter house Monastic conference- or boardroom

Chi-rho Monogram formed of χρ, the first letters of 'Christ' in Greek

Clerestory Upper storey of a church's nave walls, with windows

Cloister Enclosed quadrangle connecting monastic church with domestic offices

Corbel Projecting stone supporting beam or other weight

Crenellation Battlemented parapet

Crypt Sub-chamber of church, usually underground

Curtain wall A wall that is not load-bearing, usually linking towers round a castle

Decorated Richly decorated style of Gothic architecture, mainly fourteenth century

Dissolution The suppression of English and Welsh monasteries by Henry VIII, 1536–40

Dolmen Prehistoric burial chamber with upright stones supporting a large capstone

Early English Style of Gothic architecture with earliest pointed windows, mainly thirteenth century

Forum Roman market-place

Frater Monastic refectory or dining room

Garderobe Medieval lavatory or privy

Gothic Style of architecture prevailing from twelfth to sixteenth centuries. It succeeded Romanesque (Norman) and is chiefly characterized by pointed arches

Hood-mould Projecting moulding which protects door from rainwater

Hypocaust Roman under-floor heating system

Ingeniator Medieval military architect

Iron age Historical period following Bronze Age, approx. 500 BC–AD 43

Keep The main dwelling-tower of a castle

Knapped flint Flint dressed with smooth side for building purposes

Lancet Narrow, pointed window

Lavatorium Place for washing hands before meals in monastery

Machicolation Projecting gallery on castle wall with holes in floor for dropping molten lead etc. on attackers

Mausoleum A large and elaborate tomb – often a family monument

Megalith A very large stone, either standing or part of a prehistoric structure

Moss-troopers Freebooters in Scottish Border region, seventeenth century

Motte Artificial mound on which Norman castles were built

Mullion Vertical division between lights of a window

Municipium A Roman provincial town

Nave The main body of a church, between west door and transept

Neolithic New Stone Age (approx. 3500–1800 BC)

Newel Central post of spiral staircase

Ogee An S-shaped curve

Oppidum A Roman town

Oriel Projecting upper-floor window supported by brackets or corbel

Palaestra Roman gymnasium or wrestling school

Palisade Fence of wooden stakes

Pediment Shallow gable on classical buildings

Peel-Tower Sixteenth-century fortified house in northern Britain, with no direct access from ground floor to upper part

Perpendicular Style of Gothic architecture, approx. 1350–1530

Pilaster A column attached to a wall

Pilgrimage of Grace The popular uprising in northern England, 1536–7, against the dissolution of the monasteries

Piscina Basin for washing sacred vessels

Portcullis Iron grille lowered to protect castle gateway

Portico Central feature of classical building, with columns and pediment

Preceptory House of Knights Templar or Hospitallers, usually headquarters of estate

Recusant A religious dissenter – usually Roman Catholic refusing to attend compulsory Church of England services

Refectory Monastic dining hall

Romanesque Norman architecture, characterized by round arches

Glossary

Shell-keep A tower within a circular wall on a mound

Solar Upper living-room on sunny side of castle or medieval house

Squint Small opening in wall of church giving view of altar from outside, often used by lepers

Tracery Intersecting ornamental stone ribwork in church windows

Transept The part of a church that forms the cross shape, between nave and chancel

Transitional The period in which Norman architecture was giving way to Gothic

Transom Cross-beam or horizontal division of a window

Tuscan column Roman interpretation of the Greek Doric column, unfluted

Undercroft A vaulted basement or underground chamber

Voussoir Wedge-shaped stone in an arch

Ward Court of a castle (same as **Bailey**)

Select Bibliography

It would be unhelpful to readers for me to list the countless guidebooks and topographical works from which I have gathered information for this book. I acknowledge my indebtedness to all authors and compilers of such works, and especially to the excellent official guides to individual monuments in the care of English Heritage and the National Trust. There are very few books specifically about ruins, but I list below those and some other specialized works on which I have chiefly relied.

R. J. Atkinson, *Stonehenge*, Penguin Books, Harmondsworth, 1979

Brian Bailey, *The National Trust Book of Ruins*, Weidenfeld & Nicolson, London, 1984

Bede, *Ecclesiastical History of the English Nation*, Dent, London, 1975

Maurice Beresford and John G. Hurst, *Deserted Medieval Villages*, Lutterworth Press, Cambridge, 1971

Frank Bottomley, *The Abbey Explorer's Guide*, Kaye & Ward, Tadworth, Surrey, 1981

David J. Breeze and Brian Dobson, *Hadrian's Wall*, Allen Lane, Harmondsworth, 1976

Rotha Mary Clay, *The Medieval Hospitals of England*, Frank Cass, London, 1966

James Forde-Johnston, *A Guide to the Castles of England and Wales*, Constable, London, 1981

Antonia Fraser, *Mary Queen of Scots*, Weidenfeld & Nicolson, London, 1969

Sheppard Frere, *Britannia: A History of Roman Britain*, Routledge & Kegan Paul, London, 1967

Plantagenet Somerset Fry, *Castles*, David & Charles, Newton Abbot, Devon, 1980

Jacquetta Hawkes, *A Guide to the Prehistoric and Roman Monuments in England and Wales*, Chatto & Windus, London, 1951

Paul Johnson, *The National Trust Book of British Castles*, Weidenfeld & Nicolson, London, 1978

Bryan Little, *Abbeys and Priories in England and Wales*, Batsford, London, 1979

Rose Macaulay, *Pleasure of Ruins*, Thames & Hudson, London, 1953

J. D. Mackie, *A History of Scotland*, Penguin Books, Harmondsworth, 1978

Richard Muir, *The Lost Villages of Britain*, Michael Joseph, London, 1982

Nikolaus Pevsner and others, *The Buildings of England* (46 vols.), Penguin Books, Harmondsworth, 1951–74

John Prebble, *The Lion in the North*, Secker & Warburg, London 1971

M. W. Thompson, *Ruins: Their Preservation and Display*, British Museum, London, 1981

John Timbs and Alexander Gunn, *Abbeys, Castles and Ancient Halls of England and Wales* (3 vols.), Frederick Warne, Dorking, Surrey, n.d.

Margaret Wood, *The English Medieval House*, Dent, London, 1965

Index of Names

Index of Places

Index